T0128002

Get the eBook FREE!

(PDF, ePub, Kindle, and liveBook all included)

We believe that once you buy a book from us, you should be able to read it in any format we have available. To get electronic versions of this book at no additional cost to you, purchase and then register this book at the Manning website.

Go to https://www.manning.com/freebook and follow the instructions to complete your pBook registration.

That's it!
Thanks from Manning!

Object Design Style Guide

MATTHIAS NOBACK
FOREWORD BY ROSS TUCK

MANNING
SHELTER ISLAND

Manning Publications Co.
20 Baldwin Road
PO Box 761
Shelter Island, NY 11964

Development editor:	Elesha Hyde
Technical development editor:	Tanya Wilke
Review editor:	Aleksandar Dragosavljević
Production editor:	Deirdre Hiam
Copyeditor:	Andy Caroll
Proofreader:	Keri Hales
Technical proofreader:	Justin Coulston
Typesetter:	Gordan Salinovic
Cover designer:	Marija Tudor

ISBN 9781617296857
Printed in the United States of America

To my daughter Julia:
Don't let anyone tell you that you can't do something because you're a girl.

To women everywhere:
I hope you'll never feel discouraged in any way to become a programmer.

To programmers everywhere:
Let's make our teams as welcoming as possible for anyone who wants to join us.

contents

1 Programming with objects: A primer 1

4 *Manipulating objects   102*

foreword

All programmers can appreciate the value of a good name. A name is a promise: it tells you what you can and can't expect. It helps you make a decision and move on.

But a Good Name, with capital letters, is more than just a contract. A Good Name shares something about the soul of what's described. It gives you a glimpse of the creator's intention, its *raison d'être*. The name Walkie-Talkie tells you both the what and the why of the thing. The name doesn't need to be accurate: fire ants aren't made of fire but they might as well be. A Good Name reveals.

I'm happy to say that the book you are now holding has an exceptionally Good Name.

You may be familiar with the style guides often used by journalists, such as the *AP Stylebook* or *The Chicago Manual of Style*. Like those books, this one offers both guidelines and guidance on achieving a clear, consistent tone across a larger team.

In following this model, Matthias Noback's goal is humble and direct. There are no new concepts, no fancy tools, no radical breakthroughs. Matthias has simply documented what he was already doing. He has captured his approach to designing systems and distilled it into the elements of his style.

These elements are discussed in terms of existing patterns, some of which you may have heard of elsewhere. What I find wonderful in this book is the realization that these patterns seldom live in isolation. What seems reasonable on the page will often fail in the IDE without the guarantees offered by other practices. For example, consider how difficult unit tests are without dependency injection.

And so, this *Object Design Style Guide* is greater than the sum of its parts. Taken together, these patterns interlock and strengthen each other. Deeper treatments of each topic exist elsewhere, but what Matthias has done is take a collection of best practices and turn them into a cohesive, recognizable style.

Publishing your own style may seem strange, even arrogant. After all, why should we follow this style rather than yours or mine? The most brutal argument suggests that, like coding standards that dictate where the brackets and spaces go, it doesn't matter which style we follow, only that we follow one. This one just has the virtue of already being documented.

Yet I believe the intent is not to constrain the reader but to provide a reference point. Innovation happens within constraints, they say. Iterate on this style, improve on it, start here—but make it your own, because your circumstances are unique. After all, the only thing worse than a newspaper written like a love letter would be a love letter written like a newspaper.

If you remain unconvinced, this book at least offers you the chance to see a high-level practitioner at work. There is a remarkable honesty and vulnerability on display. There is no secret sauce, no technique withheld in these pages. What you see here is how Matthias approaches his daily work—nothing more, nothing less.

Indeed, in the process of reviewing this book, I was struck several times by the memory of watching over his shoulder as he codes, listening to him weigh each concern and select a tool. I imagined myself pointing at something that seemed out of place in his familiar style, and Matthias just smiling. "Oh yes," he'd say, "that was the interesting part."

I hope you enjoy that same experience as much as I have.

—Ross Tuck
rosstuck.com

preface

Between learning how to program and learning about advanced design patterns and principles, there isn't much educational material for object-oriented programmers. The recommended books are hard to read, and it often proves difficult to apply the theory to your everyday coding problems. Besides, most developers don't have a lot of time to read a book. What's left is a gap in programming education materials.

Even without reading books, you will grow as a programmer over time. You'll learn how to make better design choices. You'll collect a set of basic rules that you can pretty much always apply, freeing mental capacity to focus on other interesting areas of the code that need improving. So what can't be learned from reading software books can, in fact, be learned through years and years of struggling with code.

I wrote this book to close part of the education-materials gap and to give you some suggestions that will help you write better object-oriented code. These will be mostly short and simple suggestions. Technically, there won't be a lot to master. But I find that following these suggestions (or "rules") helps move your focus from trivial to more interesting aspects of the code that deserve more of your attention. If everyone on your team follows the same suggestions, the code in your project will have a more uniform style.

So I boldly claim that the object design rules provided in this book will improve the quality of your objects, and of your entire project. This fits well with the other goal I had in mind: that this book can be used as part of an on-boarding process for new team members. After telling them about the coding standard for the project and showing them the style guide for commit messages and code reviews, you can hand out this book and explain how your team aims for good object design in all areas of the project.

I wish you good luck on your object design journey, together with your team, and I'll do my very best to reach the goals that I've just set.

acknowledgments

Before we get to it, let me thank some people here. First of all, I'd like to thank the 125 people who bought the book before it was even finished. This was very encouraging! Thanks for your feedback, too, in particular from Сергей Лукьяненко, Iosif Chiriluta, Nikola Paunovic, Niko Mouk, Damon Jones, and Mo Khaledi. A special mention goes to Rémon van de Kamp, who provided quite a list of insightful comments.

A big thank you goes to Ross Tuck and Laura Cody for performing a thorough review of this book. Thanks to your suggestions, the arguments are better, the progression smoother, and the risk of misunderstanding lower.

All of this happened before Manning Publications adopted this book and worked on a new release with me. Mike Stephens, thanks for accepting my proposal. It has been an absolutely wonderful experience. Every conversation I've had with any staff member was very helpful: Deirdre Hiam, production editor; Andy Carroll, copyeditor; Keri Hales, proofreader; Aleksandar Dragosavljević, review editor; Tanya Wilke, technical development editor; and Justin Coulston, technical proofreader. Thanks so much for all of your hard work on this project!

I would also like to thank all of the reviewers: Angel R. Rodriguez, Bruno Sonnino, Carlos Ezequiel Curotto, Charles Soetan, Harald Kuhn, Joseph Timothy Lyons, Justin Coulston, Maria Gemini, Patrick Regan, Paul Grebenc, Samantha Berk, Scott Steinman, Shayn Cornwell, and Steve Westwood.

In particular, I want to thank Elesha Hyde, the development editor of this project. She did a great job at managing the process, as well as providing invaluable input to increase the educational value of this book.

about this book

Who should read this book

This book is for programmers with at least some basic knowledge of an object-oriented programming language. You should understand the language's possibilities regarding class design. That is, I expect you to know what it means to define a class, instantiate it, extend it, mark it as `abstract`, define a method, call it, define parameters and parameter types, define return types, define properties and their types, etc.

I also expect you to have some actual experience with all of this, even if it's not much. I think you should be able to read this book if you've just finished a basic programming course, but also if you've been working with classes for years.

How this book is organized: A roadmap

Writing a book means taking a huge amount of material and shaping it into something relatively small and manageable. This is why creativity, without any constraints, is expected to produce chaos. If you mix in some constraints, the chances of success are much larger. Setting a number of constraints for yourself will help you make most of the micro-decisions along the way, preventing you from getting stuck.

Here are the constraints I introduced for this book:

- *No chapter titles will have the name of a principle or pattern in them.* It should be clear what the advice is, without having to remember what all that jargon meant.

- *Sections will be short.* I don't want this to be a heavy book that takes months to finish. I want the programming advice to be readily available, instead of being buried deep inside oracle-like philosophical mumblings. The advice should be clear and easy to follow.
- *Chapters will have useful summaries.* If you want to quickly reread a piece of advice, or refer to it, you shouldn't be forced to read the whole chapter again. Useful summaries should conclude every chapter.
- *Code samples should come with suggestions for testing.* Good object design makes testing an object easier, and at the same time, the design of an object can improve by testing it in the right way. So it makes sense to show suggestions for (unit) testing next to suggestions for object design.

I also chose to use the following conventions:

- I use the word "client" to represent the place where the class or method gets called. Sometimes I use the term "call site."
- I use the word "user" to represent the programmer who uses your class by instantiating it and calling methods on it. Note that this usually isn't the user of the application as a whole.
- In code samples, I abbreviate statements with `//  ...` and expressions with `/*  ...  */`. I sometimes use `//` or `/*  ...  */` to add some more context to the examples.

The book starts with a chapter about programming with objects (chapter 1). This chapter also offers a very brief introduction to unit testing. It helps us settle on terminology and provides an overview of some important object-oriented concepts.

The actual style guide starts with chapter 2. We first make a distinction between two types of objects: services, and other objects. Then we discuss how service objects should be created, and that they shouldn't be manipulated after instantiation. In chapter 3 we take a look at other objects, how they should be created, and how, in some cases, they can be manipulated afterwards (chapter 4).

Chapter 5 covers some general guidelines for writing methods, allowing you to add behavior to objects. There will be two kinds of things a client can do with an object: retrieve information from it (chapter 6), or let it perform a task (chapter 7). These two use cases of an object come with different implementation rules. Chapter 8 shows how you can make a distinction between write and read models, which helps you divide the responsibilities of making changes and providing information over multiple objects.

Chapter 9 provides some advice for when it comes to changing the behavior of a service object. It shows how you can change, or enhance, the behavior of services by composing existing objects into new objects or by making behavior configurable.

Chapter 10 is a field guide to objects. It shows you around the different areas of an application, and points out the different types of objects you may encounter in these areas.

The books ends with chapter 11, where I provide a brief overview of topics you can look into if you want to know more about object design, including some recommendations for further reading.

Although this book will provide a steady learning path from beginning to end, it's also supposed to be useful as a reference guide. If you're looking for advice on a certain topic, feel free to skip to the corresponding chapter.

About the code

The code samples are written in a fictional object-oriented language that's optimized to be read by a large number of object-oriented programmers. This language does not really exist, so the code in this book can't be executed in any runtime environment. I'm confident that the code samples will be easy to understand if you have experience with a language like PHP, Java, or C#. If you want to know more about the properties of the imagined language used in this book, take a look at this book's appendix.

Some code samples will have accompanying unit test code. I assume the availability of an xUnit-style test framework (PHPUnit, JUnit, NUnit, etc.). I rely on a limited set of features when it comes to making assertions, checking for exceptions, or creating test doubles. This should make all the code samples easily portable to your own favorite testing frameworks and libraries.

liveBook discussion forum

Purchase of *Object Design Style Guide* includes free access to a private web forum run by Manning Publications where you can make comments about the book, ask technical questions, and receive help from the author and from other users. To access the forum, go to https://livebook.manning.com/book/object-design-style-guide/discussion. You can also learn more about Manning's forums and the rules of conduct at https://livebook.manning.com/#!/discussion.

Manning's commitment to our readers is to provide a venue where a meaningful dialogue between individual readers and between readers and the author can take place. It is not a commitment to any specific amount of participation on the part of the author, whose contribution to the forum remains voluntary (and unpaid). We suggest you try asking the author some challenging questions lest his interest stray! The forum and the archives of previous discussions will be accessible from the publisher's website as long as the book is in print.

about the author

Matthias Noback is a professional web developer (since 2003). He lives in Zeist, The Netherlands, with his girlfriend, son, and daughter.

Matthias has his own web development, training, and consultancy company called Noback's Office. He has a strong focus on backend development and architecture, and he's always looking for better ways to design software.

Since 2011, he's been blogging about all sorts of programming-related topics on matthiasnoback.nl. Other books by Matthias are *A Year with Symfony* (Leanpub, 2013), *Microservices for Everyone* (Leanpub, 2017), and *Principles of Package Design* (Apress, 2018). You can reach Matthias by email (info @matthiasnoback.nl) or on Twitter (@matthiasnoback).

about the cover illustration

The figure on the cover of *Object Design Style Guide* is a woman from the island of Ulijan off the coast of Croatia. The illustration is taken from a French book of dress customs, *Encyclopedie des Voyages* by Jacques Grasset de Saint-Sauveur (1757–1810), published in 1796. Travel for pleasure was a relatively new phenomenon at the time, and illustrated guides such as this one were popular, introducing both the tourist and the armchair traveler to the inhabitants of other far-off regions of the world, as well as to the more familiar regional costumes of France and Europe.

The diversity of the drawings in the *Encyclopedie des Voyages* speaks vividly of the uniqueness and individuality of the world's countries and peoples just 200 years ago. This was a time when the dress codes of two regions, sometimes separated by just a few dozen miles, identified people as belonging to one or the other, and when members of a social class or trade or tribe could be easily distinguished by what they were wearing.

Dress codes have changed since then, and the diversity by region, so rich at the time, has slowly faded away. Today it is often hard to tell the inhabitants of one continent apart from another. But diversity by nationality, ethnicity, and geography still exists in our modern world and should be recognized and honored, and this is what we at Manning celebrate with our series of historical covers that bring back to life the richness of dress codes from two centuries ago.

Programming
with objects: A primer

This chapter covers

- Working with objects
- Unit testing
- Dynamic arrays

Before we get into the actual style guide, this chapter covers some of the fundamental aspects of programming with objects. We'll briefly go over some important concepts and establish a shared terminology that we can build on in the following chapters.

We'll be covering the following topics in this chapter:

- *Classes and objects*—Creating objects based on classes, using a constructor, static versus object methods, static factory methods for creating new instances, and throwing exceptions inside a constructor (section 1.1).
- *State*—Defining private and public properties, assigning values to them, constants, and mutable versus immutable state (section 1.2).
- *Behavior*—Private and public methods, passing values as arguments, and `NullPointerExceptions` (section 1.3).
- *Dependencies*—Instantiating them, locating them, and injecting them as constructor arguments (section 1.4).

1

- *Inheritance*—Interfaces, abstract classes, overriding implementations, and final classes (section 1.5).
- *Polymorphism*—Same interface, different behavior (section 1.6).
- *Composition*—Assigning objects to properties and building more advanced objects (section 1.7).
- *Return statements and exceptions*—Returning a value from a method, throwing an exception inside a method, catching exceptions, and defining custom exception classes (section 1.9).
- *Unit testing*—Arrange-Act-Assert, testing for failures, and using test doubles to replace dependencies (section 1.10).
- *Dynamic arrays*—Using them to create lists or maps (section 1.11).

If you are somewhat familiar with all of these topics, feel free to skip this chapter and jump to chapter 2. If some topics are unknown to you, take a look at the corresponding sections. If you are just beginning as an object-oriented programmer, I recommend reading this whole chapter.

1.1   Classes and objects

The runtime behavior of an object is defined by its class definition. Using a given class, you can create any number of objects. The following listing shows a simple class, with no state or behavior, which can be instantiated.

Listing 1.1   A minimum viable class

```
class Foo
{
    // There's nothing here
}

object1 = new Foo();
object2 = new Foo();

object1 == object2 // false
```

Two instances of the same class should not be considered the same.

Once you have an instance, you can call methods on it.

Listing 1.2   Calling a method on an instance

```
class Foo
{
    public function someMethod(): void
    {
        // Do something
    }
}

object1 = new Foo();
object1.someMethod();
```

A regular method,like `someMethod()`, can only be called on an *instance* of the class. Such a method is called an *object method*. You can also define methods that can be called *without* an instance. These are called *static methods*.

Listing 1.3   Defining a static method

```
class Foo
{
    public function anObjectMethod(): void
    {
        // ...
    }

    public static function aStaticMethod(): void
    {
        // ...
    }
}
object1 = new Foo();
object1.anObjectMethod();    ◁

Foo.aStaticMethod();    ◁
```

anObjectMethod() can only be called on an instance of SomeClass.

aStaticMethod() can be called without an instance.

Besides object and static methods, a class can also contain a special method: the *constructor*. This method will be called before a reference to the object gets returned. If you need to do anything to prepare the object before it's going to be used, you can do it inside the constructor.

Listing 1.4   Defining a constructor method

```
class Foo
{
    public function __construct()
    {
        // Prepare the object
    }
}
object1 = new Foo();    ◁
```

__construct() will be implicitly called before a Foo instance gets assigned to object1.

You can prevent an object from being fully instantiated by throwing an *exception* inside the constructor, as shown in the following listing. You can read more about exceptions in section 1.9.

Listing 1.5   Throwing an exception inside the constructor

```
class Foo
{
    public function __construct()
    {
```

```
        throw new RuntimeException();
    }
}
```

It won't be possible to instantiate Foo because its constructor always throws an exception.

```
try {
    object1 = new Foo();
} catch (RuntimeException exception) {
    // `object1` will be undefined here
}
```

The standard way to instantiate a class is using the new operator, as we just saw. It's also possible to define a static *factory method* on the class itself, which returns a new instance of the class.

Listing 1.6   Defining a static factory method

```
class Foo
{
    public static function create(): Foo
    {
        return new Foo();
    }
}

object1 = Foo.create();
object2 = Foo.create();
```

The create() method has to be defined as static because it should be called on the class, not on an instance of that class.

1.2   State

An object can contain data. This data will be stored in *properties*. A property will have a *name* and a *type*, and it can be populated at any moment after instantiation. A common place for assigning values to properties is inside the constructor.

Listing 1.7   Defining properties and assigning values

```
class Foo
{
    private int someNumber;
    private string someString;

    public function __construct()
    {
        this.someNumber = 10;
        this.someString = 'Hello, world!';
    }
}

object1 = Foo.create();
```

After instantiation, someNumber and someString will contain 10 and 'Hello, world!' respectively.

The data contained in an object is also known as its *state*. If that data is going to be hardcoded, as in the previous example, you might as well make it part of the property definition or define a constant for it.

Listing 1.8   Defining constants

```
class Foo
{
    private const int someNumber = 10;        ◁─┐
    private someString = 'Hello, world!';
}
```

> Your programming language may have a different syntax. For example, in Java you would use "final private int someNumber."

On the other hand, if the initial value of a property should be *variable*, you can let the client provide a value for it as a constructor argument. By adding a parameter to the constructor, you force clients to provide a value when instantiating the class.

Listing 1.9   Adding a constructor argument

```
class Foo
{
    private int someNumber;

    public function __construct(int initialNumber)
    {
        this.someNumber = initialNumber;
    }
}

object1 = new Foo(); // doesn't work    ◁─┐
object2 = new Foo(20);                  ◁─┘
```

> It won't be possible to instantiate Foo without providing a value for initialNumber.

> This should work; it assigns the initial value of 20 to the someNumber property of the new Foo instance.

Marking the someNumber and someString properties as private makes them available to instances of Foo only. This is called *scoping*. Alternative scopes for properties are protected (see section 1.5) and public. By making a property public, you make it accessible to any client.

Listing 1.10   Defining and using a public property

```
class Foo
{
    public const int someNumber;

    public string someString;

    // ...
}

object1 = new Foo();
number = object1.someNumber;    ◁─┐
object2.someString = 'Cliché';  ◁─┘
```

> Because someNumber is defined as a constant, we can't change its value, but we can at least retrieve it.

> someString is not a constant, but it's public, so we can change it.

Private should be your default scope

In general, a `private` scope is preferable and should be your default choice. Limiting access to object data helps the object keep its implementation details to itself. It ensures that clients won't rely on any specific piece of data owned by the object, and that they will always talk to the object through explicitly defined public methods (find out more about methods in section 1.3). We'll discuss this topic in more detail in later chapters; for instance, in sections 6.3 and 9.8.

Property scoping (as well as method scoping; see section 1.3), is class-based, meaning that if a property is `private`, *any* instance of the same class has access to this property on any instance of the same class, including itself.

Listing 1.11   Accessing another instance's private property

```
class Foo
{
    private int someNumber;

    // ...

    public function getSomeNumber(): int
    {
        return this.someNumber;          Foo, of course, has access to its
    }                                    own someNumber property.

    public function getSomeNumberFrom(Foo other): int
    {
        return other.someNumber;    Foo also has access to other's
    }                               private property someNumber.
}

object1 = new Foo();
object2 = new Foo();
                                          This will return the value of
object2.getSomeNumberFrom(object1);       object1's someNumber property.
```

When the value of an object's property can change during the lifetime of the object, it's considered a *mutable* object. If none of an object's properties can be modified after instantiation, the object is considered an *immutable* object. The following listing shows examples of both cases.

Listing 1.12   Mutable vs. immutable objects

```
class Mutable
{
    private int someNumber;

    public function __construct(int initialNumber)
    {
```

```
            this.someNumber = initialNumber;
        }

    public function increase(): void
    {
        this.someNumber = this.someNumber + 1;
    }
}

class Immutable
{
    private int someNumber;

    public function __construct(int initialNumber)
    {
        this.someNumber = initialNumber;
    }

    public function increase(): Immutable
    {
        return new Immutable(someNumber + 1);
    }
}

object1 = new Mutable(10);
object1.increase();

object2 = new Immutable(10);
object2 = object2.increase();
```

Calling increase() on Mutable will change the state of object1 by changing the value of its someNumber property.

Calling increase() on Immutable doesn't change the state of object2. Instead, we receive a new instance with the value of someNumber increased.

In section 4.4 we'll take a closer look at mutable objects and how to make them immutable.

1.3 Behavior

Besides state, an object also has behaviors that its clients can make use of. These behaviors are defined as methods on the object's class. The `public` methods are the ones accessible to clients of the object. They can be called any time after the object has been created.

Some methods will return something to the caller. In that case an explicit type will be declared as the *return type*. Some methods will return nothing. In that case the return type will be `void`.

Listing 1.13 An object's behaviors are defined as public methods

```
class Foo
{
    public function someMethod(): int
    {
        return /* ... */;
    }

    public function someOtherMethod(): void
```

```
    {
        // ...
    }
}

object1 = new Foo();
value = object1.someMethod();   ◄─────┐
                                      │
object1.someOtherMethod();   ◄────────┘
```

someMethod() returns an integer, which we can capture in a variable.

someOtherMethod() doesn't return anything specific, so a client can't capture its return value.

A class can also contain `private` method definitions. This works in the same way as with private properties. Any instance of a given class can call private methods on any other instance of the same class, including itself. Usually though, private methods are used to represent smaller steps in a larger process.

Listing 1.14   Private methods

```
class Foo
{
    public function someMethod(): int
    {
        value = this.stepOne();

        return this.stepTwo(value);
    }

    private function stepOne(): int
    {
        // ...
    }

    private function stepTwo(int value): int
    {
        // ...
    }
}
```

Just like you can define constructor parameters, you can define method parameters. A caller then has to provide a specific value as an argument when calling the method. The method itself can use the value to determine what to do, it can pass it on to collaborating objects, or it can use it to change the value of a property.

Listing 1.15   Several ways in which method arguments can be used

```
class Foo
{
    private int number;

    public function setNumber(int newNumber): void   ◄──┐
    {                                                    │
        this.number = newNumber;
    }
```

Here, newNumber will become the new value of the number property.

```
private function multiply(int other): int
{
    return this.number * other;
}
```
In this case, other will be multiplied by the current value of the number property.

```
private function someOtherMethod(Bar bar): void
{
    bar.doSomething();
}
}
```
Here, another object gets passed as an argument, so Foo can call a method on it.

Check for `null` arguments

Some languages allow a client to pass `null` as an argument even if the type of a parameter has been explicitly declared. So in the example in listing 1.15, the provided argument for `bar` may be `null`, even though it's typed as `Bar`. Trying to call `doSomething()` on `bar` would then cause a `NullPointerException` to be thrown. This is why you always have to check for `null`, or preferably, let a compiler or static analyzer warn you against potential `NullPointerExceptions`.

The fictional programming language used in this book by default *does not allow* `null` to be passed as an argument. In examples where we want to allow it, we explicitly have to declare it using a question mark (?) after the type declaration of a method parameter. This also works for property types and return types:

```
class Foo
{
    private string? foo;

    private function someOtherMethod(Bar? bar): Baz?
    {
        // ...
    }
}
```

1.4   Dependencies

If object `Foo` needs object `Bar` to perform part of its job, `Bar` is called a *dependency* of `Foo`. There are different ways to make sure that `Foo` has access to the `Bar` dependency.

- It could instantiate `Bar` itself.
- It could fetch a `Bar` instance from a known location.
- It could get a `Bar` instance injected upon construction.

The following listing shows an example of each option.

Listing 1.16   Different ways for `Foo` to get access to a `Logger` instance

```
class Foo
{
    public function someMethod(): void
```

```
    {
        logger = new Logger();        ◁──┐ Foo instantiates a
        logger.debug('...');              │ Logger when needed.
    }
}

class Foo
{
    public function someMethod(): void
    {
        logger = ServiceLocator.getLogger();    ◁──┐ Foo fetches a Logger instance
        logger.debug('...');                        │ from a known location.
    }
}

class Foo
{
    private Logger logger;

    public function __construct(Logger logger)
    {
        this.logger = logger;        ◁──────┐ Foo has an instance of Logger provided
    }                                        │ to it as a constructor argument.

    public function someMethod(): void
    {
        this.logger.debug('...');
    }
}
```

We'll take a closer look at how to deal with dependencies in section 2.2. For now, it's good to know that fetching dependencies from a known location is called *service location*, and that retrieving dependencies as constructor arguments is called *dependency injection*.

1.5   *Inheritance*

It's possible to define only part of a class and let others expand on it. For instance, you can have a class with no properties and no methods, but only method signatures. Such a class is usually called an *interface*, and many object-oriented languages allow you to define it as such. A class can then implement the interface and provide the actual implementations of the methods that were defined in the interface.

Listing 1.17   Bar and Baz "implementing" the Foo interface

```
interface Foo                          The Foo interface declares
{                                      a foo() method but doesn't
    public function foo(): void;       provide an implementation.
}                              ◁──────┘

class Bar implements Foo       ◁──┐ Bar is an incorrect implementation
{                                 │ of Foo, because it doesn't have an
}                                 │ implementation for the foo() method.
```

```
class Baz implements Foo
{
    public foo(): void
    {
        // ...
    }
}
```

Baz is a correct implementation of Foo, because it provides an implementation for the foo() method.

An interface doesn't define any implementation, but an *abstract class* does. It allows you to provide the implementation for some methods and only the signatures for some other methods. An abstract class can't be instantiated, but first has to be extended by a class that provides implementations for the abstract methods.

Listing 1.18   Baz extends the abstract `Foo` class

```
abstract class Foo
{
    abstract public function foo(): void;

    public function bar(): void
    {
        // ...
    }
}
```

The foo() method is abstract and has to be defined by a subclass.

Foo provides an actual implementation for the bar() method.

```
class Baz extends Foo
{
    public function foo(): void
    {
    }
}
```

Baz is a correct implementation of Foo, because it provides an implementation for the previously abstract foo() method.

Finally, a class could provide a full implementation for all its methods but allow other classes to extend and override some of its methods.

Listing 1.19   `Bar` extends the `Foo` class and changes part of its behavior

```
class Foo
{
    public function bar(): void
    {
        // do something
    }
}

class Bar extends Foo
{
    public function bar(): void
    {
        // do something else
    }
}
```

Foo is a regular class, without any abstract methods.

Bar extends Foo, which is now its parent class. It can change the behavior of its bar() method.

Foo is a regular class, without any abstract methods.

Classes that extend from another class have access to `public` and `protected` methods of the parent class.

Listing 1.20   Access to `public` and `protected` methods

```
class Foo
{
    public function foo(): void
    {
        // do something
    }

    protected function bar(): void
    {
    }

    private function baz(): void
    {
    }
}

class Bar extends Foo
{
    public function someMethod(): void
    {
        $this->foo();

        $this->bar();

        //$this->baz();
    }
}
```

bar() is available because it's a protected method.

foo() is available because it's a public method.

baz() is not available because it's a private method.

Subclasses can only override `protected` and `public` methods of a parent class too.

Listing 1.21   Overriding `public` and `protected` methods

```
class Foo
{
    public function foo(): void
    {
        // do something
    }

    protected function bar(): void
    {
    }

    private function baz(): void
    {
    }
}
```

```
class Bar extends Foo
{
    public function foo(): void      ◁─┐  foo() can be overridden
    {                                  │  because it's a public method.
        // ...
    }

    protected function bar(): void   ◁─┐  bar() can be overridden because
    {                                  │  it's a protected method.
        // ...
    }

    private function baz(): void     ◁─┐  baz() can't be overridden
    {                                  │  because it's a private method.
        // does not work
    }
}
```

In this book, inheritance plays a small role, even though it's supposed to be a very important feature of object-oriented programming. In practice, using inheritance mostly leads to a confusing design. In this book, we'll use inheritance mainly in two situations:

- When defining interfaces for dependencies
- When defining a hierarchy of objects, such as when defining custom exceptions that extend from built-in exception classes

In most other cases we'd want to actively prevent developers to extend from our classes. You can do so by adding the `final` keyword in front of the class. You can read more about it in section 9.7.

Listing 1.22 Bar can't be extended

```
final class Bar
{
    // ...
}
                                          │  Bar is marked as final,
class Baz extends Bar // won't work  ◁─┘  so Baz can't extend it.
{
    // ...
}
```

1.6 *Polymorphism*

Polymorphism is one of the foundations of object-oriented programming. Polymorphism means that if a parameter has a certain class as its type, any object that is an instance of that class can be provided as a valid argument. For example, any instance of `Foo` can be passed as an argument to the `bar()` method in the following listing.

Listing 1.23 Any Foo instance will be accepted by bar()

```
class Foo
{
    // ...
}

final class Bar
{
    public function bar(Foo foo): void
    {
        foo.someMethod();
    }
}
```

Since one instance of Foo could have been configured in a different way, or otherwise have a different internal state than another instance of Foo, every instance of Foo could in theory behave differently. This means that you can change the behavior of bar() without changing the code in bar().

Even more variation in behavior can be introduced by subclasses. We've already looked at inheritance and how you can use it to change the behavior of a parent class by overriding (part of) its behavior in a subclass. Any object that is an instance of a subclass of Foo also counts as an instance of Foo itself. This makes any instance of that subclass of Foo a valid argument for Foo-type parameters as well.

As you'll learn in chapter 9, using subclasses to change the behavior of objects is often not recommended. In most situations it's better to use polymorphism with an interface parameter type. This looks the same in code (see the following listing), but now Foo is an interface.

Listing 1.24 Any Foo instance will be accepted by bar()

```
interface Foo        ◁—— Foo is an interface now.
{
    // ...
}

final class Bar
{
    public function bar(Foo foo): void
    {
        foo.someMethod();
    }
}
```

1.7   *Composition*

Besides being an example of polymorphism, listing 1.25 also shows how an object of instance Foo can be used by another object (of type Bar) to perform part of its job. If Foo is a service, it can also be provided to Bar as a constructor argument. Bar could then assign the Foo object to one of its properties.

Listing 1.25 The provided `Foo` instance gets assigned to a property

```
final class Bar
{
    private Foo foo;

    public function __construct(Foo foo)
    {
        this.foo = foo;
    }
}
```

Assigning an object to another object's property is called *object composition*. You are building up a more complicated object out of simpler objects. Object composition can be combined with polymorphism to compose your object out of other objects, whose (interface) type you know, but not the actual class.

Composition can be used with a service object, making part of its behavior configurable. It can also be used with other types of objects, like entities (sometimes known as *models*), where composition is used for related child elements. For example, an `Order` object that contains `Line` objects could use composition to establish the relationship between an order and its lines. In that case, a client might provide not a single `Line` object, but a collection (array) of `Line` objects.

Listing 1.26 An `Order` object assigns multiple `Line` objects to its property

```
final class Order
{
    private array lines;

    public function __construct(array lines)
    {
        this.lines = lines;          ◁———┐  Each element in lines
    }                                     │  is a Line object.
}
```

1.8 Class organization

Programming languages offer varying options for organizing classes: directories, namespaces, components, modules, packages, etc. Sometimes the language even offers ways to keep classes private to the module or package they are in. Just like with property and method scopes, this can help reduce the potential coupling surface between modules. This book doesn't contain specific rules for organizing classes into larger groups—it focuses on design rules for the classes themselves. If you're interested in component-level organization principles, take a look at one of my other books, *Principles of Package Design* (Apress, 2018).

1.9   *Return statements and exceptions*

When you call a method, it will normally be executed statement by statement from the top until a `return` statement is encountered, or the end of the method is reached. If at some point you want to prevent further execution of a method, you can insert a `return` statement, making sure that the rest of the method will be skipped.

> **Listing 1.27   A `return` statement will prevent further execution of a method**

```
final class Foo
{
    public function someMethod(): void
    {
        if (/* should we stop here? */) {
            return;                          ◁─┐  A method with a void return
        }                                        type returns nothing.

        // ...
    }

    public function someOtherMethod(): bool
    {
        if (/* should we stop here? */) {
            return false;                    ◁─┐  A method with a specific return
        }                                        type can return a specific value.

        // ...

        return true;
    }
}
```

Another way to stop execution of a method is to *throw an exception* in it. An exception is a special kind of object that, when instantiated, collects information about where the object was instantiated and what happened before (the so-called *stack trace*). Normally an exception indicates some kind of failure, such as

- The wrong method arguments were provided.
- A map has no value for the given key.
- Some external service is unreachable.

The following listing shows how to throw an exception.

> **Listing 1.28   Throwing an exception also prevents further execution of the method**

```
final class Foo
{
    public function someMethod(): void
    {
        if (/* should we stop here? */) {
            throw new RuntimeException(           You can provide a custom
                'Something is wrong'        ◁─┘   message for an exception.
```

```
        );
    }

    // ...
    }
}
```

As soon as it becomes clear that the method won't be able to perform its job correctly, it should throw an exception. The difference from a simple `return` statement is that the method doesn't return anything when it throws an exception. In fact, execution stops and can only be picked up by a client that has wrapped the method call inside a `try/catch` block. The following listing shows how that works.

Listing 1.29   A client can recover from an exception if it uses a `try/catch` block

```
foo = new Foo();

try {
    foo.someMethod();
} catch (Exception) {
    // ...
}
```

If someMethod() throws an exception, catch() will have caught it, and we can continue doing other things.

Programming languages come with their own built-in set of exception classes. They form some kind of hierarchy, like `RuntimeException extends Exception`, `InvalidArgumentException extends LogicException`. You can also define your own exception classes. They should always extend one of the built-in exception classes. The following listing shows an example.

Listing 1.30   Defining a custom exception

```
final class CanNotFindFoo extends RuntimeException
{
    // ... 1((CO25-1))
}

final class Foo
{
    public function someMethod(): void
    {
        if (/* should we stop here? */) {
            throw new CanNotFindFoo();
        }

        // ...
    }
}
```

Exceptions are an important aspect of object design. They are part of the complete set of behaviors that a client can expect from an object. We'll talk about exceptions in more detail later, such as in section 5.2.

1.10   *Unit testing*

Defining objects by writing classes is not enough. Objects serve a purpose: they will be used to perform a particular task, or to provide an answer to a specific question. To be reliable, an object needs to behave in the way clients expect. Of course, you can write a bit of code, then compile and run your application, and then find out if what you wrote provides the expected outcome. But a more solid approach would be to write a script that instantiates your object, calls one of its methods, and compares the result to some written expectation.

Unit-testing frameworks support this type of "scripted" approach. A framework will look for classes of a specific type, also called *test* classes. It will then instantiate each test class, and call each of the methods that are marked as a test (methods with the @test annotation).

The basic structure of each test method is Arrange-Act-Assert:

1 Arrange—Bring the object that we're testing (also known as the SUT, or Subject Under Test) into a certain known state.
2 Act—Call one of its methods.
3 Assert—Make some assertions about the end state.

The following listing shows a simple class with some accompanying unit tests.

Listing 1.31   A simple class with some unit tests

```
final class Foo
{
    private int someNumber;

    public function __construct(int startWith)
    {
        this.someNumber = startWith;
    }

    public function increment(): void
    {
        this.someNumber++;
    }

    public function someNumber(): int
    {
        return this.someNumber;
    }
}

final class FooTest
{
    /**
     * @test
     */
    public function you_can_start_with_a_given_number(): void
    {
```

```
        // Arrange
        foo = new Foo(10);              No actual action is performed
                                        here. We just verify the
        // Act          ⊲──────         expected state of the object.

        // Assert
        assertEquals(10, foo.someNumber());
    }

    /**
     * @test
     */
    public function you_can_increment_the_number(): void
    {
        // Arrange
        foo = new Foo(10);
                                        Here we call increment(), which is the
                                        action. Afterwards, we verify that the
        // Act                          object is in the expected state.
        foo.increment();  ⊲──────

        // Assert
        assertEquals(11, foo.someNumber());
    }
}
```

If in the second test the return value of `someNumber()` is the expected value, namely 11, everything is fine. The execution flow will continue and give back control to the test framework. If, however, `someNumber()` hasn't been fully implemented yet, or has been implemented incorrectly, the call to `assertEquals()` will cause an exception to be thrown. If, for example, `someNumber()` returns 20, the test framework will record that this test has *failed*. Once you have fixed the problem and run the test again, the test will *pass*.

`assertEquals()` and related assertions, such as `assertTrue()`, `assertNull()`, and so on, are usually built into the testing framework. They can be used to compare the return value of a successful method call. But sometimes you'll want to verify that a method call *fails* in a controlled way. For instance, if you wanted to put a restriction on the initial number provided to the constructor of `Foo` (for example, "it should be greater than or equal to 0"), you'd want to verify in a unit test that providing a negative number causes `Foo` to throw an exception. The following listing shows how you could do this using plain code.

> Listing 1.32 Testing for failures

```
final class Foo
{
    private int someNumber;

    public function __construct(int startWith)
    {
        if (startWith < 0) {
```

```
                throw new InvalidArgumentException(
                    'A negative starting number is not allowed'
                );
            }
            this.someNumber = startWith;
        }

        // ...
    }

    final class FooTest
    {
        /**
         * @test
         */
        public function you_cannot_start_with_a_negative_number(): void
        {
            try {
                new Foo(-10);
                throw new RuntimeException(
                    'The constructor should have failed'
                );
            } catch (Exception exception) {
                if (exception.className != InvalidArgumentException.className) {
                    throw new RuntimeException(
                        'We expected a different type of exception'
                    );
                }

                assertContains('negative', exception.getMessage());
            }
        }

        // ...
    }
```

If instantiating Foo with a negative number doesn't throw an exception, we should mark the test as failed.

If a caught exception's class doesn't match the expected exception class, mark the test as failed.

Finally, we verify that the exception's message contains the expected keyword.

This is a lot of boilerplate code for every failure scenario you want to test. Luckily, testing frameworks usually have some tooling for testing exceptions—something like the expectException() utility function shown in the following listing.

Listing 1.33   A utility function for testing for failures

```
    final class FooTest
    {
        /**
         * @test
         */
        public function you_cannot_start_with_a_negative_number(): void
        {
            expectException(
                InvalidArgumentException.className,
                'negative',
                function () {
```

The expected exception class

The expected message keyword

An anonymous function that calls the method that's expected to fail

```
                new Foo(-10);
            }
        );
    }

    // ...
}
```

If the object you're testing has a dependency, you may not want to use the real dependency when testing. For example, maybe that dependency would make changes to a database, or start sending out emails. Every test run would produce these undesired side effects. In a situation like this, we'll want to replace the actual dependency with a stand-in object that looks like the real dependency but replaces part of its original behavior. The following listing shows an example of this.

Listing 1.34 Using a test double

```
interface Mailer 1((CO28-1))
{
    public function sendWelcomeEmail(UserId userId): void;
}

final class ActualMailer implements Mailer          ◁─────┐
{
    public function sendWelcomeEmail(UserId userId): void      Define an
    {                                                          interface for the
        // Send an actual email                                dependency, and
    }                                                          provide a stand-in
}                                                              implementation
                                                               for it.
final class StandInMailer implements Mailer         ◁─────┘
{
    public function sendWelcomeEmail(UserId userId): void
    {
        // Do nothing
    }
}

class Foo
{
    private Mailer mailer;

    public function __construct(Mailer mailer)
    {
        this.mailer = mailer;
    }
}                                                   In a test, we can instantiate
// In a test:                                       Foo, providing the stand-in
foo = new Foo(new StandInMailer());         ◁─────  as a constructor argument.
```

If you also want to verify that Foo actually called sendWelcomeEmail(), you can use a special kind of stand-in, called a *mock*. Testing frameworks usually offer special tooling for setting up such a mock and making the required assertions. The following listing shows an example of mocking without the use of special tooling.

Listing 1.35 Using a simple mock to verify that a method was actually called

```
final class MockMailer implements Mailer
{
    private bool hasBeenCalled = false;

    public function sendWelcomeEmail(UserId userId): void
    {
        this.hasBeenCalled = true;        ◁────  The only thing this mock does is record
    }                                             the fact that its sendWelcomeEmail()
                                                  method was called.
    public function hasBeenCalled(): bool
    {
        return this.hasBeenCalled;
    }
}

class Foo
{
    private Mailer mailer;

    public function __construct(Mailer mailer)
    {
        this.mailer = mailer;
    }

    public function someMethod(): void
    {
        this.mailer.sendWelcomeEmail();
    }
}

// In a test:
mockMailer = new MockMailer();            We provide the mock
foo = new Foo(mockMailer);        ◁────   as a dependency.

foo.someMethod();                                 At the end of the test, we verify
                                                  that the mock has in fact received
assertTrue(mockMailer.hasBeenCalled());   ◁────   a call to sendWelcomeEmail().
```

We'll talk in more detail about test doubles in sections 6.6 and 7.7.

There's a lot more to say about testing and how you should approach it, but it goes beyond the scope of this book.[1] In this section, I wanted to show some of the basic techniques used in unit testing. There will be more detailed examples and discussions later in this book.

---

[1] Other good books on this topic include *Test-Driven Development: By Example* by Kent Beck (Addison-Wesley Professional, 2002); *Growing Object-Oriented Software, Guided by Tests* by Steve Freeman and Nat Pryce (Addison-Wesley Professional, 2009); and *XUnit Test Patterns* by Gerard Meszaros (Addison-Wesley Professional, 2007).

1.11 *Dynamic arrays*

This book is a style guide for object design. Most code samples will therefore focus on classes, properties, and methods. The code inside the methods is less important, so I've tried to make that code as simple as possible. However, for some examples I needed data structures like maps and lists. Using dedicated List or Map classes and explicitly specifying the types of the keys or values of their elements would make the code samples too verbose, so I decided to use something known as a *dynamic array* instead.

A dynamic array is a data structure that can be used to create both lists and maps. A *list* is a collection of values with a particular order. A list can be looped over, and you can retrieve a specific value by its index, which will be an integer starting with 0.

Listing 1.36 A dynamic array used as a list

```
emptyList = [];

listOfStrings = ['foo', 'bar'];

// Looping over a list:
foreach (listOfStrings as key => value) {
    // First time: key = 0, value = 'foo'
    // Second time: key = 1, value = 'bar'
}

// Alternatively, if the key is irrelevant:
foreach (listOfStrings as value) {
    // First time: value = 'foo'
    // Second time: value = 'bar'
}

// Retrieving the value at a specific index:
fooString = listOfStrings[0];
barString = listOfStrings[1];

// Adding items to the list:
listOfStrings[] = 'baz';
```

A *map* is also a collection of values, but the values have no particular order. Instead, each value can be added to the map with a particular key, which is a string. Using the key, you can later retrieve the value from the map. The following listing shows an example of how a dynamic array can be used as a map.

Listing 1.37 A dynamic array used as a map

```
emptyMap = [];

mapOfStrings = [
    'foo' => 'bar',
    'bar' => 'baz'
];
```

```
// Looping over a map:
foreach (mapOfStrings as key => value) {
    // First time: key = 'foo', value = 'bar'
    // Second time: key = 'bar', value = 'baz'
}

// Retrieving the value at a specific index:
fooString = mapOfStrings['foo'];
barString = mapOfStrings['bar'];

// Adding items to the map:
mapOfStrings['baz'] = 'foo';
```

These arrays are called *dynamic* because you don't have to declare a type for the keys or the values they contain, and because you don't have to provide an initial size for them. A dynamic array will grow automatically whenever you try to add a new value to it.

Summary

- Objects can be instantiated based on a given class.
- A class defines properties, constants, and methods.
- Private properties and methods are accessible to instances of the same class. Public properties and methods are accessible to any client of an object.
- An object is immutable if all of its properties can't be modified, and if all objects contained in those properties are immutable themselves.
- Dependencies can be created on the fly, fetched from a known location, or injected as constructor arguments (which is called *dependency injection*).
- Using inheritance you can override the implementation of certain methods of a parent class. An interface can declare methods but leave their implementations entirely to a class that implements the interface.
- Polymorphism means that code can use another object's methods as defined by its type (usually an interface), but that the runtime behavior can be different depending on the specific instance that is provided by the client.
- When an object assigns other objects to its properties, it's called composition.
- Unit tests specify and verify the behaviors of an object.
- While testing, you may replace an object's actual dependencies with stand-ins known as test doubles (such as stubs and mocks).
- Dynamic arrays can be used to define lists or maps without specifying types for its keys and values.

Creating services

This chapter covers

- Instantiating service objects
- Injecting and validating dependencies and configuration values
- Promoting optional constructor arguments to required ones
- Making implicit dependencies explicit
- Designing services to be immutable

In the following two chapters, we'll discuss different types of objects and the guidelines for instantiating them. Roughly speaking, there are two types of objects, and they both come with different rules. In this chapter we'll consider the first type of objects: services. The creation of other objects will be the topic of chapter 3.

2.1 Two types of objects

In an application there will typically be two types of objects:

- Service objects that either perform a task or return a piece of information
- Objects that will hold some data, and optionally expose some behavior for manipulating or retrieving that data

25

Objects of the first type will be created once, and then be used any number of times, but nothing can be changed about them. They have a very simple lifecycle. Once they've been created, they can run forever, like little machines with specific tasks. These objects are called *services*.

The second type of objects are used by the first type to complete their tasks. These objects are the materials that the services work with. For instance, a service may retrieve such an object from another service, and it would then manipulate the object and hand it over to another service for further processing (figure 2.1). The lifecycle of a material object may therefore be more complicated than that of a service: after it has been created, it could optionally be manipulated, and it may even keep an internal event log of everything that has happened to it.

Service objects are do-ers, and they often have names indicating what they do: controller, renderer, calculator, etc. Service objects can be constructed by using the `new` keyword to instantiate their class, e.g., `new FileLogger()`.

In this chapter we'll discuss all the relevant aspects of instantiating a service. You'll learn how to deal with its dependencies, what you can and can't do inside its constructor, and to instantiate it once and make it reusable many times.

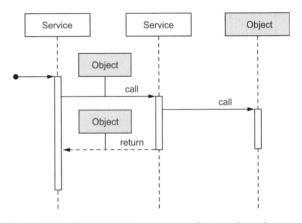

Figure 2.1   This UML-style sequence diagram shows how services will call other services, passing along other types of objects as method arguments or return values. Inside a service method, such an object may be manipulated, or a service may retrieve data from it.

Exercises

1 Which of the following are likely to be the class name of a service object?

    a `User`
    b `EventDispatcher`
    c `UserRepository`
    d `Route`

2 Which of the following are likely to be the class name of some other object?

    a `DiscountCalculator`
    b `Product`
    c `TemplateRenderer`
    d `Credentials`

2.2 Inject dependencies and configuration values as constructor arguments

A service usually needs other services to do its job. Those other services are its dependencies, and they should be injected as constructor arguments. The following `File-Logger` class is an example of a service with its dependency.

Listing 2.1 The `FileLogger` service

```
interface Logger
{
    public function log(string message): void;
}

final class FileLogger implements Logger
{
    private Formatter formatter;                        Formatter is a
                                                        dependency of
    public function __construct(Formatter formatter)  ◁─ FileLogger.
      {
          this.formatter = formatter;
      }

    public function log(string message): void
      {
          formattedMessage = this.formatter.format(message);

          // ...
      }
}

logger = new FileLogger(new DefaultFormatter());
logger.log('A message');
```

Making every dependency available as a constructor argument will make the service ready for use immediately after instantiation. No further setup will be required, and you can't accidentally forget to provide a dependency.

Sometimes a service needs some configuration values, like a location for storing files or credentials for connecting to an external service. Inject such configuration values as constructor arguments too, as in the following listing.

Listing 2.2 `FileLogger` has a dependency and needs a configuration value

```
final class FileLogger implements Logger
{
    // ...
                                                  logFilePath is a configuration value
    private string logFilePath;                   that tells the FileLogger to which file
                                                  the messages should be written.
    public function __construct(          ◁─
        Formatter formatter,
        string logFilePath
```

```
    ) {
        // ...

        this.logFilePath = logFilePath;
    }

    public function log(string message): void
    {
        // ...

        file_put_contents(
            this.logFilePath,
            formattedMessage,
            FILE_APPEND
        );
    }
}
```

These configuration values may be globally available in your application in some kind of parameter bag, settings object, or other large data structure, along with other configuration values. Instead of injecting the whole configuration object, make sure you only inject the values that the service actually needs.

Exercises

3 Rewrite the constructor of `FileCache` to receive only the configuration values it needs, instead of the application's entire configuration object:

```
final class FileCache implements Cache
{
    private AppConfig appConfig;

    public function __construct(AppConfig appConfig)
    {
        this.appConfig = appConfig;
    }

    public function get(string cacheKey): string
    {
        directory = this.appConfig.get('cache.directory');

        // ...
    }
}
```

2.2.1 *Keeping together configuration values that belong together*

A service shouldn't get the entire global configuration object injected—only the values that it needs. However, some of these values will always be used together, and injecting them separately would break their natural cohesion. Take a look at the following example, where an API client gets the credentials for connecting to the API injected as separate constructor arguments.

Listing 2.3   Using separate constructor arguments for username and password

```
final class ApiClient
{
    private string username;
    private string password;

    public function __construct(string username, string password)
    {
        this.username = username;
        this.password = password;
    }
}
```

To keep these values together, you can introduce a dedicated configuration object. Instead of injecting the username and password separately, inject a Credentials object that contains both.

Listing 2.4   Username and password are now together in a `Credentials` object

```
final class Credentials
{
    private string username;
    private string password;

    public function __construct(string username, string password)
    {
        this.username = username;
        this.password = password;
    }

    public function username(): string
    {
        return this.username;
    }

    public function password(): string
    {
        return this.password;
    }
}

final class ApiClient
{
    private Credentials credentials;

    public function __construct(Credentials credentials)
    {
        this.credentials = credentials;
    }
}
```

Exercises

4   Rewrite the constructor of the `MySQLTableGateway` class in such a way that the connection information can be passed as an object:

```
final class MySQLTableGateway
{
    public function __construct(
        string host,
        int port,
        string username,
        string password,
        string database,
        string table
    ) {
        // ...
    }
}
```

2.3   *Inject what you need, not where you can get it from*

If a framework or library is complicated enough, it will offer you a special kind of object that holds every service and configuration value you could ever want to use. Common names for such a thing are service locator, manager, registry, or container.

What's a service locator?

A service locator is itself a service, from which you can retrieve other services. The following example shows a service locator that has a `get()` method. When called, the locator will return the service with the given identifier, or throw an exception if the identifier is invalid.

Listing 2.5   A simplified implementation of a service locator

```
final class ServiceLocator
{
    private array services;

    public function __construct()
    {
        this.services = [
            'logger' => new FileLogger(/* ... */)    ◁——  You can have
        ];                                                  any number of
    }                                                       services here.

    public function get(string identifier): object
    {
        if (!isset(this.services[identifier])) {
            throw new LogicException(
```

```
                    'Unknown service: ' . identifier
            );
        }

        return this.services[identifier];
    }
}
```

In this sense, a service locator is like a map; you can retrieve services from it as long as you know the correct key. In practice, this key is often the name of the service class or interface that you want to retrieve.

The implementation of a service locator is usually more advanced than the preceding example. A service locator often knows how to instantiate all the services of an application, and it will take care of providing the right constructor arguments when doing so. It will also reuse already instantiated services, which can improve runtime performance.

Because a service locator gives you access to all of the available services in an application, it may be tempting to inject a service locator as a constructor argument and be done with it, as in the following listing.

Listing 2.6 Using a `ServiceLocator` to retrieve dependencies

```
final class HomepageController
{                                           Instead of injecting the dependencies we need, we
    private ServiceLocator locator;         inject the whole ServiceLocator, from which we can
                                                  later retrieve any specific dependency.
    public function __construct(ServiceLocator locator)
    {
        this.locator = locator;
    }

    public function execute(Request request): Response
    {
        user = this.locator.get(EntityManager.className)
            .getRepository(User.className)
            .getById(request.get('userId'));

        return this.locator.get(ResponseFactory.className)
            .create()
            .withContent(
                this.locator.get(TemplateRenderer.className)
                    .render(
                        'homepage.html.twig',
                        [
                            'user' => user
                        ]
                    ),
                'text/html'
            );
    }
}
```

This results in a lot of extra function calls in the code, obscuring what `Homepage-Controller` really does. Furthermore, because services aren't injected as dependencies, `HomepageController` needs to know how to retrieve them. Finally, this service now has access to many other services that can be retrieved from the service locator. Eventually this service will end up fetching all kinds of unrelated things from the service locator because it doesn't push the programmer to look for a better design alternative.

To prevent all these problems, we can apply the following rule: Whenever a service needs another service in order to perform its task, it should declare the latter explicitly as a dependency and get it injected as a constructor argument. The `ServiceLocator` in the preceding example is not a true dependency of `HomepageController`; it's used to *retrieve* the actual dependencies. So instead of declaring `ServiceLocator` as a dependency, the controller should declare the actual dependencies that it needs as constructor arguments, and expect them to be injected.

Listing 2.7   Injecting the actual dependencies as constructor arguments

```
final class HomepageController
{
    private EntityManager entityManager;
    private ResponseFactory responseFactory;
    private TemplateRenderer templateRenderer;

    public function __construct(
        EntityManager entityManager,
        ResponseFactory responseFactory,
        TemplateRenderer templateRenderer
    ) {
        this.entityManager = entityManager;
        this.responseFactory = responseFactory;
        this.templateRenderer = templateRenderer;
    }

    public function execute(Request request): Response
    {
        user = this.entityManager.getRepository(User.className)
            .getById(request.get('userId'));

        return this.responseFactory
            .create()
            .withContent(
                this.templateRenderer.render(
                    'homepage.html.twig',
                    [
                        'user' => user
                    ]
                ),
                'text/html'
            );
    }
}
```

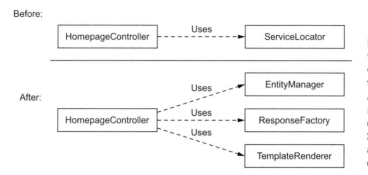

Figure 2.2 **In the initial version, `Homepage-Controller` only seemed to have one dependency. After we get rid of the `ServiceLocator` dependency, it's clear that `HomepageController` actually has three dependencies.**

The resulting dependency graph, shown in figure 2.2, is much more honest about the actual dependencies of the class.

We should make another iteration here. We only need `EntityManager` because we fetch the user repository from it. We should make the repository an explicit dependency instead.

Listing 2.8 The actual dependency is `UserRepository`, not `EntityManager`

```
final class HomepageController
{
    private UserRepository userRepository;
    // ...

    public function __construct(
        UserRepository userRepository,
        /* ... */
    ) {
        this.userRepository = userRepository
        // ...
    }

    public function execute(Request request): Response
    {
        user = this.userRepository
            .getById(request.get('userId'));
        // ...
    }
}
```

What if I need the service and the service I retrieve from it?

Consider the following code that needs both the `EntityManager` and `User-Repository` dependencies:

```
user = this.entityManager
    .getRepository(User.className)
    .getById(request.get('userId'));
user.changePassword(newPassword);
this.entityManager.flush();
```

(continued)

If we follow the advice to inject `UserRepository` instead of `EntityManager`, we'll end up with an extra dependency, because we'll still need `EntityManager` for flushing (persisting) the entity.

Situations like this usually require a redistribution of responsibilities. The object that can retrieve a `User` entity might just as well be able to persist any changes that are made to it. In fact, such an object would follow an established pattern, the *Repository* pattern. Since we already have a `UserRepository` class, it would make sense to add a `flush()`, or (now that we have the opportunity to choose another name) `save()` method to it:

```
user = this.userRepository.getById(request.get('userId'));
user.changePassword(newPassword);
this.userRepository.save(user);
```

Exercises

5   How can you know if you're injecting the right dependency into the constructor of a service object?

   a   If the service calls any method on it.
   b   If the service retrieves a dependency from it.
   c   If the service doesn't retrieve a dependency from it, but uses the dependency directly.

2.4 *All constructor arguments should be required*

Sometimes you may feel like a dependency is optional; the object could function very well without it. An example of such an optional dependency could be the `Logger` we just saw. You may consider logging to be a secondary concern for the task at hand.

   To make it an optional dependency of a service, you can make it an optional constructor argument, as in the following listing.

Listing 2.9 `Logger` as an optional constructor argument

```
final class BankStatementImporter
{
    private Logger? logger;

    public function __construct(Logger? logger = null)      logger can be null
    {                                                       or an instance of
        this.logger = logger;                           ◁── Logger.
    }

    public function import(string bankStatementFilePath): void
```

```
    {
        // Import the bank statement file

        // Every now and then log some information for debugging...
    }
}
importer = new BankStatementImporter();
```

BankStatementImporter can be instantiated without a Logger instance.

However, this unnecessarily complicates the code inside the BankStatementImporter class. Whenever you want to log something, you first have to check if a Logger instance has indeed been provided (if you don't, and no Logger has been injected, you'll get a fatal error):

```
public function import(string bankStatementFilePath): void
{
    // ...

    if (this.logger instanceof Logger) {
        this.logger.log('A message');
    }
}
```

To prevent this kind of workaround for optional dependencies, every dependency should be a required one.

　　The same goes for configuration values. You may feel like the user of a FileLogger doesn't really *have* to provide a path to write log messages to if a sensible default path exists. You could add a default value for the corresponding constructor argument as follows.

Listing 2.10　The client doesn't have to provide a value for `logFilePath`

```
final class FileLogger implements Logger
{
    public function __construct(
        string logFilePath = '/tmp/app.log'
    ) {
        // ...
    }
}
logger = new FileLogger();
```

If the user omits the logFilePath argument, /tmp/app.log will be used.

However, when someone instantiates this FileLogger class, it won't be immediately clear to which file the log messages will be written. The situation gets worse if the default value is buried deeper in the code, as in the following example.

Listing 2.11　The default value for `logFilePath` is hidden in `log()`

```
final class FileLogger implements Logger
{
    private string? logFilePath;
```

```
    public function __construct(string? logFilePath = null)
    {
        this.logFilePath = logFilePath;
    }

    public function log(string message): void
    {
        // ...

        file_put_contents(
            this.logFilePath != null ? this.logFilePath : '/tmp/app.log',
            formattedMessage,
            FILE_APPEND
        );
    }
}
```

To figure out which file path a `FileLogger` actually uses, the user must dive into the code of the `FileLogger` class itself. Also, the default path is now an implementation detail that could easily change without the user noticing.

Instead, you should always let the user of the class provide any configuration value the object needs. If you do this for all classes, you can find out how an object has been configured simply by looking at how it's instantiated.

In summary, whether constructor arguments are used to inject dependencies or to provide configuration values, constructor arguments should always be required and not have default values.

2.5   *Only use constructor injection*

Another trick that's used to optionally inject dependencies is to add a setter to the class, which can be called if the user decides they want to use the dependency. An example of this approach is the `setLogger()` method of `BankStatementImporter`, which allows the client to inject a `Logger` service into it after it has been constructed.

Listing 2.12   A `Logger` can be provided later by calling `setLogger()`

```
final class BankStatementImporter
{
    private Logger? logger;

    public function __construct()
    {
    }

    public function setLogger(Logger logger): void
    {
        this.logger = logger;
    }

    // ...
```

```
}

importer = new BankStatementImporter();

importer.setLogger(logger);
```

This solution comes with the same problem described earlier: it complicates the code inside the class. Furthermore, setter injection violates two rules that we'll cover later:

- It shouldn't be possible to create an object in an incomplete state.
- Services should be immutable, that is, impossible to change after they have been fully instantiated.

In short, don't use setter injection; only use constructor injection.

2.6 *There's no such thing as an optional dependency*

The previous sections can be summarized as: "There's no such thing as an optional dependency." You either need the dependency, or you don't. Still, suppose you really consider logging to be a secondary concern. Now that I've advised you to use only constructor injection and make all constructor arguments required, what can you do about it? In many cases you can resort to using a stand-in object that looks just like the real thing but doesn't do anything, like the following `NullLogger` implementation of the `Logger` interface.

> **Listing 2.13 An implementation of the `Logger` interface that does nothing**

```
final class NullLogger implements Logger
{
    public function log(string message): void
    {
        // Do nothing
    }
}

importer = new BankStatementImporter(new NullLogger());
```

Such a harmless object is often called a *null object*, or sometimes a *dummy*.

If the injected optional dependency isn't a service, but a configuration value of some sort, you can use a similar approach. The configuration value should still be a required argument, but you should provide a way for the user to obtain a sensible default value.

> **Listing 2.14 A default `Configuration` object can easily be obtained**

```
final class MetadataFactory
{
    public function __construct(Configuration configuration)
    {
```

```
        // ...
    }
}

metadataFactory = new MetadataFactory(
    Configuration.createDefault()
);
```

> Instead of making MetadataFactory's configuration argument optional, provide a Configuration class with a sensible default state.

Exercises

6   The `CsvImporter` class has an optional dependency on an object that imple-
    ments the `EventDispatcher` interface. Rewrite the `CsvImporter` class, promot-
    ing `EventDispatcher` to a required dependency. Provide a convenient
    alternative for users who don't want to inject a full-blown `EventDispatcher`.

```
interface EventDispatcher
{
    public function dispatch(string eventName): void;
}

final class CsvImporter
{
    private EventDispatcher? eventDispatcher;

    public function __construct(EventDispatcher? eventDispatcher)
    {
        this.setEventDispatcher(eventDispatcher);
    }

    public function setEventDispatcher(
        EventDispatcher eventDispatcher
    ): void {
        this.eventDispatcher = eventDispatcher;
    }
}
```

2.7   *Make all dependencies explicit*

If all of your dependencies and configuration values have been properly injected as
constructor arguments, there may still be room for *hidden dependencies*. They are
hidden, because they can't be recognized by taking a quick look at the constructor
arguments.

2.7.1   *Turn static dependencies into object dependencies*

In some applications, it's possible to retrieve globally available dependencies using
static accessors. Anywhere in your code, you can make calls like `ServiceRegistry`
`.get()` or `Cache.get()`. Every time a service retrieves its dependencies like this,
rewrite the service to receive these dependencies as injected constructor arguments
instead. This has the extra advantage of making the all dependencies explicit.

Listing 2.15 Inject a `Cache` instance instead of using its static methods

```
// Before:
final class DashboardController
{
    public function execute(): Response
    {
        recentPosts = [];

        if (Cache.has('recent_posts')) {
            recentPosts = Cache.get('recent_posts');
        }

        // ...
    }
}


// After:
final class DashboardController
{
    private Cache cache;

    public function __construct(Cache cache)
    {
        this.cache = cache;
    }

    public function execute(): Response
    {
        recentPosts = [];

        if (this.cache.has('recent_posts')) {
            recentPosts = this.cache.get('recent_posts');
        }

        // ...
    }
}
```

2.7.2 *Turn complicated functions into object dependencies*

Sometimes dependencies are hidden because they are functions, not objects. These functions are often part of the standard library of the language, such as `json_encode()` or `simplexml_load_file()`, and there's a lot of functionality behind these functions. If you had to write the code for them yourself, you would have to introduce lots of classes to deal with the complexity, and you would eventually inject the whole thing as a dependency into your service. This would make it a true object dependency of the service, instead of a hidden dependency, which a function usually is.

You can promote these functions to become true service dependencies by introducing a custom class that wraps the function call. The wrapper class is a great starting place to add custom logic around the standard library function, such as providing default arguments or improving the way it handles errors.

Listing 2.16   JsonEncoder wraps the `json_encode()` call

```
// Before:

final class ResponseFactory
{
    public function createApiResponse(array data): Response
    {
        return new Response(
            json_encode(data, JSON_THROW_ON_ERROR | JSON_FORCE_OBJECT),   <─┐
            [                                                               │
                'Content-Type' => 'application/json'              json_encode() is a
            ]                                                     hidden dependency.
        );
    }
}

// After:

final class JsonEncoder
{
    /**
     * @throws RuntimeException
     */
    public function encode(array data): string
    {
        try {                                              From now on, a call
            return json_encode(                            to json_encode() will
                data,                                      always have the
                JSON_THROW_ON_ERROR | JSON_FORCE_OBJECT   <─┘ right arguments.
            );
        } catch (RuntimeException previous) {                               <─┐
            throw new RuntimeException(                                       │
                'Failed to encode data: ' . var_export(data, true),          │
                0,
                previous                         We can throw our own exception
            );                                   now, providing more information
        }                                        that will help us with debugging.
    }
}

final class ResponseFactory
{
    private JsonEncoder jsonEncoder;

    public function __construct(JsonEncoder jsonEncoder)   <─┐
    {                                                         A JsonEncoder
        this.jsonEncoder = jsonEncoder;                       instance can now be
    }                                                         injected as an actual,
                                                              explicit dependency.
    public function createApiResponse(data): Response
    {
        return new Response(
            this.jsonEncoder.encode(data),
            [
```

```
                           'Content-Type' => 'application/json'
                 ]
             );
        }
    }
}
```

Promoting the job of JSON encoding to a true object dependency of `Response-Factory` makes it easier for the user of this class to form a picture of what it does, simply by looking at its list of constructor arguments. Introducing an object dependency is also the first step toward making the behavior of the service reconfigurable without touching its code. We'll get back to this topic in chapter 9.

Should all functions be promoted to object dependencies?

Not all functions have to wrapped in objects and be injected as dependencies. For instance, functions that could easily be written inline (`array_keys()`, `strpos()`, etc.) definitely don't need to be wrapped.

To determine whether or not you should extract an object dependency, you could ask the following questions:

- Will you want to replace or enhance the behavior provided by this dependency at some point?
- Is there a certain level of complexity to the behavior of this dependency, such that you couldn't achieve the same result with just a few lines of custom code?
- Is the function dealing with objects instead of just primitive-type values?

If the answers are mostly yes, you'd likely want to turn the function call into an object dependency. An added benefit of doing so is that it will be easier to describe in a test what behavior you expect from it. This will help you replace the function call with another one, with some custom code, or maybe even with an entire library that exposes the same behavior.

2.7.3 Make system calls explicit

A subset of functions and classes provided by the language will also count as implicit dependencies: functions that reach out to the world outside. Examples are a `DateTime` class and functions like `time()` and `file_get_contents()`.

Consider the following `MeetupRepository` class, which depends on the system clock to get the current time.

Listing 2.17 `MeetupRepository` depends on the current time

```
final class MeetupRepository
{
    private Connection connection;
```

```
    public function __construct(Connection connection)
    {
        this.connection = connection;
    }

    public function findUpcomingMeetups(string area): array
    {
        now = new DateTime();

        return this.findMeetupsScheduledAfter(now, area);
    }

    public function findMeetupsScheduledAfter(
        DateTime time,
        string area
    ): array {
        // ...
    }
}
```

Instantiating a DateTime object with no arguments will implicitly ask the system what the current time is.

The current time isn't something that this service could derive from either the provided method arguments, or from any of its dependencies, so it's a hidden dependency. Since there is no service available to get the current time, you have to define your own, as in the following listing.

Listing 2.18 `Clock` can be used to retrieve the current time

```
interface Clock
{
    public function currentTime(): DateTime;
}
```

A suitable name for this new service, which can tell us the current time, would simply be "Clock."

```
final class SystemClock implements Clock
{
    public function currentTime(): DateTime
    {
        return new DateTime();
    }
}
```

The standard implementation for this service will use the system's clock to return a DateTime object representing the current time.

```
final class MeetupRepository
{
    // ...
    private Clock clock;

    public function __construct(
        Clock clock,
        /* ... */
    ) {
        this.clock = clock;
    }

    public function findUpcomingMeetups(string area): array
```

```
    {
        now = this.clock.currentTime();
        // ...
    }
}
```

> Instead of "creating" the current time on the spot, we can now ask the Clock service for it.

```
meetupRepository = new MeetupRepository(new SystemClock());
meetupRepository.findUpcomingMeetups('NL');
```

By moving the system call ("What's the current time?") outside of the `Meetup-Repository` class, we have improved the testability of the `MeetupRepository` class itself. If we had run tests in the original situation, the class would have used the actual current time. This makes the result of the test dependent on the date and time when the test runs. That's likely to make the test unstable, and cause it to fail after a certain date. Instead of applying patches to the problem, we can now use the `Clock` interface and replace the "current time" based on the system's clock with a "fixed time" that's completely under our control, something like the following.

Listing 2.19 A `Clock` implementation where time is fixed

```
final class FixedClock implements Clock
{
    private DateTime now;

    public function __construct(DateTime now)
    {
        this.now = now;
    }

    public function currentTime(): DateTime
    {
        return this.now;
    }
}

meetupRepository = new MeetupRepository(
    new FixedClock(
        new DateTime('2018-12-24 11:16:05')
    )
);
meetupRepository.findUpcomingMeetups('NL');
```

> The FixedClock implementation of the Clock interface can be used in tests. When instantiating it, we have to provide a DateTime object that represents the current time.

> When testing MeetupRepository, we pass in a FixedClock as a constructor argument. This will make the test results fully deterministic.

Passing in a `Clock` object as a constructor argument allows the `MeetupRepository` to request the current time. But we could also let the client of `MeetupRepository` provide the current time as a method argument of `findUpcomingMeetups()`. Then there would no longer be a need for the `Clock` dependency.

Listing 2.20   You can also pass the current time as a method argument

```
final class MeetupRepository
{
    public function __construct(/* ... */)        ◁──┐ The Clock dependency
    {                                                 │ is no longer needed.
        // ...
    }

    public function findUpcomingMeetups(
        string area,
        DateTime now                      ◁──┐ The current time will be provided
    ): array {                                │ by clients of this method.
        // ...
    }
}
```

We should now revise our initial assessment that retrieving the current time is something we need an object dependency for. Passing the current time as a method argument turns it into contextual information that is needed to perform the task of finding upcoming meetups.

Exercises

7   A UUID is a random number that can be used to refer uniquely to objects in your application. Creating a new UUID relies on the system's random device. The following code creates a new UUID using a package dedicated to this:

```
final class CreateUser
{
    public function create(string username): void
    {
        userId = Uuid.create();

        user = new User(userId, username);
        // ...
    }
}
```

What's wrong with this code?

a Uuid is a static dependency and should be turned into an object dependency.

b The Uuid object is a dependency of the service, and should therefore be injected as a constructor argument.

c Uuid is a configuration value, and should therefore be injected as a constructor argument.

d Uuid.create() involves a call to something outside the application, so it should be created by a service dependency.

2.8   *Task-relevant data should be passed as method arguments instead of constructor arguments*

As you know, a service should get all of its dependencies and configuration values injected as constructor arguments. But information about the task itself, including any relevant contextual information, should be provided as method arguments.

As a counterexample, consider an `EntityManager` that can only be used to save one entity to the database.

Listing 2.21   An `EntityManager` that can only be used to save a single object

```
final class EntityManager
{
    private object entity;

    public function __construct(object entity)
    {
        this.entity = entity;
    }

    public function save(): void
    {
        // ...
    }
}

user = new User(/* ... */);
comment = new Comment(/* ... */);

entityManager = new EntityManager(user);
entityManager.save();

entityManager = new EntityManager(comment);
entityManager.save();
```

To save another entity, we'd have to instantiate another **EntityManager.**

This wouldn't be a very useful class, because you'd have to instantiate it again for every job you have for it.

Having an entity as a constructor argument may look like an obviously bad choice of design. A more subtle, and more common scenario would be a service that gets the current `Request` or the current `Session` object injected as a constructor argument.

Listing 2.22   `ContactRepository` depends on a `Session` object

```
final class ContactRepository
{
    private Session session;

    public function __construct(Session session)
    {
        this.session = session;
    }
```

```
    public function getAllContacts(): array
    {
        return this.select()
            .where([
                'userId' => this.session.getUserId(),
                'companyId' => this.session.get('companyId')
            ])
            .getResult();
    }
}
```

This `ContactRepository` service can't be used to get the contacts of a different user or company than the one known to the current `Session` object. That is, it can only run in one context.

Injecting part of the job details as constructor arguments gets in the way of making the service reusable, and the same goes for contextual data. All of this information should be passed as method arguments, in order to make the service reusable for different jobs.

A guiding question to help you decide whether something should be passed as a constructor argument or as a method argument is, "Could I run this service in a batch, without requiring it to be instantiated over and over again?" Depending on your programming language, you may already be used to the idea that your service will be instantiated once and should be prepared for reuse. However, if you use PHP, any object that gets instantiated will usually last only as long as it takes to process an HTTP request and return a response. In that case, when designing your services, you should always ask yourself, "If memory was not wiped after every web request, could this service be used for subsequent requests, or would it have to be reinstantiated?"

Take another look at the `EntityManager` service we saw earlier. It would be impossible to save multiple entities in a batch without instantiating the service again, so `entity` should become a parameter of the `save()` method, instead of being a constructor argument.

> ### Listing 2.23 `entity` should be a method argument

```
final class EntityManager
{
    public function save(object entity): void
    {
        // ...
    }
}
```

The same goes for `ContactRepository`. It couldn't be used in a batch to get the contacts for different users and different companies. `getAllContacts()` should have extra arguments for the current company and user ID, as follows.

Listing 2.24 UserId and CompanyId should be passed as method arguments

```
final class ContactRepository
{
    public function getAllContacts(
        UserId userId,
        CompanyId companyId
    ): array {
        return this.select()
            .where([
                'userId' => userId,
                'companyId' => companyId
            ])
            .getResult();
    }
}
```

In fact, the word "current" is a useful signal that this information is contextual information that needs to be passed as method arguments: "the current time," "the currently logged in user ID," "the current web request," etc.

Exercises

8 What's wrong with the following code?

```
final Translator
{
    private string userLanguage;

    public function __construct(string userLanguage)
    {
        this.userLanguage = userLanguage;
    }

    public function translate(string messageKey): string
    {
        // ...
    }
}
```

  a The userLanguage constructor argument should have a default value, in case there is no logged-in user.
  b The current user's language should be retrieved from a service, which should be injected as a constructor argument.
  c userLanguage should be passed as an argument when calling translate().
  d Passing in userLanguage as a constructor argument makes it harder for Translator to be reused.

2.9   *Don't allow the behavior of a service to change after it has been instantiated*

As we saw earlier, when you inject optional dependencies into a service after instantiation, you will change the behavior of a service. This makes the service unpredictable. The same goes for methods that don't inject dependencies but allow you to influence the behavior of the service from outside. An example would be the `ignoreErrors()` method of the `Importer` class in the following listing.

Listing 2.25   Calling `ignoreErrors()` changes the behavior of `Importer`

```
final class Importer
{
    private bool ignoreErrors = true;

    public function ignoreErrors(bool ignoreErrors): void
    {
        this.ignoreErrors = ignoreErrors;
    }

    // ...
}

importer = new Importer();
                                         When we use Importer now, it
// ...                           ◁───    will ignore errors.

importer.ignoreErrors(false);
                                         When we use it now, it
// ...                           ◁───    won't ignore errors.
```

Make sure that this can't happen. All dependencies and configuration values should be there from the start, and it shouldn't be possible to reconfigure the service after it has been instantiated.

Another example is an `EventDispatcher` in the following listing. It allows the list of active listeners to be reconfigured after it has been instantiated.

Listing 2.26   The behavior of `EventDispatcher` can change after instantiation

```
final class EventDispatcher
{
    private array listeners = [];
                                         You can add a new event listener
    public function addListener(  ◁───   for the given type of event.
        string event,
        callable listener
    ): void {
        this.listeners[event][] = listener;
    }
                                         You can also remove
    public function removeListener(  ◁─  an existing listener.
```

```
        string event,
        callable listener
    ): void {
        foreach (this.listenersFor(event) as key => callable) {
            if (callable == listener) {
                unset(this.listeners[event][key]);
            }
        }
    }

    public function dispatch(object event): void
    {
        foreach (this.listenersFor(event.className) as callable) {
            callable(event);
        }
    }

    private function listenersFor(string event): array
    {
        if (isset(this.listeners[event])) {
            return this.listeners[event];
        }

        return [];
    }
}
```

Any listener that hasn't been removed yet will be called.

Allowing event listeners to be added and removed on the fly makes the behavior of `EventDispatcher` unpredictable because it can change over time. In this case, we should turn the array of event listeners into a constructor argument and remove the `addListener()` and `removeListener()` methods, as is done in the following listing.

Listing 2.27   Listeners can only be configured at construction time

```
final class EventDispatcher
{
    private array listeners;

    public function __construct(array listenersByEventName)
    {
        this.listeners = listenersByEventName;
    }

    // ...
}
```

Because `array` isn't a very specific type and could contain anything (if you use a dynamically typed programming language), you should validate the `listenersBy-EventName` argument before assigning it. We'll take a closer look at validating constructor arguments later in this chapter.

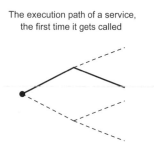

The execution path of a service, the first time it gets called

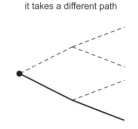

The second time it gets called, it takes a different path

Figure 2.3   Allowing the behavior of a service to be modified after instantiation causes it to behave unpredictably for some clients, because it may suddenly take a different execution path.

If you don't allow a service to be modified after instantiation, and you also don't allow it to have optional dependencies, the resulting service will behave predictably over time, and won't suddenly start to follow different execution paths based on who called a method on it (see figure 2.3).

"In the type of applications I build, I actually need mutable services."
Good point. My background is mostly in web application development. Web applications really don't need mutable services—the full set of behaviors of a service can always be defined at construction time.

You may be working on other types of applications, where you do need a service like an event dispatcher that allows you to add and remove listeners or subscribers after construction time. For instance, if you're creating a game, or some other kind of interactive application with a UI, and a user opens a new window, you'd want to register event listeners for its UI elements. Later on, when the user closes the window, you'd want to remove those listeners again. In those cases, services really do need to be mutable. However, if you're designing such mutable services, I encourage you to think about ways to not let objects reconfigure other objects' behaviors using public methods like addListener() and removeListener().

2.10   *Do nothing inside a constructor, only assign properties*

Creating a service means injecting constructor arguments, thereby preparing the service for use. The real work will be done inside one of the object's methods. Inside a constructor, you may sometimes be tempted to do more than just assign properties, to make the object truly ready for use. Take, for example, the following FileLogger class. Upon construction, it will prepare the log file for writing.

Listing 2.28   FileLogger creates a log file directory if necessary

```
final class FileLogger implements Logger
{
    private string logFilePath;

    public function __construct(string logFilePath)
```

```
    {
        logFileDirectory = dirname(logFilePath);
        if (!is_dir(logFileDirectory)) {
            mkdir(logFileDirectory, 0777, true);
        }

        touch(logFilePath);

        this.logFilePath = logFilePath;
    }

    // ...
}
```

⟵ Create the directory if it doesn't exist yet.

But instantiating a `FileLogger` will leave a trace on the filesystem, even if you never actually use the object to write a log message.

It's considered good object manners to not do anything inside a constructor. The only thing you should do in a service constructor is validate the provided constructor arguments, and then assign them to the object's properties.

Listing 2.29   The constructor of `FileLogger` doesn't create the directory

```
final class FileLogger implements Logger
{
    private string logFilePath;

    public function __construct(string logFilePath)
    {
        this.logFilePath = logFilePath;
    }

    public function log(string message): void
    {
        this.ensureLogFileExists();

        // ...
    }

    private function ensureLogFileExists(): void
    {
        if (is_file(this.logFilePath)) {
            return;
        }

        logFileDirectory = dirname(this.logFilePath);
        if (!is_dir(logFileDirectory)) {
            mkdir(logFileDirectory, 0777, true);
        }

        touch(this.logFilePath);
    }
}
```

⟵ Only copy values into properties.

Pushing the work outside of the constructor, deeper into the class, is one possible solution. In this case, however, we will only find out if it's possible to write to the log file when the first message is written to it. Most likely, we will want to hear about such problems sooner. What we could do instead is push the work outside of the constructor: we don't want it to happen after constructing the FileLogger, but before. Maybe a LoggerFactory could take care of that.

Listing 2.30   The `LoggerFactory` will create the log file directory

```
final class FileLogger implements Logger
{
    private string logFilePath;

    public function __construct(string logFilePath)          We expect that the log file
    {                                                        path has already been
        if (!is_writable(logFilePath)) {                     properly set up, so all we
            throw new InvalidArgumentException(              do here is a safety check.
                'Log file path "{logFilePath}" should be writable'
            );
        }
        this.logFilePath = logFilePath;
    }

    public function log(string message): void
    {
        // ...                          No need for a call to
    }                                   ensureLogFileExists()
}                                       or anything.

final class LoggerFactory
{
    public function createFileLogger(string logFilePath): FileLogger
    {
        if (!is_file(logFilePath)) {
            logFileDirectory = dirname(logFilePath);
            if (!is_dir(logFileDirectory)) {
                mkdir(logFileDirectory, 0777, true);
            }

                                    The task of creating the log directory and
            touch(logFilePath);     file should be moved to the bootstrap
        }                           phase of the application itself.

        return new FileLogger(logFilePath);
    }
}
```

Note that moving the log file setup code outside the constructor of FileLogger changes the contract of the FileLogger itself. In the initial situation, you could pass in any log file path, and FileLogger would take care of everything (creating the directory if necessary, and checking that the file path itself is writable). In the new situation, FileLogger accepts a log file path and expects that its containing directory already exists. We can push out even more to the bootstrap phase of the application and rewrite the contract of FileLogger to state that the client has to provide a file path to a file that already exists and is writable. The following listing shows what this would look like.

Listing 2.31 **LoggerFactory takes care of everything FileLogger needs**

```
final class FileLogger implements Logger
{
    private string logFilePath;

    /**
     * @param string logFilePath Absolute path to a log file that
     *                           already exists and is writable.
     */
    public function __construct(string logFilePath)
    {
        this.logFilePath = logFilePath;
    }

    // ...
}

final class LoggerFactory
{
    public function createFileLogger(string logFilePath): FileLogger
    {
        if (!is_file(logFilePath)) {
            logFileDirectory = dirname(logFilePath);
            if (!is_dir(logFileDirectory)) {
                mkdir(logFileDirectory, 0777, true);
            }

            touch(logFilePath);
        }

        if (!is_writable(logFilePath)) {
            throw new InvalidArgumentException(
                'Log file path "{logFilePath}" should be writable'
            );
        }

        return new FileLogger(logFilePath);
    }
}
```

> **Besides taking care of the directory, LoggerFactory now also makes sure that the log file exists and is writable.**

Let's take a look at another, more subtle example of an object that does something in its constructor. Take a look at the following Mailer class , which calls one of its dependencies inside the constructor.

Listing 2.32 `Mailer` does something inside its constructor

```
final class Mailer
{
    private Translator translator;
    private string defaultSubject;

    public function __construct(Translator translator)
    {
        this.translator = translator;

        // ...

        this.defaultSubject = this.translator
            .translate('default_subject');
    }

    // ...
}
```

What happens if you change the order of assignments?

Listing 2.33 Changing the order of assignments in the `Mailer` constructor

```
final class Mailer
{
    private Translator translator;
    private string defaultSubject;

    public function __construct(
        Translator translator,
        string locale
    ) {
        this.defaultSubject = this.translator
            .translate('default_subject', locale);

        // ...

        this.translator = translator;
    }

    // ...
}
```

Now you'll get a fatal error for calling `translate()` on `null`. This is why the rule that you may only assign properties in service constructors comes with the consequence that the assignments could happen in any order. If the assignments have to happen in a specific order, you know that you're doing something in your constructor.

The constructor of this `Mailer` class is also an example of how contextual data, namely the current user's locale, is sometimes passed as a constructor argument. As you know, contextual information should be passed as a method argument instead.

Exercises

9 Take a look at the following `MySQLTableGateway` class. It connects to the database using the provided `ConnectionConfiguration`.

```
final class MySQLTableGateway
{
    private Connection connection;

    public function __construct(
        ConnectionConfiguration connectionConfiguration,
        string tableName
    ) {
        this.tableName = tableName;

        this.connect(connectionConfiguration);
    }

    private function connect(
        ConnectionConfiguration connectionConfiguration
    ): void {
        this.connection = new Connection(
            // ...
        );
    }

    public function insert(array data): void
    {
        this.connection.insert(this.tableName, data);
    }
}
```

Rewrite this class to make sure that the constructor doesn't do anything, except assign values to properties.

2.11 Throw an exception when an argument is invalid

When a client of a class provides an invalid constructor argument, the type checker will usually warn you, such as when the argument requires a `Logger` instance and the client provides a `bool` value. However, there are other types of arguments where only relying on the type system will be insufficient. For instance, in the following `Alerting` class, one of the constructor arguments should be an `int`, representing a configuration flag.

Listing 2.34 `Alerting` requires an `int` constructor argument

```
final class Alerting
{
    private int minimumLevel;
```

```
    public function __construct(int minimumLevel)
    {
        this.minimumLevel = minimumLevel;
    }
}

alerting = new Alerting(-99999999);
```

By accepting any `int` for `minimumLevel`, you can't be sure that the provided value is realistic and can be used by the remaining code in a meaningful way. Instead, the constructor should check that the value is valid, and if it isn't, throw an exception. Only after the argument has been validated should it be assigned, as follows.

Listing 2.35   Validate a constructor argument before assigning it

```
final class Alerting
{
    private int minimumLevel;

    public function __construct(int minimumLevel)
    {
        if (minimumLevel <= 0) {
            throw new InvalidArgumentException(
                'Minimum alerting level should be greater than 0'
            );
        }
        this.minimumLevel = minimumLevel;
    }
}

alerting = new Alerting(-99999999);        ⟵──┐ This will throw an
                                               InvalidArgumentException.
```

By throwing an exception inside the constructor, you can prevent the object from being constructed based on invalid arguments.

> **NOTE** Instead of throwing custom exceptions, it's quite common to use reusable assertion functions for validating method and constructor arguments. We will talk about these in more detail in section 3.7.

Choosing not to throw an exception could also be an option, if that won't break the object's behavior in a later stage. Consider the following `Router` class.

Listing 2.36   `Router` doesn't throw an exception

```
final class Router
{
    private array controllers;
    private string notFoundController;

    public function __construct(
        array controllers,
```

```
        string notFoundController
    ) {
        this.controllers = controllers;

        this.notFoundController = notFoundController;
    }

    public function match(string uri): string
    {
        foreach (this.controllers as pattern => controller) {
            if (this.matches(uri, pattern)) {
                return controller;
            }
        }

        return this.notFoundController;
    }

    private function matches(string uri, string pattern): bool
    {
        // ...
    }
}

router = new Router(
    [
        '/' => 'homepage_controller'
    ],
    'not-found'
);

router.match('/');
```

> **Should we check if the controllers array is empty?** ← (pointing to `this.controllers = controllers;`)

> **This will return homepage_controller.** ← (pointing to `router.match('/');`)

Should you validate the controllers argument here, to verify that it contains at least one URI pattern/controller name pair? Actually, you don't have to, because the behavior of the Router won't be broken if the controllers array is empty. If you accept an empty array, and the client calls match(), it will just return the "not found" controller, because there are no matching patterns found for the given URI (nor any other URI). This is the behavior you'd expect from a router, so it shouldn't be considered a sign of broken logic.

However, you should validate that all the keys and values in the controllers array are strings. This will help you identify programming mistakes early on. Consider the following example.

Listing 2.37 Router should validate the controllers array

```
final class Router
{
    // ...

    public function __construct(array controllers)
```

```
    {
        foreach (array_keys(controllers) as pattern) {
            if (!is_string(pattern)) {
                throw new InvalidArgumentException(
                    'All URI patterns should be provided as strings'
                );
            }
        }
        foreach (controllers as controller) {
            if (!is_string(controller)) {
                throw new InvalidArgumentException(
                    'All controllers should be provided as strings'
                );
            }
        }
        this.controllers = controllers;
    }

    // ...
}
```

Alternatively, you can use an assertion library or custom assertion functions to validate the contents of `controllers` (we'll discuss assertion functions in more detail in section 3.7) or use the type system to check the types for you, as in the following listing. Because the `addController()` method has explicit string types for its arguments, calling this method on every key/value pair in the provided controllers array will be the equivalent of asserting that all keys and values in the array are strings.

Listing 2.38   An alternative for validating the `controllers` array

```
final class Router
{
    private array controllers = [];

    public function __construct(array controllers)
    {
        foreach (controllers as pattern => controller) {      ◁——  Don't assign
            this.addController(pattern, controller);                 controllers directly;
        }                                                            let addController()
    }                                                                take care of that.

    private function addController(
        string pattern,
        string controller
    ): void {
        this.controllers[pattern] = controller;
    }

    // ...
}
```

Exercises

10 The constructor of the following `EventDispatcher` class doesn't properly verify that the provided `eventListeners` argument has the mandatory structure. Rewrite the constructor to throw an exception whenever a client supplies an invalid value to it.

```
final class EventDispatcher
{
    private array eventListeners;

    public function __construct(array eventListeners)
    {
        this.eventListeners = eventListeners;
    }

    public function dispatch(object event): void
    {
        eventName = event.className;

        listeners = isset(this.eventListeners[eventName]) ?
            this.eventListeners[eventName] : [];

        foreach (listeners as listener) {
            listener(event);
        }
    }
}
```

2.12 Define services as an immutable object graph with only a few entry points

Once the application framework calls your controller (be it a web controller or a controller for a command-line application), you can consider every dependency to be known. For instance, the web controller needs a repository to fetch some objects from, it needs the templating engine to render a template, it needs a response factory to create a response object, etc. All these dependencies have their own dependencies, which, when carefully listed as constructor arguments, can be created at once, resulting in an often pretty large graph of objects.

If the framework decides to call a different controller, it will use a different graph of dependent objects to perform its task. The controller itself is also a service with dependencies, so you can consider controllers to be the entry points of the application's object graph, as shown in figure 2.4.

Most applications have something like a service container that describes how all of the application's services can be constructed, what their dependencies are, how they can be constructed, and so on. The container behaves as a service locator too. You can ask it to return one of its services so you can use it. You already saw how a service locator can be used, in section 2.3, when we discussed the rule that you should inject the

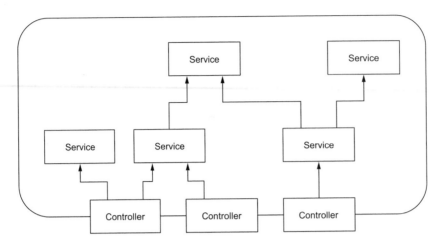

Figure 2.4   The graph contains all the services of an application, with controller services marked as entry point services. These are the only services that can be retrieved directly; all other services are only available as injected dependencies.

dependencies that you need, not a service locator that allows you to retrieve those dependencies.

Given the following,

- All the services in an application form one large object graph.
- The entry points will be the controllers.
- No service will need the service locator to retrieve services.

we should conclude that the service container only needs to provide public methods for retrieving controllers. The other services defined in the container can and should remain private, because they will only be needed as injected dependencies for controllers.

Translated to code, this means we could use a service container as a service locator to retrieve a controller from. All the other service instantiation logic that's needed to produce the controller objects can stay behind the scenes, in `private` methods.

Listing 2.39   Public methods for entry points, private ones for dependencies

```
final class ServiceContainer
{
    public function homepageController(): HomepageController
    {
        return new HomepageController(
            this.userRepository(),
            this.responseFactory(),
            this.templateRenderer()
        );
    }

    private function userRepository(): UserRepository
```

```
    {
        // ...
    }

    private function responseFactory(): ResponseFactory
    {
        // ...
    }

    private function templateRenderer(): TemplateRenderer
    {
        // ...
    }

    // ...
}

if (uri == '/') {                                    ←——  The framework could use a router to find the
    controller = serviceContainer.homepageController();    right controller for the current request. It can
    response = controller.execute(request);                then fetch the controller from the service
    // ...                                                  locator and let it handle the request.
} elseif (/* ... */) {                               ←——  Retrieve and call
    // ...                                                  another controller.
}
```

A service container allows for reuse of services, which is why, starting with the controller as an entry point, not every branch of the object graph will be completely standalone. For example, another controller may use the same `TemplateRenderer` instance as `HomepageController` (see figure 2.5). This is why it's important to make services behave as predictably as possible. If you apply all the previously discussed rules, you will end up with an object graph that can be instantiated once, and then reused many times.

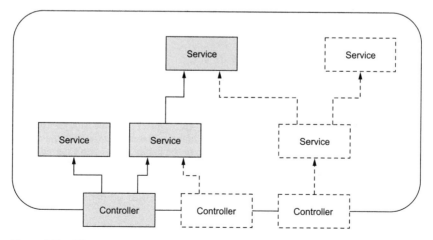

Figure 2.5 Different entry points use different branches of the object graph.

Summary

- Services should be created in one go, providing all their dependencies and configuration values as constructor arguments. All service dependencies should be explicit, and they should be injected as objects. All configuration values should be validated. When a constructor receives an argument that is in any way invalid, it should throw an exception.
- After construction, a service should be immutable; its behavior shouldn't be changed by calling any of its methods.
- All services of an application combined will form a large, immutable object graph, often managed by a service container. Controllers are the entry points of this graph. Services can be instantiated once and reused many times.

Answers to the exercises

1 Correct answers: **b** and **c**.

2 Correct answers: **b** and **d**.

3 Suggested answer:

```
final class FileCache implements Cache
{
    private string cacheDirectory;

    public function __construct(string cacheDirectory)
    {
        this.cacheDirectory = cacheDirectory;
    }

    // ...
}
```

4 Suggested answer:

```
final class MySQLTableGateway
{
    public function __construct(
        ConnectionConfiguration connectionConfiguration,
        string table
    ) {
        // ...
    }
}
```

The name of the table isn't part of the information needed to make the connection to the database, so it isn't moved to the new ConnectionConfiguration object.

5 Correct answer: **c**. An injected dependency should be used directly, not to fetch the actual dependency.

6 First, make `eventDispatcher` a required argument, and remove the `setEvent-Dispatcher()` method:

```
final class CsvImporter
{
    private EventDispatcher eventDispatcher;

    public function __construct(EventDispatcher eventDispatcher)
    {
        this.eventDispatcher = eventDispatcher;
    }
}
```

Then provide a "dummy" implementation of EventDispatcher, which clients can inject if they don't actually want to use event dispatching:

```
final class EventDispatcherDummy implements EventDispatcher
{
    public function dispatch(string eventName): void
    {
        // do nothing
    }
}
```

7 Correct answer: **d**. Although Uuid.create() is a static method, it isn't a static dependency that could be injected as a constructor argument instead (it's actually a named constructor). Uuid is also not a configuration value, since its actual value will be unique every time you create a new instance of it by calling Uuid.create().

8 Correct answers: **c** and **d**. The user's language is contextual information that should be provided as a method argument. It should not be injected as a constructor argument, nor should it be retrieved from an injected service. Passing it on to translator will also save that service from relying on implicit contextual information.

9 Suggested answer:

```
final class MySQLTableGateway
{
    private ConnectionConfiguration connectionConfiguration;      ⟵  Store the connection configuration in a
                                                                      property so you can later use it to
                                                                      connect to the database.
    public function __construct(
        ConnectionConfiguration connectionConfiguration,
        string tableName
    ) {
        this.connectionConfiguration = connectionConfiguration;
        this.tableName = tableName;
    }

    private function connect(): void                              Check if
    {                                                             you aren't
        if (this.connection instanceof Connection) {             connected
            return;                             ⟵                already.
        }
```

```
        this.connection = new Connection(
            // ...
        );
    }
```

> Use this.connectionConfiguration to set up the actual connection.

```
    public function insert(array data): void
    {
        this.connect();

        this.connection.insert(this.tableName, data);
    }
}
```

> Whenever a connection is needed, you first call connect().

10 Suggested answer:

```
public function __construct(array eventListeners)
{
    foreach (eventListeners as eventName => listeners) {
        if (!is_string(eventName)) {
            throw new InvalidArgumentException(
                'eventName should be a string'
            );
        }
        if (!is_array(listeners)) {
            throw new InvalidArgumentException(
                'listeners should be an array'
            );
        }
        foreach (listeners as listener) {
            if (!is_callable(listener)) {
                throw new InvalidArgumentException(
                    'listener should be a callable'
                );
            }
        }
    }

    this.eventListeners = eventListeners;
}
```

Here's an alternative, which relies more on the type checker of the interpreter:

```
private array eventListeners = [];

public function __construct(array eventListeners)
{
    foreach (eventListeners as eventName => listeners) {
        this.addListeners(eventName, listeners);
    }
}
```

> This gradually collects values for the eventListeners property, so you have to initialize it as an empty array.

```
private function addListener(string eventName, array listeners): void
{
    foreach (listeners as listener) {
        if (!is_callable(listener)) {
            throw new InvalidArgumentException(
                'listener should be a callable'
            );
        }
    }

    this.eventListeners[eventName] = listeners;
}
```

The parameter types enforce that the key of each value in the original eventListeners array is a string, and that the corresponding value is an array.

This gradually collects values for the eventListeners property, so you have to initialize it as an empty array.

Creating other objects

This chapter covers

- Instantiating other types of objects
- Preventing objects from being incomplete
- Protecting domain invariants
- Using named constructors
- Using assertions

I mentioned earlier that there are two types of objects: services and other objects. The second type of objects can be divided into more specific subtypes, namely *value objects* and *entities* (sometimes known as "models"). Services will create or retrieve entities, manipulate them, or pass them on to other services. They will also create value objects and pass them on as method arguments, or create modified copies of them. In this sense, entities and value objects are the materials that services use to perform their tasks.

In chapter 2 we looked at how a service object should be created. In this chapter, we'll look at the rules for creating these other objects.

3.1 Require the minimum amount of data needed to behave consistently

Take a look at the following Position class.

Listing 3.1 The Position class

```
final class Position
{
    private int x;
    private int y;

    public function __construct()
    {
        // empty
    }

    public function setX(int x): void
    {
        this.x = x;
    }

    public function setY(int y): void
    {
        this.y = y;
    }

    public function distanceTo(Position other): float
    {
        return sqrt(
            (other.x - this.x) ** 2 +
            (other.y - this.y) ** 2
        );
    }
}

position = new Position();
position.setX(45);
position.setY(60);
```

Until we've called both setX() and setY(), the object is in an inconsistent state. We can notice this if we call distanceTo() before calling setX() or setY(); it won't give a meaningful answer.

Since it's crucial to the concept of a position that it have both x and y parts, we have to enforce this by making it impossible to create a Position object without providing values for both x and y.

Listing 3.2 Position has required constructor arguments for *x* and *y*

```
final class Position
{
    private int x;
```

```
    private int y;

    public function __construct(int x, int y)
    {
        this.x = x;
        this.y = y;
    }

    public function distanceTo(Position other): float
    {
        return sqrt(
            (other.x - this.x) ** 2 +
            (other.y - this.y) ** 2
        );
    }
}

position = new Position(45, 60);
```

x and y have to be provided, or you won't be able to get an instance of Position.

This is an example of how a constructor can be used to protect a *domain invariant*, which is something that's always true for a given object, based on the domain knowledge you have about the concept it represents. The domain invariant that's being protected here is, "A position has both an x and a y coordinate."

Exercises

1   What's wrong with the Money object used here?

```
money = new Money()
money.setAmount(100);
money.setCurrency('USD');
```

a It uses setters for providing the minimum required data.
b It has no dependencies.
c Apparently it has default constructor arguments.
d It can exist in an inconsistent state.

3.2   *Require data that is meaningful*

In the previous example, the constructor would accept any integer, positive or negative and to infinity in both directions. Now consider another system of coordinates, where positions consist of a latitude and a longitude, which together determine a place on earth. In this case, not every possible value for latitude and longitude would be considered meaningful.

Listing 3.3 The `Coordinates` class

```
final class Coordinates
{
    private float latitude;
    private float longitude;

    public function __construct(float latitude, float longitude)
    {
        this.latitude = latitude;
        this.longitude = longitude;
    }

    // ...
}

meaningfulCoordinates = new Coordinates(45.0, -60.0);

offThePlanet = new Coordinates(1000.0, -20000.0);
```

> **Nothing stops us from creating a Coordinates object that doesn't make any sense.**

Always make sure that clients can't provide data that is meaningless. What counts as meaningless can be phrased as a domain invariant too. In this case, the invariant is, "The latitude of a coordinate is a value between −90 and 90 inclusive. The longitude of a coordinate is a value between −180 and 180 inclusive."

When you're designing your objects, let yourself be guided by these domain invariants. Collect more invariants as you go, and incorporate them in your unit tests. As an example, the following listing uses the `expectException()` utility described in section 1.10.

Listing 3.4 Verifying the domain invariants of `Coordinates`

> **A keyword that should be in the exception's message**

```
expectException(
    InvalidArgumentException.className,
    'Latitude',
    function() {
        new Coordinates(90.1, 0.0);
    }
);
expectException(
    InvalidArgumentException.className,
    'Longitude',
    function() {
        new Coordinates(0.0, 180.1);
    }
);
// and so on...
```

> **The type of the expected exception**

> **An anonymous function that should cause the exception to be thrown**

To make these tests pass, throw an exception in the constructor as soon as something about the provided arguments looks wrong.

Listing 3.5   Throwing exceptions for invalid constructor arguments

```
final class Coordinates
{
    // ...

    public function __construct(float latitude, float longitude)
    {
        if (latitude > 90 || latitude < -90) {
            throw new InvalidArgumentException(
                'Latitude should be between -90 and 90'
            );
        }
        this.latitude = latitude;

        if (longitude > 180 || longitude < -180) {
            throw new InvalidArgumentException(
                'Longitude should be between -180 and 180'
            );
        }
        this.longitude = longitude;
    }
}
```

Although the exact order of the statements in your constructor shouldn't matter (as we discussed earlier), it's still recommended that you perform the checks directly above their associated property assignments. This will make it easy for the reader to understand how the two statements are related.

In some cases it's not enough to verify that every constructor argument is valid on its own. Sometimes you may need to verify that the provided constructor arguments are meaningful together. The following example shows the ReservationRequest class, which is used to keep some information about a hotel reservation.

Listing 3.6   The ReservationRequest class

```
final class ReservationRequest
{
    public function __construct(
        int numberOfRooms,
        int numberOfAdults,
        int numberOfChildren
    ) {
        // ...
    }
}
```

Discussing the business rules for this object with a domain expert, you may learn about the following rules:

- There should always be at least one adult (because children can't book a hotel room on their own).

- Everybody can have their own room, but you can't book more rooms than there are guests. (It wouldn't make sense to allow people to book rooms where nobody will sleep.)

So it turns out that numberOfRooms and numberOfAdults are related, and can only be considered to be meaningful together. We have to make sure that the constructor takes both values and enforces the corresponding business rules, as in the following listing.

Listing 3.7 Validating the meaningfulness of constructor arguments

```
final class ReservationRequest
{
    public function __construct(
        int numberOfRooms,
        int numberOfAdults,
        int numberOfChildren
    ) {
        if (numberOfRooms > numberOfAdults + numberOfChildren) {
            throw new InvalidArgumentException(
                'Number of rooms should not exceed number of guests'
            );
        }

        if (numberOfAdults < 1) {
            throw new InvalidArgumentException(
                'numberOfAdults should be at least 1'
            );
        }

        if (numberOfChildren < 0) {
            throw new InvalidArgumentException(
                'numberOfChildren should be at least 0'
            );
        }
    }
}
```

In other cases, constructor arguments may at first sight appear to be related, but a redesign could help you avoid multi-argument validations. Consider the following class, which represents a business deal between two parties, where there's a total amount of money that has to be divided between two parties.

Listing 3.8 The Deal class

```
final class Deal
{
    public function __construct(
        int totalAmount,
        int amountToFirstParty,
        int amountToSecondParty
```

```
    ) {
        // ...
    }
}
```

You should at least validate the constructor arguments separately (the total amount should be larger than 0, etc.). But there's also an invariant that spans all the arguments: the sum of what both parties get should be equal to the total amount. The following listing shows how you could verify this rule.

Listing 3.9   Deal validates the sum of the amounts for both parties

```
final class Deal
{
    public function __construct(
        int totalAmount,
        int amountToFirstParty,
        int amountToSecondParty
    ) {
        // ...

        if (amountToFirstParty + amountToSecondParty
            != totalAmount) {
            throw new InvalidArgumentException(/* ... */);
        }
    }
}
```

As you may have noted, this rule could be enforced in a much simpler way. You could say that the total amount itself doesn't even have to be provided, as long as the client provides positive numbers for amountToFirstParty and amountToSecondParty. The Deal object could figure out on its own what the total amount of the deal was by summing these values. The need to validate the constructor arguments together disappears.

Listing 3.10   Removing the superfluous constructor argument

```
final class Deal
{
    private int amountToFirstParty;
    private int amountToSecondParty;

    public function __construct(
        int amountToFirstParty,
        int amountToSecondParty
    ) {
        if (amountToFirstParty <= 0) {
            throw new InvalidArgumentException(/* ... */);
        }
        this.amountToFirstParty = amountToFirstParty;

        if (amountToSecondParty <= 0) {
```

```
            throw new InvalidArgumentException(/* ... */);
        }
        this.amountToSecondParty = amountToSecondParty;
    }

    public function totalAmount(): int
    {
        return this.amountToFirstParty
            + this.amountToSecondParty;
    }
}
```

Another example where it would seem that constructor arguments have to be validated together is the following class, which represents a line.

Listing 3.11 The `Line` class

```
final class Line
{
    public function __construct(                We only care about the
        bool isDotted,                          distance if the line is a
        int distanceBetweenDots                 dotted line. For solid lines,
    ) {                                         there's no distance to be
        if (isDotted && distanceBetweenDots <= 0) {   dealt with.
            throw new InvalidArgumentException(
                'Expect the distance between dots to be positive.'
            );
        }

        // ...
    }
}
```

However, this could more elegantly be dealt with by providing the client with two distinct ways of defining a line: dotted and solid. Different types of lines could be constructed with different constructors.

Listing 3.12 `Line` now offers different ways for lines to be constructed

```
final class Line
{
    private bool isDotted;
    private int distanceBetweenDots;

    public static function dotted(int distanceBetweenDots): Line
    {
        if (distanceBetweenDots <= 0) {
            throw new InvalidArgumentException(
                'Expect the distance between dots to be positive.'
            );
        }
```

```
        line = new Line(/* ... */);
        line.distanceBetweenDots = distanceBetweenDots;
        line.isDotted = true;

        return line;
    }

    public static function solid(): Line
    {
        line = new Line();

        line.isDotted = false;

        return line;
    }
}
```

No need to worry about
distanceBetweenDots here!

These static methods are *named constructors,* and we'll take a closer look at them in section 3.9.

If you make sure that every object has the minimum required data provided to it at construction time, and that this data is correct and meaningful, you will only encounter complete and valid objects in your application. It should be safe to assume that you can use every object as intended. There should be no surprises and no need for extra validation rounds.

3.3 *Don't use custom exception classes for invalid argument exceptions*

So far we've been throwing a generic InvalidArgumentException whenever a method argument doesn't match our expectations. We could use a custom exception class that extends from InvalidArgumentException. The advantage of doing so is that we could catch specific types of exceptions and deal with them in specific ways.

Listing 3.13 `SpecificException` can be caught and dealt with

```
final class SpecificException extends InvalidArgumentException
{
}

try {
    // try to create the object
} catch (SpecificException exception) {
    // handle this specific problem in a specific way
}
```

However, you should rarely need to do that with invalid argument exceptions. An invalid argument means that the client is using the object in an invalid way. Usually this will be caused be a programming mistake. In that case, you'd better fail hard and not try to recover, but fix the mistake instead.

For `RuntimeExceptions` on the other hand, it often makes sense to use custom exception classes because you may be able to recover from them, or to convert them into user-friendly error messages. We'll discuss custom runtime exceptions and how to create them in section 5.2.

3.4 *Test for specific invalid argument exceptions by analyzing the exception's message*

Even if you only use the generic `InvalidArgumentException` class to validate method arguments, you still need a way to distinguish between them in a unit test. Let's take another look at the `Coordinates` class and constructor.

Listing 3.14 The `Coordinates` class

```
final class Coordinates
{
    // ...

    public function __construct(float latitude, float longitude)
    {
        if (latitude > 90 || latitude < -90) {
            throw new InvalidArgumentException(
                'Latitude should be between -90 and 90'
            );
        }
        this.latitude = latitude;

        if (longitude > 180 || longitude < -180) {
            throw new InvalidArgumentException(
                'Longitude should be between -180 and 180'
            );
        }
        this.longitude = longitude;
    }
}
```

We want to verify that clients can't pass in the wrong arguments, so we can write a few tests, like the following ones.

Listing 3.15 Tests for the domain invariants of Coordinates

```
// Latitude can't be more than 90.0
expectException(
    InvalidArgumentException.className,
    function() {
        new Coordinates(90.1, 0.0);
    }
);
// Latitude can't be less than -90.0
expectException(
    InvalidArgumentException.className,
    function() {
        new Coordinates(-90.1, 0.0);
    }
);

// Longitude can't be more than 180.0
expectException(
    InvalidArgumentException.className,
    function() {
        new Coordinates(-90.1, 180.1);
    }
);
```

In the last test case, the InvalidArgumentException that gets thrown from the constructor isn't the one we'd expect it to be. Because the test case reuses an invalid value for latitude (–90.1) from the previous test case, trying to construct a Coordinates object will throw an exception telling us that "Latitude should be between –90.0 and 90.0." But the test was supposed to verify that the code would reject invalid values for longitude. This leaves the range check for longitude uncovered in a test scenario, even though all the tests succeed.

To prevent this kind of mistake, make sure to always verify that the exception you catch in a unit test is in fact the expected one. A pragmatic way to do this is to verify that the exception message contains certain predefined words.

Listing 3.16 Verifying that the exception message contains a specific string

```
expectException(
    InvalidArgumentException.className,
    'Longitude',                        ◁──────  This word is supposed to be
    function() {                                 in the exception message.
        new Coordinates(-90.1, 180.1);
    }
);
```

Adding this expectation about the exception message to the test in listing 3.15 will make the test fail. It will pass again once we provide the constructor with a sensible value for latitude.

3.5 Extract new objects to prevent domain invariants from being verified in multiple places

You'll often find the same validation logic repeated in the same class, or even in different classes. As an example, take a look at the following User class and how it has to validate an email address in multiple places, using a function from the language's standard library.

Listing 3.17 The User class

```
final class User
{
    private string emailAddress;

    public function __construct(string emailAddress)
    {
        if (!is_valid_email_address(emailAddress)) {    ⟵┐ Validates that the provided
            throw new InvalidArgumentException(            email address is valid
                'Invalid email address'
            );
        }
        this.emailAddress = emailAddress;
    }

    // ...

    public function changeEmailAddress(string emailAddress): void
    {
        if (!is_valid_email_address(emailAddress)) {    ⟵┐ Validates it again, if it's
            throw new InvalidArgumentException(            going to be updated
                'Invalid email address'
            );
        }
        this.emailAddress = emailAddress;
    }
}
                                            ┌─ The constructor will catch
expectException(                    ⟵──────┘  invalid email addresses.
    InvalidArgumentException.className,
    'email',
    function () {
        new User('not-a-valid-email-address');
    }
);                                          ┌─ Creates a valid
                                            │  User object first
user = new User('valid@emailaddress.com');  ⟵─┘

                                    ┌─ changeEmailAddress() will also
expectException(            ⟵──────┘  catch invalid email addresses.
```

```
        InvalidArgumentException.className,
        'email',
        function () use (user) {
            user.changeEmailAddress('not-a-valid-email-address');
        }
);
```

Although you could easily extract the email address validation logic into a separate method, the better solution is to introduce a new type of object that represents a valid email address. Since we expect all objects to be valid the moment they are created, we can leave out the "valid" part from the class name and implement it as follows.

Listing 3.18   The `EmailAddress` class

```
final class EmailAddress
{
    private string emailAddress;

    public function __construct(string emailAddress)
    {
        if (!is_valid_email_address(emailAddress)) {
            throw new InvalidArgumentException(
                'Invalid email address'
            );
        }
        this.emailAddress = emailAddress;
    }
}
```

Wherever you encounter an `EmailAddress` object, you will know it represents a value that has already been validated:

```
final class User
{
    private EmailAddress emailAddress;

    public function __construct(EmailAddress emailAddress)
    {
        this.emailAddress = emailAddress;
    }

    // ...

    public function changeEmailAddress(EmailAddress emailAddress): void
    {
        this.emailAddress = emailAddress;
    }
}
```

Wrapping values inside new objects called *value objects* isn't just useful for avoiding repeated validation logic. As soon as you notice that a method accepts a primitive-type value (`string`, `int`, etc.), you should consider introducing a class for it. The guiding question for deciding whether or not to do this is, "Would any `string`, `int`, etc., be acceptable here?" If the answer is no, introduce a new class for the concept.

You should consider the value object class itself to be a type, just like `string`, `int`, etc., are types. By introducing more objects to represent domain concepts, you're effectively extending the type system. Your language's compiler or runtime will be able to support you much better, because it can do type-checking for you and make sure that only the right types end up being used when passing method arguments and returning values.

Exercises

3   A country code can be represented as a two-character string, but not every two-character string will be a valid country code. Create a value object class that represents a valid country code. For now, assume that the list of known country codes is `NL` and `GB`.

3.6   *Extract new objects to represent composite values*

When creating all these new types, you'll find that some of them naturally belong together and always get passed together from method call to method call. For example, an amount of money always comes with the currency of the amount, as in the following listing. If a method received just an amount, it wouldn't know how to deal with it.

Listing 3.19   Amount and Currency

```
final class Amount
{
    // ...
}

final class Currency
{
    // ...
}

final class Product
{
    public function setPrice(           ◁──────┐
        Amount amount,
        Currency currency
    ): void {
        // ...
    }
}                                              Amount and Currency
                                               always go together.
final class Converter
{
    public function convert(            ◁──────┘
```

```
        Amount localAmount,
        Currency localCurrency,
        Currency targetCurrency
    ): Amount {
        // ...
    }
}
```

In this last example, the return type is actually quite confusing. An `Amount` will be returned, and the currency of this amount is expected to match the given `target-Currency`. But this is not evident by looking at the types used in this method.

Whenever you notice that values belong together (or can always be found together), wrap those values into a new type. In the case of `Amount` and `Currency`, a good name for the combination of the two could be "money," resulting in the `Money` class.

Listing 3.20   The `Money` class

```
final class Money
{
    public function __construct(Amount amount, Currency currency)
    {
        // ...
    }
}
```

Using this type indicates that you want to keep these values together, although if you wanted to use them separately, you still could.

Adding more object types leads to more typing. Is that really necessary?

`100` has fewer characters than `new Amount(100)`, but all that extra typing gives you the benefits of using object types:

1 You can be certain that the data the object wraps has been validated.
2 An object usually exposes additional, meaningful behaviors that make use of its data.
3 An object can keep values together that belong together.
4 An object helps you keep implementation details away from its clients.

If you feel like it's a hassle to create all these objects one by one based on primitive values, you can always introduce helper methods for creating them. Here's an example:

```
// Before:

money = new Money(new Amount(100), new Currency('USD'));

// After:

money = Money.create(100, 'USD');
```

You will learn more about this style of creating objects in section 3.9.

Exercises

4 With a `Run` object, you can save the distance you covered in a run:

```
final class Run
{
    public function __construct(int distance)
    {
        // ...
    }
}
```

The problem with the current implementation is that there's no way to find out what kind of value `distance` represents. Is it measured in meters, feet, kilometers perhaps? This requires a new value object representing both the quantity and the unit of the running distance. For your implementation, assume the distance can only be measured in meters or feet.

3.7 Use assertions to validate constructor arguments

We've already seen several examples of constructors that throw exceptions when something is wrong. The general structure is always like this:

```
if (somethingIsWrong()) {
    throw new InvalidArgumentException(/* ... */);
}
```

These checks at the beginnings of methods are called "assertions," and they're basically safety checks. Assertions can be used to establish the situation, examine the materials, and signal if anything is wrong. For this reason, assertions are also called "precondition checks." Once you're past these assertions, it should be safe to perform the task at hand with the data that has been provided.

Because you'll often write the same kinds of checks in many different places, it'll be convenient to use an assertion library instead.[1] Such a library contains many assertion functions that will cover almost all situations. These are some examples:

```
Assertion.greaterThan(value, limit);
Assertion.isCallable(value);
Assertion.between(
    value,
    lowerLimit,
    upperLimit
);
// and so on...
```

---

[1] If you use PHP, take a look at the `beberlei/assert` or `webmozart/assert` package.

The question is always, "Should you verify that these assertions work in a unit test for your object?" The guiding question is, "Would it be theoretically possible for the language runtime to catch this case?" If the answer is yes, don't write a unit test for it.

For example, a dynamically typed language like PHP doesn't have a way to set the type of an argument to a `list of <class name>`. Instead, you'd have to rely on the pretty generic `array` type. To verify that a given array is indeed a flat list of objects of a certain type, you would use an assertion, as in the following listing.

Listing 3.21 `EventDispatcher` uses an assertion function in its constructor

```
final class EventDispatcher
{
    public function __construct(array eventListeners)
    {
        Assertion.allIsInstanceOf(
            eventListeners,
            EventListener.className
        );

        // ...
    }
}
```

Since this is an error condition that a more evolved type system could catch, you don't have to write a unit test that catches the `AssertionFailedException` thrown by `allIsInstanceOf()`. However, if you have to inspect a given value and check that it's within a certain range, or if you have to verify the number of items in a list, etc., you will have to write a unit test that shows you've covered the edge cases. Revisiting a previous example, the domain invariant that a given latitude is always between −90 and 90 inclusive should be verified with a test.

Listing 3.22 Add unit tests for domain invariants

```
expectException(
    AssertionFailedException.className,
    'latitude',
    function() {
        new Coordinates(-90.1, 0.0)
    }
);
// and so on...
```

Don't collect exceptions

Although the tools sometimes allow it, you shouldn't save up assertion exceptions and throw them as a list. Assertions are not meant to provide the user with a convenient list of things that are wrong. They are meant for the programmer, who needs to know that they are using a constructor or method in the wrong way. As soon as you notice anything wrong, just make the object scream.

If you want to supply the user with a list of things that are wrong about the data they provided (by submitting a form, sending an API request, etc.) you should use a *data transfer object* (DTO) and validate it instead. We'll discuss this type of object at the end of this chapter.

Exercises

5 You can use the following assertion functions:

```
Assertion.greaterThan(value, limit);
Assertion.between(
    value,
    lowerLimit,
    upperLimit
);
Assertion.lessThan(value, limit);
```

Rewrite the constructor of `PriceRange` to use the appropriate assertion functions.

```
final class PriceRange
{
    public function __construct(int minimumPrice, int maximumPrice)
    {
        if (minimumPrice < 0) {
            throw new InvalidArgumentException(
                'minimumPrice should be 0 or more'
            );
        }
        if (maximumPrice < 0) {
            throw new InvalidArgumentException(
                'maximumPrice should be 0 or more'
            );
        }
        if (maximumPrice <= minimumPrice) {
            throw new InvalidArgumentException(
                'maximumPrice should be greater than minimumPrice'
            );
        }

        this.minimumPrice = miminumPrice;
        this.maximumPrice = maximumPrice;
    }
}
```

3.8 Don't inject dependencies; optionally pass them as method arguments

Services can have dependencies, and they should be injected as constructor arguments. But other objects shouldn't get any dependencies injected, only values, value objects, or lists of them. If a value object still needs a service to perform some task, you could optionally inject it as a method argument, as in the next listing.

Listing 3.23 Money needs the `ExchangeRateProvider` service

```
final class Money
{
    private Amount amount;
    private Currency currency;

    public function __construct(Amount amount, Currency currency)
    {
        this.amount = amount;
        this.currency = currency;
    }

    public function convert(
        ExchangeRateProvider exchangeRateProvider,        ◁─────┐  ExchangeRateProvider
        Currency targetCurrency                                  │  is a method argument,
    ): Money {                                                   │  not a constructor
        exchangeRate = exchangeRateProvider.getRateFor(          │  argument.
            this.currency,
            targetCurrency
        );

        return exchangeRate.convert(this.amount);
    }
}
```

It may sometimes feel a bit strange to pass a service as a method argument, so it makes sense to consider alternative implementations too. Maybe we shouldn't pass the ExchangeRateProvider service, but only the information we get from it: ExchangeRate. This would require Money to expose both its internal Amount and Currency objects, but that may be a reasonable price to pay for not injecting the dependency. This results in a situation like the following.

Listing 3.24 Alternative implementation: don't pass `ExchangeRateProvider`

```
final class ExchangeRate
{
    public function __construct(
        Currency from,
        Currency to,
        Rate rate
    ) {
        // ...
```

```
        }

    public function convert(Amount amount): Money
    {
        // ...
    }
}

money = new Money(/* ... */);
exchangeRate = exchangeRateProvider.getRateFor(
    money.currency(),
    targetCurrency
);
converted = exchangeRate.convert(money.amount());
```

We retrieve ExchangeRate up front.

Then we use it to convert the amount we have.

After moving things around one more time, we could settle for a solution that involves only exposing Money's internal Currency object, not its Amount, as is done in the following listing. (We will get back to the topic of exposing object internals in section 6.3.)

Listing 3.25 Passing ExchangeRate instead of ExchangeRateProvider

```
final class Money
{
    public function convert(ExchangeRate exchangeRate): Money
    {
        Assertion.equals(
            this.currency,
            exchangeRate.fromCurrency()
        );

        return new Money(
            exchangeRate.rate().applyTo(this.amount),
            exchangeRate.targetCurrency()
        );
    }
}

money = new Money(/* ... */);
exchangeRate = exchangeRateProvider.getRateFor(
    money.currency(),
    targetCurrency
);
converted = money.convert(exchangeRate);
```

You could argue that this solution expresses more clearly the domain knowledge we have about money and exchange rates. For example, the converted amount will be in the target currency of the exchange rate, and its "source" currency will be the same currency as the currency of the original amount.

In some cases, the need for passing around services as method arguments could be a hint that the behavior should be implemented as a service instead. In the case of converting an amount of money to a given currency, we might as well create a service and let it do the work, collecting all the relevant information from the Amount and Currency objects provided to it.

Listing 3.26   Alternative implementation: ExchangeService does all the work

```
final class ExchangeService
{
    private ExchangeRateProvider exchangeRateProvider;

    public function __construct(
        ExchangeRateProvider exchangeRateProvider
    ) {
        this.exchangeRateProvider = exchangeRateProvider;
    }

    public function convert(
        Money money,
        Currency targetCurrency
    ): Money {
        exchangeRate = this.exchangeRateProvider
            .getRateFor(money.currency(), targetCurrency);

        return new Money(
            exchangeRate.rate().applyTo(money.amount()),
            targetCurrency
        );
    }
}
```

Which solution you choose will depend on how close you want to keep the behavior to the data, whether or not you think it's too much for an object like Money to know about exchange rates too, or how much you want to avoid exposing object internals.

Exercises

6   Given the following User class, how should you provide the PasswordHasher service to it?

```
interface PasswordHasher
{
    public function hash(string password): string
}

final class User
{
    private string username;
    private string hashedPassword;

    public function __construct(string username)
    {
        this.username = username;
    }
```

```
public function setPassword(
    string plainTextPassword
): void {
    this.hashedPassword = /* ... */;
}
}
```

Here we'd like to use the
PasswordHasher service
to hash the password.

a By adding an extra constructor argument:

```
private PasswordHasher hasher;

public function __construct(
    string username,
    PasswordHasher hasher
) {
    this.hasher = hasher;
}

public function setPassword(
    string plainTextPassword
): void {
    this.hashedPassword = this.hasher.hash(
        plainTextPassword
    );
}
```

b By adding a `setPasswordHasher(PasswordHasher passwordHasher)` to the class:

```
private PasswordHasher hasher;

public function setPasswordHasher(PasswordHasher hasher): void
{
    this.hasher = hasher;
}

public function setPassword(
    string plainTextPassword
): void {
    this.hashedPassword = this.hasher.hash(
        plainTextPassword
    );
}
```

c By adding `PasswordHasher` as a method argument:

```
public function setPassword(
    string plainTextPassword,
    PasswordHasher hasher
): void {
    this.hashedPassword = hasher.hash(
        plainTextPassword
    );
}
```

(continued)

   d By making the `PasswordHasher` globally available:

```
public function setPassword(
    string plainTextPassword
): void {
    this.hashedPassword = PasswordHasher.getInstance()
        .hash(
            plainTextPassword
        );
}
```

3.9   *Use named constructors*

For services, it's fine to use the standard way of defining constructors (`public function __construct()`). However, for other types of objects, it's recommended that you use *named constructors*. These are `public static` methods that return an instance. They could be considered object factories.

3.9.1   *Create from primitive-type values*

A common case for using named constructors is constructing an object from one or more primitive-type values. This results in methods like `fromString()`, `fromInt()`, etc. As an example, take a look at the following `Date` class.

Listing 3.27   The `Date` class wraps a date `string`

```
final class Date
{
    private const string FORMAT = 'd/m/Y';
    private DateTime date;

    private function __construct()
    {
        // do nothing here
    }

    public static function fromString(string date): Date
    {
        object = new Date();

        DateTime = DateTime.createFromFormat(        We'd still have to assert that
            Date.FORMAT,                             createFromFormat() doesn't
            date                                     return false.
        );

        object.date = DateTime;

        return object;
    }
}

date = Date.fromString('1/4/2019');
```

It's important to add a regular, but `private`, constructor method, so that clients won't be able to bypass the named constructor you offer to them, which would possibly leave the object in an invalid or incomplete state.

> **Wait, does this work?**
>
> It may seem strange that this `public static fromString()` method can create a new object instance and manipulate the `date` property of the new instance. After all, this property is `private`, so that shouldn't be allowed, right?
>
> Scoping of methods and properties is usually class-based, not instance-based, so private properties can be manipulated by any object, as long as it's of the exact same class. The `fromString()` method in this example counts as a method of the same class, which is why it can manipulate the `date` property directly, without the need for a setter.

3.9.2 Don't immediately add toString(), toInt(), etc.

When you add a named constructor that creates an object based on a primitive-type value, you may feel the need for symmetry and want to add a method that can convert the object back to the primitive-type value. For instance, having a `fromString()` constructor may lead you to automatically provide a `toString()` method too. Make sure you only do this once there is a proven need for it.

3.9.3 Introduce a domain-specific concept

When you discuss the concept of a "sales order" with your domain expert, they would never speak about "constructing" a sales order. Maybe they would talk about "creating" a sales order, or they might use a more specific term like "placing" a sales order. Look out for these words and use them as method names for your named constructors.

Listing 3.28 In real life, sales orders aren't "constructed," but "placed"

```
final class SalesOrder
{
    public static function place(/* ... */): SalesOrder
    {
        // ...
    }
}

salesOrder = SalesOrder.place(/* ... */);
```

3.9.4 Optionally use the private constructor to enforce constraints

Some objects may offer multiple named constructors, because there are different ways in which you can construct them. For example, if you want a decimal value with a certain precision, you could choose an integer value with a positive integer precision as the normalized way of representing such a number. At the same time, you may want to allow clients to use their existing values, which are strings or floats, as input for working with such a decimal value. Using a private constructor helps to ensure that whatever construction method is chosen, the object will end up in a complete and consistent state. The following listing shows an example.

Listing 3.29 Protecting domain invariants inside a private constructor

```
final class DecimalValue
{
    private int value;
    private int precision;

    private function __construct(int value, int precision)
    {
        this.value = value;

        Assertion.greaterOrEqualThan(precision, 0);
        this.precision = precision;
    }

    public static function fromInt(
        int value,
        int precision
    ): DecimalValue {
        return new DecimalValue(value, precision);
    }

    public static function fromFloat(
        float value,
        int precision
    ): DecimalValue {
        return new DecimalValue(
            (int)round(value * pow(10, precision)),
            precision
        );
    }

    public static function fromString(string value): DecimalValue
    {
        result = preg_match('/^(\d+)\.(\d+)/', value, matches);
        if (result == 0) {
            throw new InvalidArgumentException(/* ... */);
        }

        wholeNumber = matches[1];
        decimals = matches[2];

        valueWithoutDecimalSign = wholeNumber . decimals;

        return new DecimalValue(
            (int)valueWithoutDecimalSign,
            strlen(decimals)
        );
    }
}
```

In summary, the using named constructors offers two main advantages:

- They can be used to offer several ways to construct an object.
- They can be used to introduce domain-specific synonyms for creating an object.

Besides creating entities and value objects, named constructors can be used to offer convenient ways to instantiate custom exceptions. We'll discuss these later, in section 5.2.

Exercises

7 The following `Date` class can be instantiated by passing in a string in the right format, which will then be converted to a `DateTime` instance. But what if the client already has a `DateTime` instance available? How can we build in an option for the client to pass their instance directly to the `Date` object, instead of through an intermediate `string` representation?

```
final class Date
{
    private DateTime date;

    public function __construct(string date)
    {
        this.date = DateTime.createFromFormat(
            'd/m/Y',
            date
        );
    }
}
```

a Remove the `string` type from the constructor's `date` parameter to allow clients to pass in a `DateTime` instance without any type errors.

b Add two named constructors to the class: `fromString(string date): Date` and `fromDateTime(DateTime dateTime): Date`.

c Make the `string date` parameter optional, and add a second optional `DateTime dateTime` parameter to the constructor.

d Create a new class that extends from `Date` and overrides the constructor to accept a `DateTime` instance instead of a string.

3.10 *Don't use property fillers*

Applying all the object design rules in this book will lead to objects that are in complete control of what goes into them, what stays inside, and what a client can do with them. A technique that works completely against this object design style is property filler methods, which look like the following `fromArray()` method.

Listing 3.30 `Position` has a property filler called `fromArray()`

```
final class Position
{
    private int x;
    private int y;
```

```
    public static function fromArray(array data): Position
    {
        position = new Position();
        position.x = data['x'];
        position.y = data['y'];
        return position;
    }
}
```

This kind of method could even be turned into a generic utility that would copy values from the data array into the corresponding properties using reflection. Though it may look convenient, the object's internals are now out in the open, so always make sure that the construction of an object happens in a way that's fully controlled by the object itself.

> **NOTE** At the end of this chapter, we'll look at an exception to this rule. For *data transfer objects*, a property filler could be a way to map, for example, form data onto an object. Such an object doesn't need to protect its internal data as much as an entity or a value object has to.

3.11   *Don't put anything more into an object than it needs*

It's common to start designing an object by thinking about what needs to go in. For services, you may end up injecting more dependencies than you need, so you should inject dependencies only when you need them. The same is true for other types of objects: don't require more data than is strictly needed to implement the object's behavior.

One type of object that often ends up carrying around more data than needed is an event object, representing something that has happened somewhere in the application. An example of such an event is the following ProductCreated class.

Listing 3.31   The `ProductCreated` class represents an event

```
final class ProductCreated
{
    public function __construct(
        ProductId productId,
        Description description,
        StockValuation stockValuation,
        Timestamp createdAt,
        UserId createdBy,
        /* ... */
    ) {
        // ...
    }
}

this.recordThat(                      ⟵──┐ Inside the
    new ProductCreated(                   │ Product entity
        /* ... */            ⟵──┐ Passes along all the data that
    )                           │ was available when creating
);                              │ the product
```

If you don't know which event data will be important for yet-to-be-implemented event listeners, don't add anything. Just add a constructor with no arguments at all, and add more data when the data is needed. This way, you will provide data on a need-to-know basis.

How do you know what data should actually go into an object's constructor? By designing the object in a test-driven way. This means that you first have to know how an object is going to be used.

3.12 Don't test constructors

Writing tests for your objects, specifying their desired behavior, will let you figure out which data is actually needed at construction time and which data can be provided later. It will also help you figure out which data needs to be exposed later on and which data can stay behind the scenes, as implementation details of the object.

As an example, let's take another look at the Coordinates class we saw earlier.

Listing 3.32 The constructor of Coordinates

```
final class Coordinates
{
    // ...

    public function __construct(float latitude, float longitude)
    {
        if (latitude > 90 || latitude < -90) {
            throw new InvalidArgumentException(
                'Latitude should be between -90 and 90'
            );
        }
        this.latitude = latitude;

        if (longitude > 180 || longitude < -180) {
            throw new InvalidArgumentException(
                'Longitude should be between -180 and 180'
            );
        }
        this.longitude = longitude;
    }
}
```

How can we test that the constructor works? What about the following test?

Listing 3.33 A first try at testing the constructor of Coordinates

```
public function it_can_be_constructed(): void
{
    coordinates = new Coordinates(60.0, 100.0);

    assertIsInstanceOf(Coordinates.className, coordinates);
}
```

This isn't very informative. In fact, it's impossible for the assertion to fail unless the constructor has thrown an exception, which is an execution flow we're explicitly not testing here.

What is the task of the constructor? Judging from the code, it's to assign the given constructor arguments to internal object properties. So how can we be sure that this has worked? We could add getters, which would allow us to find out what's inside the object's properties, as follows.

> **Listing 3.34   Extra getters for testing the `Coordinates` constructor**

```
final class Coordinates
{
    // ...

    public function latitude(): float
    {
        return this.latitude;
    }

    public function longitude(): float
    {
        return this.longitude;
    }
}
```

The next listing shows how we could use those getters in a unit test.

> **Listing 3.35   Using the new getters in a unit test**

```
public function it_can_be_constructed(): void
{
    coordinates = new Coordinates(60.0, 100.0);

    assertEquals(60.0, coordinates.latitude());
    assertEquals(100.0, coordinates.longitude());
}
```

But now we've introduced a way for internal data to get out of the object, for no other reason than to test the constructor.

Look back at what we've done here: We've been testing constructor code after we wrote it. We've been testing this code, knowing what's going on in there, meaning the test is very close to the implementation of the class. We've been putting data into an object, without even knowing if we'll ever need that data again. In conclusion, we've done too much, too soon, without a healthy dose of distance from the object's implementation.

The only thing we can and should do at this point is test that the constructor doesn't accept invalid arguments. We've discussed this before: you should verify that providing values for latitude and longitude outside of their acceptable ranges triggers an exception, making it impossible to construct the `Coordinates` object.

Further down the road, we'll talk more about exposing data, but for now take the following advice:

- Only test a constructor for ways in which it should fail.
- Only pass in data as constructor arguments when you need it to implement real behavior on the object.
- Only add getters to expose internal data when this data is needed by some other client than the test itself.

Once you start adding actual behavior to the object, you will implicitly test the happy path for the constructor anyway, because when doing so you'll need a fully instantiated object.

Exercises

8 What's wrong with the following code for the `Product` entity?

```
final class Product
{
    private int id;
    private string name;

    public function __construct(int id, string name)
    {
        this.id = id;
        this.name = name;
    }

    public function id(): int
    {
        return this.id;
    }

    public function name(): string
    {
        return this.name;
    }
}

public function it_can_be_constructed(): void
{
    product = new Product(1, 'Some name');

    assertEquals(1, product.id());
    assertEquals('Some name', product.name());
}
```

This is the only test for the Product class.

- a It has getters.
- b The getters seem to be there only to test the constructor.
- c The properties aren't nullable.

3.13   *The exception to the rule: Data transfer objects*

The rules described in this chapter apply to entities and value objects; we care a lot about the consistency and validity of the data that ends up inside such objects. These objects can only guarantee correct behavior if the data they use is correct too.

There's another type of object that I haven't mentioned so far, to which most of the previous rules don't apply. It's a type of object that you will find at the edges of an application, where data coming from the world outside is converted into a structure that the application can work with. The nature of this process requires it to behave a little differently from entities and value objects.

This special type of object is known as a *data transfer object* (DTO):

- A DTO can be created using a regular constructor.
- Its properties can be set one by one.
- All of its properties are exposed.
- Its properties contain only primitive-type values.
- Properties can optionally contain other DTOs, or simple arrays of DTOs.

3.13.1   *Use public properties*

Since a DTO doesn't protect its state and exposes all of its properties, there is no need for getters and setters. This means it's quite sufficient to use `public` properties for them. Because DTOs can be constructed in steps and don't require a minimum amount of data to be provided, they don't need constructor methods.

DTOs are often used as command objects, matching the user's intention and containing all the data needed to fulfill their wish. An example of such a command object is the following `ScheduleMeetup` command, which represents the user's wish to schedule a meetup with the given title on the given date.

Listing 3.36   The `ScheduleMeetup` DTO

```
final class ScheduleMeetup
{
    public string title;
    public string date;
}
```

The way you can use such an object is, for example, by populating it with the data submitted with a form, and then passing it to a service, which will schedule the meetup for the user. An example implementation can be found in the following listing.

Listing 3.37   Populating the `ScheduleMeetup` DTO and passing it to a service

```
final class MeetupController
{
    public function scheduleMeetupAction(Request request): Response
    {
```

```
                  formData = /* ... */;                          ◁─────┐  Extract the form
                                                                       │  data from the
Create the    ┌─▷ scheduleMeetup = new ScheduleMeetup();               │  request body.
command       │   scheduleMeetup.title = formData['title'];
object using  │   scheduleMeetup.date = formData['date'];
this data.    │
              │   this.scheduleMeetupService.execute(scheduleMeetup);

                  // ...
              }
          }
```

The service will create an entity and some value objects and eventually persist them. When
instantiated, these objects will throw exceptions if anything is wrong with the data that was
provided to them. However, such exceptions aren't really user-friendly; they can't even be
easily translated to the user's language. Also, because they break the application's flow,
exceptions can't be collected and returned as a list of input errors to the user.

3.13.2 *Don't throw exceptions, collect validation errors*

If you want to allow users to correct all their mistakes in one go, before resubmitting
the form, you should validate the command's data before passing the object to the service that's going to handle it. One way to do this is by adding a validate() method to
the command, which can return a simple list of validation errors. If the list is empty, it
means that the submitted data was valid.

> Listing 3.38 Validating the `ScheduleMeetup` DTO

```
final class ScheduleMeetup
{
    public string title;
    public string date;

    public function validate(): array
    {
        errors = [];

        if (this.title == '') {
            errors['title'][] = 'validation.empty_title';
        }

        if (this.date == '') {
            errors['date'][] = 'validation.empty_date';
        }

        DateTime.createFromFormat('d/m/Y', this.date);
        errors = DateTime.getLastErrors();
        if (errors['error_count'] > 0) {
            errors['date'][] = 'validation.invalid_date_format';
        }

        return errors;
    }
}
```

Form and validation libraries may offer you more convenient and reusable tools for validation. For instance, the Symfony Form and Validator components work really well with this kind of data transfer object.

3.13.3 *Use property fillers when needed*

Earlier we discussed property fillers and how they shouldn't be used when working with most objects; they expose all the object's internals. In the case of a DTO, this isn't a problem because a DTO doesn't protect its internals anyway. So, if it makes sense, you can add a property filler method to a DTO, such as to copy form data or JSON request data directly into a command object. Since filling the properties is the first thing that should happen to a DTO, it makes sense to implement the property filler as a named constructor.

> Listing 3.39   The `ScheduleMeetup` DTO has a property filler

```
final class ScheduleMeetup
{
    public string title;
    public string date;

    public static function fromFormData(
        array formData
    ): ScheduleMeetup {
        scheduleMeetup = new ScheduleMeetup();

        scheduleMeetup.title = formData['title'];
        scheduleMeetup.date = formData['date'];

        return scheduleMeetup;
    }
}
```

Exercises

9   What type of object do you need if you want to provide a list of validation errors to the user?

   a   An entity

   b   A DTO

10   What type of object would throw an exception if the data provided to it is incorrect?

   a   An entity

   b   A DTO

11   What type of object would limit the amount of data that it exposes?

   a   An entity

   b   A DTO

Summary

- Objects that are not service objects receive values or value objects, not dependencies. Upon construction, an object should require a minimum amount of data to be provided in order to behave consistently. If any of the provided constructor arguments is invalid in some way, the constructor should throw an exception about it.
- It helps to wrap primitive-type arguments inside (value) objects. This makes it easy to reuse validation rules for these values. It also adds more meaning to the code by specifying a domain-specific name for the type (class) of the value.
- For objects that aren't services, constructors should be static methods, also known as *named constructors*, which offer yet another opportunity for introducing domain-specific names in your code.
- Don't provide any more data to a constructor than is needed to make the object behave as specified by its unit tests.
- A type of object for which most of these rules don't count is a *data transfer object*. DTOs are used to carry data provided by the world outside, and they expose all their internals.

Answers to the exercises

1 Correct answers: **a** and **d**. Money is not a service, so it should not have any dependencies injected as constructor arguments. Also, based on the example, there's no way to establish whether or not the constructor has default arguments.

2 Suggested answer:

```
final class PriceRange
{
    public function __construct(int minimumPrice, int maximumPrice)
    {
        if (minimumPrice < 0) {
            throw new InvalidArgumentException(
                'minimumPrice should be 0 or more'
            );
        }
        if (maximumPrice < 0) {
            throw new InvalidArgumentException(
                'maximumPrice should be 0 or more'
            );
        }
        if (minimumPrice > maximumPrice) {
            throw new InvalidArgumentException(
                'maximumPrice should be greater than minimumPrice'
            );
        }

        this.minimumPrice = miminumPrice;
        this.maximumPrice = maximumPrice;
    }
}
```

3 Suggested answer:

```
final class CountryCode
{
    private static knownCountryCodes = ['NL', 'GB'];

    private string countryCode;

    public function __construct(string countryCode)
    {
        if (!in_array(
            countryCode,
            CountryCode.knownCountryCodes)
        ) {
            throw new InvalidArgumentException(
                'Unknown country code: ' . countryCode
            );
        }

        this.countryCode = countryCode;
    }
}
```

4 Suggested answer:

```
final class Distance
{
    private int distance;
    private string unit;

    public function __construct(int distance, string unit)
    {
        if (distance <= 0) {
            throw new InvalidArgumentException(
                'distance should be greater than 0'
            );
        }
        this.distance = distance;

        if (!in_array(unit, ['meters', 'feet'])) {
            throw new InvalidArgumentException(
                'Unknown unit: ' unit
            );
        }
        this.unit = unit;
    }
}

final class Run
{
    public function __construct(Distance distance)
    {
        // ...
    }
}
```

5 Suggested answer:

```
final class PriceRange
{
    public function __construct(int minimumPrice, int maximumPrice)
    {
        Assertion.greaterThanOrEqual(minimumPrice, 0);
        Assertion.greaterThanOrEqual(maximumPrice, 0);
        Assertion.greaterThan(maximumPrice, minimumPrice);

        this.minimumPrice = miminumPrice;
        this.maximumPrice = maximumPrice;
    }
}
```

6 Correct answer: **c.** User is not a service, but an entity, so it should not get any dependencies injected as constructor arguments or using setter methods. Also, it should not need to reach out for dependencies. Instead, any dependency that it needs to perform a task should be provided to it as a method argument.

7 Correct answer: **b.** The other options usually lead to bad design: removing types, adding multiple arguments only one of which will be used each time, and extending from a class you don't own to add behavior to it.

8 Correct answer: **b.** Getters aren't forbidden, and it's okay for a property to be null. The rule is not to add getters just for testing purposes.

9 Correct answer: **b.** As soon as an entity recognizes that a client passes invalid data to it, it will throw an exception. This leaves no room for analyzing the available data and generating a list of validation errors.

10 Correct answer: **a.** A DTO will accept any data provided to it, as long as it has the expected type. An entity will throw exceptions as soon as it receives even one piece of invalid data.

11 Correct answer: **a.** A DTO by default exposes all of its data. An entity normally protects most of its internal data.

Manipulating objects 4

This chapter covers

- Making a distinction between mutable and immutable objects
- Using modifier methods to change state or create modified copies
- Comparing objects
- Protecting against invalid state changes
- Using events to track changes in mutable objects

As you've learned in the previous chapters, services should be designed to be immutable. This means that once a service object has been created, it can never be modified. The biggest advantage is that its behavior will be predictable, and it can be reused to perform the same task using different input.

So we know that services should be immutable objects, but what about the other types of objects: entities, value objects, and data transfer objects?

4.1 *Entities: Identifiable objects that track changes and record events*

Entities are the application's core objects. They represent important concepts from the business domain, like a reservation, an order, an invoice, a product, a customer, etc. They model knowledge that developers have gained about that business domain. An entity holds the relevant data, it may offer ways to manipulate that data, and it may expose some useful information based on that data. An example of an entity is the following SalesInvoice class.

Listing 4.1 The `SalesInvoice` entity

```
final class SalesInvoice
{
    /**
     * @var Line[]
     */
    private array lines = [];

    private bool finalized = false;

    public static function create(/* ... */): SalesInvoice      ◁──── You can create
    {                                                                  a sales invoice.
        // ...
    }
                                                            You can manipulate its
                                                            state, such as by adding
    public function addLine(/* ... */): void      ◁──────── lines to it.
    {
        if (this.finalized) {
            throw new RuntimeException(/* ... */);
        }

        this.lines[] = Line.create(/* ... */);
    }
                                                     You can
    public function finalize(): void      ◁──────── finalize it.
    {
        this.finalized = true;
        // ...
    }
                                                               It exposes some useful
    public function totalNetAmount(): Money      ◁──────────── information about itself.
    {
        // ...
    }

    public function totalAmountIncludingTaxes(): Money
    {
        // ...
    }
}
```

An entity may change over time, but it should always be the same object that undergoes the changes. That's why an entity needs to be identifiable. When creating it, we give it an identifier.

Listing 4.2 `SalesInvoice` gets an identifier at construction time

```
final class SalesInvoice
{
    private SalesInvoiceId salesInvoiceId;

    public static function create(
        SalesInvoiceId salesInvoiceId
    ): SalesInvoice {
        object = new SalesInvoice();

        object.salesInvoiceId = salesInvoiceId;

        return object;
    }
}
```

This identifier can be used by the entity's repository to save the object. Later on, we can use that same identifier to retrieve it from the repository, after which it can be modified again.

Listing 4.3 Using an identifier to modify an entity you created earlier

```
salesInvoiceId = this.salesInvoiceRepository.nextIdentity();
salesInvoice = SalesInvoice.create(salesInvoiceId);
this.salesInvoiceRepository.save(salesInvoice);
```
    First, create SalesInvoice and save it.

```
salesInvoice = this.salesInvoiceRepository.getBy(salesInvoiceId);
salesInvoice.addLine(/* ... */);
this.salesInvoiceRepository.save(salesInvoice);
```
    Later, retrieve it again to make further changes to it.

Given that the state of an entity changes over time, entities are mutable objects. They come with specific rules for their implementation:

- The methods that change the entity's state should have a void return type and their names should be in the imperative form (e.g., addLine(), finalize()).
- These methods have to protect the entity against ending up in an invalid state (e.g., addLine() checks that the invoice hasn't been finalized already).
- The entity shouldn't expose all its internals to test what's going on inside. Instead, an entity should keep a change log and expose that, so other objects can find out what has changed about it, and why.

The following listing shows how SalesInvoice keeps a change log by recording internal domain events, which can be retrieved from outside by calling recordedEvents().

Listing 4.4 The `SalesInvoice` entity keeps an internal change log

```
final class SalesInvoice
{
    /**
     * @var object[]
     */
    private array events = [];
    private bool finalized = false;
    public function finalize(): void
    {
        this.finalized = true;

        this.events[] = new SalesInvoiceFinalized(/* ... */);
    }

    /**
     * @return object[]
     */
    public function recordedEvents(): array
    {
        return this.events;
    }
}

salesInvoice = SalesInvoice.create(/* ... */);          ◁——  In a test scenario ...
salesInvoice.finalize();

assertEquals(
    [
        new SalesInvoiceFinalized(/* ... */)
    ],
    salesInvoice.recordedEvents()
);
```

In a service, we can allow
event listeners to respond to
the internally recorded events.

```
salesInvoice = this.salesInvoiceRepository.getBy(salesInvoiceId);   ◁—
salesInvoice.finalize(/* ... */);
this.salesInvoiceRepository.save(salesInvoice);

this.eventDispatcher.dispatchAll(
    salesInvoice.recordedEvents()
);
```

4.2 Value objects: Replaceable, anonymous, and immutable values

Value objects are completely different. They are often much smaller, with just one or two properties. They can represent a domain concept too, in which case they represent part of an entity, or an aspect of it. For example, in the `SalesInvoice` entity, we need value objects for the ID of the sales invoice, the date on which the invoice was created, and the ID and quantity of the product on each line. The following listing shows an outline of the involved value object classes.

Listing 4.5   Value objects used by the `SalesInvoice` entity

```
final class SalesInvoiceId
{
    // ...
}

final class Date
{
    // ...
}

final class Quantity
{
    // ...
}

final class ProductId
{
    // ...
}

final class SalesInvoice
{
    public static function create(
        SalesInvoiceId salesInvoiceId,
        Date invoiceDate
    ): SalesInvoice {
        // ...
    }

    public function addLine(
        ProductId productId,
        Quantity quantity
    ): void {
        this.lines[] = Line.create(
            productId,
            quantity
        );
    }
}
```

As you saw in the previous chapter, value objects wrap one or more primitive-type values, and they can be created by providing these values to their constructors:

```
final class Quantity
{
    public static function fromInt(
        int quantity,
        int precision
    ): Quantity {
        // ...
    }
}
```

```
final class ProductId
{
    public static function fromInt(int productId): ProductId
    {
        // ...
    }
}
```

We don't need value objects to be identifiable. We don't care about the exact instance we're working with, since we don't need to track the changes that happen to a value object. In fact, we shouldn't change a value object at all. If we want to transform it to some other value, we should just instantiate a new copy, which represents the modified value. As an example, when adding two quantities, instead of changing the internal value of the original `Quantity`, we return a new `Quantity` object to represent the sum.

Listing 4.6 `add()` returns a new copy of `Quantity`

```
final class Quantity
{
    private int quantity;
    private int precision;

    private function __construct(
        int quantity,
        int precision
    ) {
        this.quantity = quantity;
        this.precision = precision;
    }

    public static function fromInt(
        int quantity,
        int precision
    ): Quantity {
        return new Quantity(quantity, precision);
    }

    public function add(Quantity other): Quantity
    {
        Assertion.same(this.precision, other.precision);

        return new Quantity(
            this.quantity + other.quantity,
            this.precision
        );
    }
}

originalQuantity = Quantity.fromInt(1500, 2); ◁

newQuantity = originalQuantity.add(Quantity.fromInt(500, 2));
```

A quantity of 1500 with a precision of 2 represents 15.00.

The modified quantity represents 15.00 + 5.00 = 20.00.

By returning a new copy instead of manipulating the existing object, we effectively make the `Quantity` value object immutable. Once created, it won't change.

Value objects don't only represent domain concepts. They can occur anywhere in the application. A value object is any immutable object that wraps primitive-type values.

4.3 Data transfer objects: Simple objects with fewer design rules

Another type of object that wraps primitive-type values is a *data transfer object*; we discussed them in the previous chapter. Although some people prefer to implement DTOs as immutable objects, this level of protection often gets in the way of other characteristics you may be after. For instance, you may want to fill the properties one by one, based on data submitted by the user. You also won't want to maintain or unit test a DTO, as it has no significant behavior (it just holds data), so you won't want it to have too many methods (such as getters and setters). In the end, you may settle on using `public` properties. If your programming language has a way to mark them as read-only/write-once (e.g., Java has a `final` keyword to accomplish this), it would be smart to use it on your DTOs.

The following listing shows an example of the DTO class `CreateSalesInvoice`, which also keeps instances of the DTO class `Line`.

Listing 4.7 DTO classes with public fields

```
final class CreateSalesInvoice
{
    /**
     * @final
     */
    public string date;

    /**
     * @var Line[]
     * @final
     */
    public array lines = [];
}

final class Line
{
    /**
     * @final
     */
    public int productId;

    /**
     * @final
     */
    public int quantity;
}
```

We don't have design rules for data transfer objects that are as strong as the rules for entities and value objects. For the latter, design quality and data integrity are more important than they are for data transfer objects. This is why the design rules in this chapter apply to entities and value objects.

Exercises

1   What type of object is represented by the following class?

```
final class UserId
{
    private int userId;

    private function __construct(int userId)
    {
        this.userId = userId;
    }

    public static function fromInt(int userId): UserId
    {
        return new UserId(userId);
    }
}
```

   a Entity
   b Value object
   c Data transfer object

2   What type of object is represented by the following class?

```
final class User
{
    private UserId userId;
    private Username username;
    private bool isActive;

    private function __construct()
    {
    }

    public static function create(
        UserId userId,
        Username username
    ): User {
        user = new User();

        user.userId = userId;
        user.username = username;

        return user;
    }
}
```

(continued)

```
    public function deactivate(): void
    {
        this.active = false;
    }
}
```

   a Entity

   b Value object

   c Data transfer object

3 What type of object is represented by the following class?

```
final class CreateUser
{
    public string username;
    public string password;
}
```

   a Entity

   b Value object

   c Data transfer object

4.4   *Prefer immutable objects*

Since an entity is designed to track changes, it is useful for it to be manipulable after construction. In general, however, you should prefer objects to be immutable. In fact, most objects that are not entities should be implemented as immutable value objects. Let's take a closer look at why you should prefer an object to be immutable.

By definition, an object can be created and then reused in different places. We can pass an object on as a method argument or a constructor argument, or we can assign an object to a property:

```
object = new Foo();

this.someMethod(object);        ◁——— Pass along the object.

this.someProperty = object;     ◁——— Assign the object to a property.

return object;                  ◁——— Maybe return the object.
```

If one call site has a reference to an object, and another call site then changes some aspect of the object, it will be quite a surprise for the first call site. How can it know that the object is still useful? Maybe the initial call site doesn't know how to deal with the new state of the object.

But even within the same call site, problems related to mutability can occur. Take a look at the following listing.

Listing 4.8 The Appointment class has mutability issues

```
final class Appointment
{
    private DateTime time;

    public function __construct(DateTime time)
    {
        this.time = time;
    }

    public function time(): string
    {
        return this.time.format('h:s');
    }

    public function reminderTime(): string
    {
        oneHourBefore = '-1 hour';

        reminderTime = this.time.modify(oneHourBefore);    ◁──  This actually modifies
                                                                 the object stored in
                                                                 the time property.
        return reminderTime.format('h:s');
    }
}

appointment = new Appointment(new DateTime('12:00'));    │  First, get the time of
                                                         │  the appointment. This
time = appointment.time();                         ◁─────┘  returns '12:00'.

reminderTime = appointment.reminderTime();    ◁───────┐  Then get the time for
                                                      │  sending a reminder.
time = appointment.time();                  ◁─────┐   │  This returns '11:00'.
                                                  │
            Finally, get the time of the          │
            appointment again. This               │
                returns '11:00' now.
```

Reading code like this, it may take a lot of time to figure out why, after requesting the time for sending a reminder, the time of the appointment itself has changed. To prevent this kind of situation, the general rule is to design every object that is not an entity to be immutable. It'll always be safe to keep a reference to an immutable object.

4.4.1 Replace values instead of modifying them

If you design objects to be immutable, they show a nice similarity with primitive-type values. Consider this example:

```
i = 1;
i++;
```

Would you consider 1 to have been changed into 2? No, we should say that the variable i previously contained 1, and now it contains 2. Integers are in fact immutable themselves. We use them, and then we discard them, but we can always use them again. Also, passing them around as method arguments or copying them into object properties isn't considered dangerous. Every time we need an integer, we create a new one from the endless supply of integers. There's no shared place in the computer's memory where we keep one instance of every integer.

The same goes for objects that are implemented as immutable values. It doesn't feel like we share them anymore. And if we need the object to be different, we don't modify the object—we create a new one. This means that if an immutable object is inside a variable or property, and we want to change something about it, we create a new object and store it in our variable or property.

To illustrate, let's say we implemented Year as an immutable object, wrapping an integer and offering a convenient method for returning a new Year instance representing the next year.

Listing 4.9   The Year class

```
final class Year
{
    private int year;

    public function __construct(int year)
    {
        this.year = year;
    }

    public function next(): Year
    {
        return new Year(this.year + 1);
    }
}

year = new Year(2019);

year.next();
assertEquals(new Year(2019), year);

year = year.next();
assertEquals(new Year(2020), year);
```

This has no effect, since next() doesn't actually change year.

Instead, we should capture the return value of next().

If we keep a Year instance in a property of a mutable object, and we want it to proceed to the next year, we should not only call next(), but we should also store its return value in the property that holds the current Year instance, as follows.

Listing 4.10   Replace values instead of modifying them

```
final class Journal
{
    private Year currentYear;
```

```
public function closeTheFinancialYear(): void
{
    // ...

    this.currentYear = this.currentYear.next();
}
}
```

How to decide if an object should be immutable

If an object is a service, it's clear: it should be immutable. If it's an entity, it's expected to change, so it should be mutable. All other types of objects should be immutable, for all the reasons mentioned in the previous section.

In practice, depending on the type of application you work on, you may still need to implement some objects as mutable, such as if your application has an interactive GUI, or if you're a game developer. If a framework forces you to let go of the rules, sometimes you have to (and sometimes you have to let go of the framework). Just make sure that your default choice is to make objects immutable.

Exercises

4 The following `ColorPalette` class represents an immutable object, which should be created once and never modified. Unfortunately, the current implementation won't result in an immutable object. Can you see what's wrong with it?

```
final class ColorPalette
{
    private Collection colors;

    private function __construct()
    {
        this.colors = new Collection();
    }

    public static function startWith(sRGB color): ColorPalette
    {
        palette = new ColorPalette();

        palette.colors.add(color);

        return palette;
    }

    public function withColorAdded(sRGB color): ColorPalette
    {
        copy = clone this;
        copy.colors = clone this.colors;

        copy.colors.add(color);
```

```
(continued)
            return copy;
        }

    public function colors(): Collection
    {
        return this.colors;
    }
}
```

    a `startWith()` internally modifies the `ColorPalette` instance, making it a mutable object.

    b `colors()` returns a mutable collection, making the `ColorPalette` instance indirectly mutable.

    c `withColorAdded()` modifies the original `ColorPalette` instance.

4.5 *A modifier on an immutable object should return a modified copy*

Based on our findings regarding immutability, immutable objects can have methods that could be considered modifiers, but they don't modify the state of the object on which we call the method. Instead, such a method returns a copy of the object, but with data that matches the method's intention. The return type of the method should be the class of that object itself, just like the return type of the `next()` method from the previous example was `Year`.

There are two basic templates for these methods. The first uses the (potentially private) constructor of the object, to create the desired copy, like the `plus()` method in the next listing.

Listing 4.11 `plus()` returns a new copy using the existing constructor

```
final class Integer
{
    private int integer;

    public function __construct(int integer)
    {
        this.integer = integer;
    }

    public function plus(Integer other): Integer
    {
        return new Integer(this.integer + other.integer);
    }
}
```

Since `Integer` already has a constructor that accepts an `int` value, we can add the existing integers and pass the resulting `int` to the constructor of `Integer`.

The other option, which can sometimes be useful for immutable objects with multiple properties, is to create an actual copy of the object using the `clone` operator, and then make the desired change to it. The `withX()` method does this in the following listing.

Listing 4.12   `withX()` uses the `clone` operator to create a copy

```
final class Position
{
    private int x;
    private int y;

    public function __construct(int x, int y)
    {
        this.x = x;
        this.y = y;
    }

    public function withX(int x): Position
    {
        copy = clone this;

        copy.x = x;

        return copy;
    }
}

position = new Position(10, 20);

nextPosition = position.withX(6);
assertEquals(new Position(6, 20), nextPosition);
```

⟵ The next position will be 4 steps to the left (6, 20).

In the previous example, `withX()` resembles a traditional setter method, which simply allows a client to replace the value of a single property. This forces the client to make the necessary calculations to find out what that new value should be. There are usually better options. Make sure you look for ways to make modifier methods a bit smarter, or at least give them a name that's domain-oriented rather than technical. You may find useful clues about how to accomplish that by looking at how clients use these methods.

For example, here's a client of the `withX()` method:

```
nextPosition = position.withX(position.x() - 4);
```

⟵ Move 4 steps to the left.

Because `Position` only has a modifier method for setting a new value for x, this client has to make its own calculations to determine which value it has to provide. But the client isn't really looking for a way to modify x; it's looking for a way to find out what the next position will be if it takes four steps to the left.

Instead of making the client do the calculations, you can let the `Position` object do it. You only need to offer a more convenient modifier method, such as `toTheLeft()` in the following listing.

Listing 4.13 `toTheLeft()` is more useful than `withX()`

```
final class Position
{
    // ...

    public function toTheLeft(int steps): Position
    {
        copy = clone this;

        copy.x = copy.x - steps;

        return copy;
    }
}

position = new Position(10, 20);

nextPosition = position.toTheLeft(4);          ⟵── The next position
assertEquals(new Position(6, 20), nextPosition);      will be (6, 20).

                                               ⟵── The original object should
assertEquals(new Position(10, 20), position);       not have been modified.
```

Exercises

5 Take a look at the following `DiscountPercentage` and `Money` value object classes.

```
final class DiscountPercentage
{
    private int percentage;

    public static function fromInt(int percentage)
    {
        discount = new DiscountPercentage();

        discount.percentage = percentage;

        return discount;
    }

    public function percentage(): int
    {
        return this.percentage;
    }
}
```

```
final class Money
{
    private int amountInCents;

    public static function fromInt(int amountInCents)
    {
        money = new Money();

        money.amountInCents = amountInCents;

        return money;
    }

    public function amountInCents(): int
    {
        return this.amountInCents;
    }
}
```

This is how you can use `Money` and `DiscountPercentage` to calculate a discounted price:

```
originalPrice = Money.fromInt(2000);          ⟵——— 20.00 euros

discountPercentage = DiscountPercentage.fromInt(10);    ⟵——— 10% discount

discount = (int)round(
    discountPercentage.percentage() / 100)    ⟵┐  Calculate the discount
     * originalPrice.amountInCents()              and subtract the discount
);                                                from the original price.
discountedPrice = Money.fromInt(
    originalPrice.amountInCents() - discount
);
```

Instead of doing this calculation outside a `Money` object, write a modifier method called `withDiscountApplied()` on the `Money` class that can perform the calculation on itself.

4.6 On a mutable object, modifier methods should be command methods

Even though almost all of your objects should be immutable, there are usually some objects that are not, namely entities. As we saw at the beginning of this chapter, an entity has methods that allow it to be manipulated.

Let's look at another example, the `Player` class, which has a current position, encoded as values for X and Y. It's a mutable object: it has a `moveLeft()` method, which updates (replaces, actually) the player's position. The `Position` object is immutable, but the `Player` object itself is mutable.

> **Listing 4.14 `Player` is mutable, `Position` is immutable**

```
final class Player
{
    private Position position;

    public function __construct(Position initialPosition)
    {
        this.position = initialPosition;
    }

    public function moveLeft(int steps): void
    {
        this.position = this.position.toTheLeft(steps);
    }

    public function currentPosition(): Position
    {
        return this.position;
    }
}
```

We can recognize mutability by the assignment operator in `moveLeft()`: the `position` property gets a new value if you call this method. Another sign is the `void` return type. These two characteristics are the trademarks of a so-called *command method*.

Methods that change the state of an object should always be command methods like this. They have a name in the imperative form, they're allowed to make a change to the object's internal data structures, and they don't return anything.

4.7   On an immutable object, modifier methods should have declarative names

Modifier methods on mutable objects are expected to change the state of the object, which nicely matches the traditional characteristics of a command method. For modifier methods of immutable objects, we need another convention.

Imagine having the same implementation of `Position` that we saw earlier, but this time `toTheLeft()` was called `moveLeft()`.

> **Listing 4.15 `moveLeft()`, instead of `toTheLeft()`**

```
final class Position
{
    // ...

    public function moveLeft(int steps): Position
    {
        // ...
    }
}
```

Given the rule that modifier methods on mutable objects are command methods, this `moveLeft()` is confusing: it has an imperative name (`moveLeft()`), but it doesn't have a `void` return type. Unless they look at the implementation, readers will be unsure whether or not calling this method will change the state of the object.

To create a good name for modifier methods on immutable objects, you can fill in the following template: "I want this ..., but ...". In the case of `Position`, this becomes "I want this position, but n steps to the left," so `toTheLeft()` seems to be a suitable method name.

Listing 4.16   `toTheLeft()` is a more suitable name

```
final class Position
{
    // ...

    public function toTheLeft(int steps): Position
    {
        // ...
    }
}
```

Following this template, you may often end up using the word "with," or using so-called participle adjectives in the past tense. For instance, "I want this quantity, but multiplied n times." Or "I want this response, but with a `Content-Type: text/html` header." These are declarative names: they don't tell you what to do, but they "declare" the result of the manipulation.

When looking for good names, also aim for domain-specific, higher-level names instead of generic names from the underlying technical domain. For example, we chose `toTheLeft()` instead of `withXDecreasedBy()`, which has a different level of abstraction.

Exercises

6   An object has the following method:

```
public setPassword(string plainTextPassword): void
```

    Is this object expected to be mutable or immutable?

    a   Mutable
    b   Immutable

7   An object has the following method:

```
public withPassword(string plainTextPassword): User
```

    Is this object expected to be mutable or immutable?

    a   Mutable
    b   Immutable

(continued)

8 An object has the following method:

```
withPassword(string plainTextPassword): void
```

Is this object expected to be mutable or immutable?

a Mutable

b Immutable

4.8   *Compare whole objects*

With mutable objects, you can write tests like the following.

Listing 4.17   A unit test for `moveLeft()`

```
public function it_can_move_to_the_left(): void
{
    position = new Position(10, 20);
    position.moveLeft(4);
    assertSame(6, position.x());
}
```

As mentioned earlier, this kind of testing usually forces additional getters to be added to the class. These getters are only needed for writing the tests; no other client might be interested in them.

  With immutable objects, you can often resort to a different kind of assertion—one that allows the object to keep its internal data and implementation details on the inside, as follows.

Listing 4.18   A unit test for `toTheLeft()`

```
public function it_can_move_to_the_left(): void
{
    position = new Position(10, 20);
    nextPosition = position.toTheLeft(4);
    assertEquals(new Position(6, 20), nextPosition);
}
```

`assertEquals()` will use a recursive method that tests for the equality of the properties of both objects, and of the objects it keeps inside those properties, and so on. Using `assertEquals()` therefore prevents value objects from having some hidden aspect that would make two objects incomparable.

4.9 When comparing immutable objects, assert equality, not sameness

The following example shows how the `Position` class from the previous example can be used in a (mutable) `Player` class.

Listing 4.19 The `Player` class

```
final class Player
{
    private Position position;

    public function __construct(Position initialPosition)
    {
        this.position = initialPosition;
    }

    public function moveLeft(int steps): void
    {
        this.position = this.position.toTheLeft(steps);
    }

    public function currentPosition(): Position
    {
        return this.position;
    }
}
```

A test for `moveLeft()` might look like the following.

Listing 4.20 A unit test for `moveLeft()`

```
function the_player_starts_at_a_position_and_can_move_left(): void
{
    initialPosition = new Position(10, 20);
    player = new Player(initialPosition);

    assertSame(initialPosition, player.currentPosition());

    player.moveLeft(4);

    assertEquals(new Position(6, 20), player.currentPosition());
}
```

We can get away with using assertSame() here—the Position object is still the *same* object we injected.

Here we have to use assertEquals().

When comparing immutable objects, tests shouldn't make a point of objects having the same reference in memory. All that matters is the thing they represent. When comparing integers, we don't compare their memory locations. We just say, "Are their values equal?" So you should always use `assertEquals()` when comparing objects.

Sometimes you'll want to compare two objects in production code rather than in a test. In that case, you can't use `assertEquals()`. What you should do will depend on your programming language. Some languages, like Java and C#, have a built-in mechanism for object comparison. Objects in those languages will inherit an `equals()` method from a generic `Object` class, which you can override to implement your own comparison logic. If you're using PHP, you should mimic this approach. Add an `equals()` method to the object that compares the data contained in both objects, as shown in the next listing.

Listing 4.21   `equals()` helps with comparing two `Position` objects

```
final class Position
{
    // ...

    public function equals(Position other): bool
    {
        return this.x == other.x && this.y == other.y;
    }
}
```

However, most value objects really don't need a custom `equals()` method, and you definitely shouldn't implement one on every immutable object without thinking about it. The rule for getters applies for the `equals()` method too: only add this method if some other client than a test uses it. Also, if you can avoid typing `other` as `object`, you should do so. In general, clients shouldn't try to compare a `Position` object to anything other than a `Position` object.

Exercises

9   How should you compare two value objects in a unit test?

   a   By comparing the return values of their getters.
   b   By using a specialized object comparison function like `assertEquals()`.
   c   By comparing the object reference (using `==`).
   d   By calling the object's `equals()` method.

10   How should you compare two value objects in production code?

   a   By comparing the return values of their getters.
   b   By using a specialized object comparison function like `assertEquals()`.
   c   By comparing the object reference (using `==`).
   d   By calling the object's `equals()` method.

4.10 *Calling a modifier method should always result in a valid object*

When we talked about creating objects earlier, we discussed concepts like meaningful data and domain invariants. The same concepts can be applied to modifier methods, and not just for modifier methods on immutable objects. The rules also apply to mutable objects.

A modifier method has to make sure that the client provides meaningful data, and it has to protect domain invariants. It does so in the same way constructors do: by making assertions about the arguments that have been provided. It can thereby prevent the object from ending up in an invalid state. For an example, look at the following add() method.

> **Listing 4.22 TotalDistanceTraveled doesn't accept a negative distance**

```
final class TotalDistanceTraveled
{
    private int totalDistance = 0;

    public function add(int distance): TotalDistanceTraveled
    {
        Assertion.greaterOrEqualThan(
            distance,
            0,
            'You cannot add a negative distance'
        );

        copy = clone this;
        copy.totalDistance += distance;

        return copy;
    }
}

totalDistanceTravelled = new TotalDistanceTraveled();
expectException(
    InvalidArgumentException.className,
    'distance',
    function () use (totalDistanceTravelled) {
        totalDistanceTravelled.add(-10);
    }
);
```

If the modifier method doesn't clone, but reuses the original constructor of the class, you can often reuse the validation logic that's already available. In fact, this can be a good reason not to use clone, but always to go through the constructor.

As an example, consider a Fraction class, which represents a fraction (e.g., 1/3, 2/5). The structure of a fraction is [numerator]/[denominator]. Both can be any whole number, but the denominator can never be 0. The constructor enforces this rule already, so the modifier method `withDenominator()` only needs to forward the call to the constructor, and the rule will be verified for the input of `withDenominator()` too.

Listing 4.23 `withDenominator()` reuses validation logic in the constructor

```
final class Fraction
{
    private int numerator;
    private int denominator;

    public function __construct(int numerator, int denominator)
    {
        Assertion.notEq(
            denominator,
            0,
            'The denominator of a fraction cannot be 0'
        );

        this.numerator = numerator;
        this.denominator = denominator;
    }

    public function withDenominator(newDenominator): Fraction
    {
        return new Fraction(this.numerator, newDenominator);     ◁──┐  Forwarding the call
    }                                                                 to the constructor
}                                                                     will also trigger any
                                                                      of its assertions.
fraction = new Fraction(1, 2);

expectException(
    InvalidArgumentException.className,
    'denominator',
    function () use (fraction) {
        fraction.withDenominator(0);
    }
);
```

Exercises

11 Point out what's wrong with the following implementation of a `Range` object:

```
final class Range
{
    private int minimum;
    private int maximum;

    private function __construct(int minimum, int maximum)
    {
        Assertion.greaterThan(maximum, minimum);

        this.minimum = minimum;
        this.maximum = maximum;
    }
```

```
public static function fromIntegers(
    int minimum,
    int maximum
): Range {
    return new Range(minimum, maximum);
}

public function withMinimum(int minimum): Range
{
    copy = clone this;
    copy.minimum = minimum;

    return copy;
}

public function withMaximum(int maximum): Range
{
    Assertion.greaterThan(maximum, this.minimum);

    copy = clone this;
    copy.maximum = maximum;

    return copy;
}
}
```

a   withMinimum() and withMaximum() create incomplete copies of the Range object.

b   The rule that "maximum should be greater than minimum" doesn't get verified in every modifier method.

4.11   A modifier method should verify that the requested state change is valid

Calling a modifier method on an object often means that the object's properties will be modified. For mutable objects like entities, such a change in the state of the object can also represent an actual *state transition*. The transition may unlock new possibilities or block options that were previously available.

As an example, consider the following SalesOrder class. Once it has been marked as "delivered," it will be impossible to cancel it, since that state transition wouldn't make sense from a business perspective. The inverse is true for an order that has been cancelled; it shouldn't be possible to deliver it after all.

Listing 4.24   SalesOrder doesn't allow certain state changes

```
final class SalesOrder
{
    // ...
```

```
    public function markAsDelivered(Timestamp deliveredAt): void
    {
        /*
         * You shouldn't be able to deliver the order if it has been
         * cancelled.
         */
    }

    public function cancel(Timestamp cancelledAt): void
    {
        /*
         * You shouldn't be able to cancel an order if it has already
         * been delivered.
         */
    }

    // and so on...
}
```

Make sure that every one of your methods prevents against making invalid state transitions. You should verify this with unit tests, like the one in the following listing.

Listing 4.25   A unit test for cancelling a delivered sales order

```
public function a_delivered_sales_order_can_not_be_cancelled(): void
{
    deliveredSalesOrder = /* ... */;
    deliveredSalesOrder.markAsDelivered(/* ... */);

    expectException(
        LogicException.className,
        'delivered',
        function () use (deliveredSalesOrder) {
            deliveredSalesOrder.cancel();
        }
    );
}
```

An appropriate exception to throw here would be a `LogicException`, but you can also introduce your own exception type, like `CanNotCancelOrder`.

If a client calls the same method twice, it requires a bit of contemplation. You could throw an exception, but in most cases it's not a big deal, and you can just ignore the call.

```
public function cancel()
{
    if (this.status.equals(Status.cancelled())) {
        return;
```

```
    }

    // ...
}
```

4.12 Use internally recorded events to verify changes on mutable objects

We've already seen how testing constructors leads to adding more getters to an object than needed, only to test that what comes in can also go out again. This isn't at all the idea of an object, which is to hide information and implementation details. The same goes for testing modifier methods.

When testing the `moveLeft()` method of the mutable `Player` object we discussed earlier, there are a few options. The first option is to use a getter to verify that the current position after moving left is the position we expect it to be.

Listing 4.27 We could test that the current position is the expected one

```
public function it_can_move_left(): void
{
    player = new Player(new Position(10, 20));
    player.moveLeft(4);

    assertEquals(new Position(6, 20), player.currentPosition());
}
```

The other, more blunt, option is to verify that the whole object is now what we expect it to be.

Listing 4.28 We could compare the whole `Player` object to the expected one

```
public function it_can_move_left(): void
{
    player = new Player(new Position(10, 20));
    player.moveLeft(4);

    assertEquals(new Player(new Position(6, 20)), player);
}
```

This second option isn't a bad solution, because at least we don't need the getter to retrieve the current position. The main issue with this test is that it covers too much ground, and we can't easily add new behavior to the `Player` object without modifying this test too (in particular, if extra constructor arguments are added over time).

Another option could be to change `moveLeft()` a bit and make it return the new position.

Listing 4.29 `moveLeft()` returns a new `Position`

```
final class Player
{
    public function moveLeft(): Position
    {
        this.position = this.position.toTheLeft(steps);

        return this.position;
    }
}

player = new Player(new Position(10, 20));
currentPosition = player.moveLeft(4);

assertEquals(new Position(6, 20), currentPosition);
```

This looks clever, but it's a violation of the rule that a modifier method on a mutable object should be a command method, and thus should have a void return type. But on top of that, this test doesn't really prove that the Player has moved to the expected position. Consider, for example, the following implementation of moveLeft(), for which the test in listing 4.29 would also pass. It returns the correct Position, but it doesn't modify the position property of Player.

Listing 4.30 A broken implementation that would pass the test

```
public function moveLeft(): Position
{
    return this.position.toTheLeft(steps);
}
```

A better way to test for changes in a mutable object is to record events inside the object that can later be inspected. These events will act like a log of the changes that happened to the object. Events are simple value objects, and you can create as many of them as needed. In the following listing, the Player class is rewritten to record PlayerMoved events and expose them through its recordedEvents() method.

Listing 4.31 Upon changing its state, `Player` records an event

```
final class Player
{
    private Position position;

    private array events = [];

    public function __construct(Position initialPosition)
    {
        this.position = initialPosition;
    }
```

```
public function moveLeft(int steps): void
{
    nextPosition = this.position.toTheLeft(steps);

    this.position = nextPosition;

    this.events[] = new PlayerMoved(nextPosition);   ◁—
}
```

After moving to the left, we record an event that can later be used to find out what has happened inside the Player object.

```
public function recordedEvents(): array
{
    return this.events;
}
}
player = new Player(new Position(10, 20));   ◁—
```

Create a new Player object and set an initial position for it.

```
player.moveLeft(4);   ◁——— Move it 4 steps to the left.

assertEquals(                     ◁—
    [
        new PlayerMoved(new Position(6, 20))
    ],
    player.recordedEvents()
);
```

Verify that the player has moved by comparing its recorded events to an expected list of events.

You can do interesting things, like only recording events if something has actually changed. For instance, maybe you allow the player to take 0 steps. If that happens, the player hasn't really moved, and the call to moveLeft() wouldn't really deserve an event to be created for it.

Listing 4.32 You may choose not to record an event

```
public function moveLeft(int steps): void
{
    if (steps == 0) {
        return;
    }

    nextPosition = this.position.toTheLeft(steps);

    this.position = nextPosition;

    this.events[] = new PlayerMoved(nextPosition);
}
```

Don't throw an exception, but also don't record an event.

After a while, assertEquals([/* ... */], player.recordedEvents()) may prove not to be flexible enough to allow the implementation of the Player object to be changed without making existing tests fail. For example, let's see what happens if we record another event to represent the moment the player took its initial position.

Listing 4.33   Player also records a `PlayerTookInitialPosition` event

```
final class PlayerTookInitialPosition
{
    // ...
}

final class Player
{
    private events;

    public function __construct(Position initialPosition)
    {
        this.position = initialPosition;

        this.events[] = new PlayerTookInitialPosition(
            initialPosition
        );
    }
}
```

This will break the existing test we had for moving to the left.

Listing 4.34   The existing test for `moveLeft()`, which will fail now

```
public function it_can_move_left(): void
{
    player = new Player(new Position(10, 20));
    player.moveLeft(4);

    assertEquals(
        [
            new PlayerMoved(new Position(6, 20))
        ],
        player.recordedEvents()
    );
}
```

> **This assertion will fail because the constructor now records a PlayerTookInitialPosition event, which will also be returned by recordedEvents().**

One thing we could do to make this test less brittle is to assert that the list of recorded events *contains* the expected event.

Listing 4.35   `assertContains ()` can compare recorded events

```
public function it_can_move_left(): void
{
    player = new Player(new Position(10, 20));
    player.moveLeft(4);

    assertContains(
        new PlayerMoved(new Position(6, 20)),
        player.recordedEvents()
    );
}
```

Take a look at the alternative implementation of `moveLeft()` in the following listing, which records an event, but doesn't actually update the player's position as stored in its `position` property. The test in listing 4.35 would also pass for this alternative, but obviously broken, implementation.

> **Listing 4.36 `moveLeft()` only records an event, but the test would still pass**

```
final class Player
{
    //...

    public function moveLeft(int steps): void
    {
        this.events[] = new PlayerMoved(nextPosition);
    }
}
```

Actually, the implementation shouldn't be considered "broken" at all. If the test passes, but the production code isn't correct, there must be something about the object's behavior that we didn't fully specify in a test. So, in a sense, the test is broken. To fix this issue, we would have to make sure that some other test forces us to update the `Player`'s `position` property. If we can't think of a good reason for doing so after all, we shouldn't worry about the `position` property at all, and simply remove it. The object's behavior will change in no observable way if we do.

> **Isn't it a bit too pushy to introduce events in every mutable object?**
>
> As mentioned at the beginning of this chapter, almost all objects will be immutable. Those few objects that are mutable will be entities. These are objects for which it's already useful to have events (they are called "domain events" then). So, in practice, adding support for recording events isn't too much to ask—it's a very natural thing to happen.
>
> This added support will likely prove useful anyway, because events are a way to respond to changes in domain objects. One type of response could be to make even more changes, or to use event data to populate search engines, build up read models, or collect useful business insights on the fly.

Since the only information the `Player` exposes to its clients is a list of internal domain events, there isn't an easy way to find out the current position of the player. In practice, that's probably not very useful; we need this information, if only to show the current position of the player on the screen. We'll get back to the topic of retrieving information from objects in chapter 6.

Exercises

12 In a unit test, what's the preferred way of finding out if a `SalesInvoice` object instantiated from the following class has been finalized?

```
final class SalesInvoice
{
    private string isFinalized = false;

    // ...

    public function finalize()
    {
        this.isFinalized = true;
    }
}
```

  a   Add a `isFinalized(): bool` method to the `SalesInvoice` class, and call it before and after a call to `finalize()`, to find out if that method did its job.

  b   Don't add a getter, but use reflection to take a peek into the private property.

  c   Collect domain events inside the entity, which can later be analyzed to find out if the invoice has indeed been finalized.

  d   Dispatch domain events and set up an event listener in the unit test, which keeps track of whether or not the invoice has been finalized.

4.13   *Don't implement fluent interfaces on mutable objects*

An object has a fluent interface when its modifier methods return `this`. If an object has a fluent interface, you can call method after method on it, without repeating the variable name of the object.

Listing 4.37   `QueryBuilder` offers a fluent interface

```
queryBuilder = QueryBuilder.create()
    .select(/* ... */)
    .from(/* ... */)
    .where(/* ... */)
    .orderBy(/* ... */);
```

However, a fluent interface can be very confusing regarding which object a method gets called on. If `QueryBuilder` is immutable, then it doesn't really matter. But who knows if it's mutable? If you look at the method signatures of `QueryBuilder` in the following listing, there's no way to find that out.

Listing 4.38   `QueryBuilder` method signatures

```
final class QueryBuilder
{
    public function select(/* ... */): QueryBuilder   <┤
```

Do these methods update the state of the object they're called on, or do they return a modified copy? Or . . . both?

```
    {
        // ...
    }

    public function from(/* ... */): QueryBuilder
    {
        // ...
    }

    // ...
}
```

Given that these method signatures look a lot like modifiers on immutable objects, we might assume that `QueryBuilder` is immutable. So we may also assume that we can safely reuse any intermediate stage of the `QueryBuilder` object, like in the next listing.

Listing 4.39   Reusing intermediate stages of a `QueryBuilder` instance

```
queryBuilder = QueryBuilder.create();

qb1 = queryBuilder
    .select(/* ... */)
    .from(/* ... */)
    .where(/* ... */)
    .orderBy(/* ... */);

qb2 = queryBuilder
    .select(/* ... */)
    .from(/* ... */)
    .where(/* ... */)
    .orderBy(/* ... */);
```

But it turns out that `QueryBuilder` isn't immutable after all, as you can see by looking at the following implementation of `where()`.

Listing 4.40   The implementation of `QueryBuilder.where()`

```
public function where(string clause, string value): QueryBuilder
{
    this.whereParts[] = clause;
    this.values[] = value;

    return this;
}
```

This method looks like a modifier of an immutable object, but it is, in fact, a regular command method. And as a very confusing bonus, it returns the current object instance after modifying it.

To avoid this confusion, don't give your mutable objects fluent interfaces. Query-Builder would be better off as an immutable object anyway. This would not leave its clients with an object in an unknown state. The following listing shows an alternative implementation of `where()` that would make `QueryBuilder` immutable.

Listing 4.41 A `where()` implementation that supports immutability

```
public function where(string clause, string value): QueryBuilder
{
    copy = clone this;

    copy.whereParts[] = clause;
    copy.values[] = value;

    return copy;
}
```

For immutable objects, having a fluent interface is not a problem. In fact, you could say that using modifier methods as they are described in this chapter gives you a fluent interface by definition, because every modifier will return a modified copy of itself. This allows for chained method calls in the same way as a regular fluent interface does (see the following listing).

Listing 4.42 Modifier methods on an immutable object form a fluent interface

```
position = Position.startAt(10, 5)
    .toTheLeft(4)
    .toTheRight(2);
```

Exercises

13 Take a look at the following sample from a `Product` entity class. Why is its `set-Price()` method so confusing?

```
final class Product
{
    // ...

    public function setPrice(Money price): Product
    {
        // ...
    }
}
```

  a The client doesn't know if the return value is the original object or a copy.
  b Being an entity, `Product` is supposed to be an immutable object, but `set-Price()` suggests that you can modify it.
  c The method looks like a modifier method on an immutable object, but `set-Price()` is not a declarative, but an imperative name.

"A third-party library has some object design issues. What do I do?"

The QueryBuilder example in this section was inspired by the actual QueryBuilder class from the Doctrine DBAL library (http://mng.bz/dx2v). It is just one example of a class that doesn't follow all the rules in this book. You're likely to encounter other classes that don't (in third-party code, and in project code itself). What to do with them?

There are different trade-offs to be made depending on how its used. For example, do you use the "badly" designed class only inside your methods, or do instances of it get passed around between methods or even objects? In the case of Query-Builder, it will likely only be used inside repository methods. This means that it can't escape and be used in other parts of your application, mitigating the design risk of using it in your project. So even if QueryBuilder has some design issues, there really is no need to rewrite it or work around it.

There may be other cases where an object is very confusing; for example, is it immutable, or mutable? A nice example is PHP's built-in DateTime class, or Java's now-deprecated java.util.Date class. Immutable alternatives have been introduced for them, but before those existed, it was a good idea to make copies of these objects before doing anything with them, or to introduce your own immutable wrapper objects. That would ensure that the mutable object never "escaped" and was modified by other clients, which could cause strange state-related issues in your application.

Summary

- Always prefer immutable objects, which can't be modified after they have been created. If you want to allow something to be changed about them, first make a copy and then make the change. Give the methods that do this declarative names, and take the opportunity to implement some useful behavior instead of simply allowing properties to be changed to new values. Make sure that after a modifier method has been called, the object is in a valid state. To do this, accept only correct data, and make sure the object doesn't make an invalid state transition.
- On mutable objects like entities, modifier methods should have a void return type. The changes that occur in such objects can be exposed by analyzing internally recorded events. As opposed to immutable objects, mutable objects shouldn't have a fluent interface.

Answers to the exercises

1. Correct answer: **b**.
2. Correct answer: **a**.
3. Correct answer: **c**.
4. Correct answer: **b**. startWith() is a constructor, and it's perfectly fine for a constructor to modify the instance it's constructing. withColorAdded() doesn't modify the original ColorPalette instance, but its copy.

5 Suggested answer:

```
final class Money
{
    // ...

    public function withDiscountApplied(
        DiscountPercentage discountPercentage
    ): Money {
        discount = (int)round(
            (discountPercentage.percentage() / 100)
            * this.amountInCents()
        );

        return Money.fromInt(
            this.amountInCents() - discount
        );
    }
}
```

6 Correct answer: **a**. If it were an immutable object, it would have a modifier method returning a modified instance of the object.

7 Correct answer: **b**. If it were a mutable object, it would have a modifier method with a void return type.

8 Correct answer: **a**. Admittedly, it's a confusing method because it mixes a declarative naming style with a command method return type (void).

9 Correct answer: **b**. Comparing the results of getters would make the test too tightly coupled to the value object. We also can't compare references, because value objects aren't supposed to share them. We should also not rely on any standard or built-in equals() method to compare objects, since we wouldn't even need to compare value objects in production code—we shouldn't add this method only for testing purposes.

10 Correct answer: **d**. See the answer to exercise 9, but in this case there seems to be an explicit need for comparing value objects in production code. Adding a custom equals() method would be recommended in this case.

11 Correct answer: **b**. It may not look like it, but withMinimum() and withMaximum() create complete copies of the Range object. Each method only overwrites the value for one property (minimum or maximum). The real problem is that withMinimum() doesn't have the assertion that withMaximum() has, leaving room for minimum to be larger than maximum.

12 Correct answer: **c**. You shouldn't add a getter just for testing; you should also not start looking around in the object's internals. Instead, use domain events to record what's going on inside the entity, and analyze it afterwards. There's no need to start dispatching events immediately either.

13 Correct answers: **a** and **c**. An entity isn't supposed to be an immutable object.

Using objects 5

This chapter covers

- Using a template to write methods
- Validating method arguments and return values
- Dealing with failure inside a method

Having instantiated an object, you're ready to use it. Objects can offer useful behaviors: they can give you information and they can perform tasks for you. Either way, these behaviors will be implemented as object methods.

Before we discuss the design rules that are specific for either retrieving information or performing tasks, we'll first discuss something these methods should have in common: a template for their implementation.

5.1   A template for implementing methods

Whenever you design a method, you should remember the following template.

Listing 5.1   A template for methods

```
[scope] function methodName(type name, ...): void|[return-type]
{
    [preconditions checks]
```

```
    [failure scenarios]

    [happy path]

    [postcondition checks]

    [return void|specific-return-type]
}
```

5.1.1   *Precondition checks*

The first step is to verify that the arguments provided by the client are correct and can be used to fulfill the task at hand. Make any number of checks, and throw exceptions when anything looks off.

Precondition checks have the following shape:

```
if (/* some precondition wasn't met */) {
    throw new InvalidArgumentException(/* ... */);
}
```

As discussed earlier, you can often use standard assertion functions for these kinds of checks.

```
Assertion.inArray(value, ['allowed', 'values']);
```

Some of these precondition checks may only be needed because the type system of the language lacks some features. For example, PHP has an array type, but no way to tell the engine that the array must consist solely of objects of a certain type. For this, you'll need to add an assertion:

```
Assertion.allIsInstanceOf(value, EventListener.className);
```

Other checks will inspect the contents of an argument and warn the client that, for instance, they provided a value in the wrong range:

```
Assertion.greaterThan(value, 0);
```

Introduce new types to get rid of precondition checks

Most of these assertions will be made to validate primitive-type arguments (int, string, etc.). As we saw in section 3.5, it often makes sense to introduce wrapper objects for these primitive-type values and move the related assertions to the constructors of these objects.

```
// Before:

public function sendConfirmationEmail(string emailAddress): void
{
    Assertion.email(emailAddress);
```

```
    // ...
}

// After:

final class EmailAddress
{
    private string emailAddress;

    public function __construct(string emailAddress)
    {
        Assertion.email(emailAddress);
        this.emailAddress = emailAddress;
    }
}

public function sendConfirmationEmail(
    EmailAddress emailAddress
): void {
    // no need to validate emailAddress anymore
}
```

This is a refactoring known as "replace primitive with object."[a]

Depending on the programming language you use, a client might still be able to provide `null` as an argument, instead of an actual `EmailAddress` object. In that case, make sure to always check for `null` arguments (or face the dreaded `NullPointer-Exception`). If possible, make this process compiler-assisted. In Java, for instance, you could use the Checker Framework for this (https://checkerframework.org/).

[a] Martin Fowler and Kent Beck, *Refactoring: Improving the Design of Existing Code, Second Edition*, Addison-Wesley Professional, 2019.

If no assertion fails, this means we accept the input arguments as they are. These precondition checks are still superficial, though, because they only inspect the values for obvious issues.

5.1.2 Failure scenarios

Even if the values "look" right and therefore pass the precondition checks, things can still go wrong. For example, even though an email address looks valid, sending an email to it might still fail. Or even though the client provides a positive integer, it might not match a record ID in the database. This means that things could still go wrong while running the remaining method code.

If something goes wrong in the method after the precondition checks, you should throw a different kind of exception. It won't be an exception indicating an invalid argument. The type of the exception should indicate that an error condition occurred that could only be detected at runtime. It's not the method itself that fails;

it's some external condition that breaks the method. The following listing shows an example of this.

Listing 5.2 getRowById () throws a RuntimeException

```
public function getRowById(int id): array              This could throw an
{                                                   InvalidArgumentException.
    Assertion.greaterThan(id, 0, 'ID should be greater than 0');  ◄────┘

    record = this.db.find(id);            ◄──────────  This could cause either an
                                                       InvalidArgumentException or a
    if (record == null) {                              RuntimeException to be thrown
        throw new RuntimeException(                    from the code that calls the
            'Could not find record with ID "{id}"'     database.
        );
    }

    return record;
}
```

This is *our* failure scenario: we couldn't find the
record, so we throw a RuntimeException.

Downstream, every method that's called may have its own precondition checks, so besides RuntimeExceptions originating from the vendor code that calls the database, we may run into an InvalidArgumentException (or its parent, LogicException). Usually we just let these exceptions "bubble up." Some higher-level application error-handling mechanism should be able to deal with these errors. What matters in this part of the method is the scenarios that the method *itself* can recognize as failure scenarios.

5.1.3 *Happy path*

The happy path, or happy part of a method, is where nothing is wrong, and the method is just performing its task. If you keep your methods small, like you should, you may find that there isn't much going on in this part. Sometimes most of the code is for dealing with failure scenarios.

5.1.4 *Postcondition checks*

Postcondition checks can be added to a method to verify that the method did what it was supposed to do. You could analyze the return value before actually returning it, or you could analyze the state of the object just before jumping out of it.

Listing 5.3 someVeryComplicatedCalculation() performs a postcondition check

```
public function someVeryComplicatedCalculation(): int
{
    // ...
    result = /* ... */;
```

```
    Assertion.greaterThan(0, result);
```
← This postcondition check is just a safety check, a.k.a. "This should never happen."

```
    return result;
}
```

In practice, most methods don't need postcondition checks. If you write tests for your methods, you already *know* that they are returning the right values, or that they are changing the object's state in the right way.

If you have strong types in your code base, and don't often use primitive-type values anymore, you will find that defining method parameters and return types with these types results in solid code that can't return something that's invalid. After all, if the return value is an object, we know that it can't exist in an invalid state.

If you're dealing with legacy code, with lots of implicit type casting and no assertions whatsoever, you may find adding postconditions a useful technique. They can then be used as safety checks, to make sure there won't be any problems downstream.

> ### Introduce new methods to get rid of postcondition checks
> You could get rid of a method's postcondition checks, just like you can remove precondition checks, by promoting primitive-type values to proper objects and returning those from your method. Another option is to wrap the method with postcondition checks in a new method that performs these checks.

5.1.5   Return value

Finally, a method may return something. In fact, only query methods should do that. We'll discuss this topic in detail in the next chapter.

Another good rule to keep in mind is to *return early*. We've encountered this rule for exceptions already: as soon as you know something is going wrong, throw an exception about it. The same applies to return values. As soon as you know what you will return, return it right away instead of keeping the value around, skipping a few more `if` clauses, and then returning it.

5.2   Some rules for exceptions

You've seen how exceptions are used for precondition and postcondition checks, as well as for failure scenarios. Let's take a look at design rules for exception classes.

5.2.1   Use custom exception classes only if needed

Adding a custom exception class can be very helpful in certain circumstances:

1   If you want to catch a specific exception type higher up

```
    try {
        // possibly throws `SomeSpecific` exception
    } catch (SomeSpecific exception) {
        // ...
    }
```

2 If there are multiple ways to instantiate a single type of exception

```
final class CouldNotDeliverOrder extends RuntimeException
{
    public static function itWasAlreadyDelivered():
        CouldNotDeliverOrder
    {
        // ...
    }

    public static function insufficientQuantitiesInStock():
        CouldNotDeliverOrder
    {
        // ...
    }
}
```

3 If you want use named constructors for instantiating the exception

```
final class CouldNotFindProduct extends RuntimeException
{
    public static function withId(
        ProductId productId
    ): CouldNotFindProduct {
        return new CouldNotFindProduct(
            'Could not find a product with ID "{productId}"'
        );
    }
}

throw CouldNotFindProduct.withId(/* ... */);
```

Using a named constructor makes the code on the client side much cleaner. The name of the exception class combined with the name of the constructor method reads like a sentence: "Could not find product for ID . . . ." The message gets assembled inside the exception class instead of at the call site.

Having a custom exception class with a named constructor like this gives you the option to add more than one named constructor, making it easier to reuse the same exception class to point out different reasons for failure.

Listing 5.4 An exception class with multiple named constructors

```
final class CouldNotPersistObject extends RuntimeException
{
    public static function becauseDatabaseIsNotAvailable():
        CouldNotPersistObject
    {
        return new CouldNotPersistObject(/* ... */);
    }

    public static function becauseMappingConfigurationIsInvalid():
        CouldNotPersistObject
    {
```

```
        return new CouldNotPersistObject(/* ... */);
    }

    // ...
}
```

5.2.2 *Naming invalid argument or logic exception classes*

Contrary to popular belief, exception class names don't need to have "Exception" in them. Instead, there are some naming helper sentences you could use. To indicate invalid arguments or logic errors, you could use the template "Invalid . . .", such as `InvalidEmailAddress`, `InvalidTargetPosition`, or `InvalidStateTransition`.

5.2.3 *Naming runtime exception classes*

For runtime exceptions, a very helpful rule is to finish the sentence, "Sorry, [I] . . . ." The words at the end will be the name of your exception class. These will be good names because they communicate how the system tried to perform the requested job, but couldn't finish it successfully. For example, `CouldNotFindProduct`, `CouldNotStoreFile`, or `CouldNotConnect`.

5.2.4 *Use named constructors to indicate reasons for failure*

If you use named constructors, you can use the name to indicate the ingredients needed to instantiate the exception, as in the following listing.

> **Listing 5.5 A named constructor receives the data that was used**

```
final class CouldNotFindStreetName extends RuntimeException
{
    public static function withPostalCode(
        PostalCode postalCode
    ): CouldNotFindStreetName {
        // ...
    }
}
```

In other cases, you may be able to use the method name to indicate the reason why something is wrong.

> **Listing 5.6 A named constructor indicates the reason for failure**

```
final class InvalidTargetPosition extends LogicException
 {
    public static function becauseItIsOutsideTheMap(
        /* ... */
    ): InvalidTargetPosition {
        // ...
    }
}
```

5.2.5 *Add detailed messages*

Providing named constructors will be useful for clients, because the constructor of the exception, not the client itself, will set up the exception's message.

Listing 5.7 The named constructor composes a detailed message

```
// Before:

final class CouldNotFindProduct extends RuntimeException
{
}

// At the call site:
throw new CouldNotFindProduct(
    'Could not find a product with ID "{productId}"'
);

// After:

final class CouldNotFindProduct extends RuntimeException
{
    public static function withId(
        ProductId productId
    ): CouldNotFindProduct {
        return new CouldNotFindProduct(
            'Could not find a product with ID "{productId}"'
        );
    }
}

// At the call site:
throw CouldNotFindProduct.withId(productId);
```

Exercises

1 Improve the arrangement of statements in the following method:

```
public function pop(): Element
{
    if (count(this.elements)) > 0) {
        lastElement = array_pop(this.elements);

        return lastElement;
    } else {
        throw new RuntimeException('There are no more elements');
    }
}
```

2 What type of exception should you throw in case of a file-not-found error?

   a `RuntimeException` or a custom subclass

   b `InvalidArgumentException` or a custom subclass

> **3** What type of exception should you throw if an integer provided by the caller was expected to be positive, but turns out to be negative?
>
>   **a** `RuntimeException` or a custom subclass
>   **b** `InvalidArgumentException` or a custom subclass

Summary

- The template for implementing methods aims at clearing the table before starting the work. You start by analyzing the provided arguments and rejecting anything that looks wrong by throwing an exception. Then you do the actual work, and deal with any failures. Finally, you wrap up, after which you may return a value to the client.
- `InvalidArgumentExceptions` should be used to signal a problem with an argument that the client provided. `RuntimeExceptions` should be used to let the client know that a problem has occurred that isn't a logical mistake.
- Define custom exception classes and named constructors to improve the quality of your exception messages and make exceptions easier to create and throw.

Answers to the exercises

1 Suggested answer:

```
public function pop(): Element            Move the check for
{                                         failure conditions to
    if (count(this.elements)) == 0) {     the top of the method.
        throw new RuntimeException('There are no more elements');
    }

    lastElement = array_pop(this.elements);   Always look for ways to
                                              get rid of the else part
    return lastElement;                       of an if statement.
}
```

2 Correct answer: **a**. The fact that a file could not be found is not something you can derive by simply looking at the contents of a provided argument, so a `RuntimeException` should be thrown.

3 Correct answer: **b**. Just by looking at the contents of the provided argument, you could know that a provided value is invalid, so an `InvalidArgumentException` should be thrown.

Retrieving information

This chapter covers

- Using query methods for retrieving information
- Using single, specific return types
- Designing an object to keep internal data to itself
- Introducing abstractions for query calls
- Using test doubles for query calls

An object can be instantiated and sometimes modified. An object may also offer methods for performing tasks or retrieving information. This chapter describes how to implement methods that return information. In chapter 7 we'll look at methods that perform a task.

6.1 Use query methods for information retrieval

Earlier, we briefly discussed command methods. These methods have a void return type and can be used to produce a side effect: change state, send an email, store a file, etc. Such a method shouldn't be used for retrieving information. If you want to retrieve information from an object, you should use a query method. Such a method does have a specific return type, and it's not allowed to produce any side effects.

Take a look at the Counter class.

Listing 6.1 The `Counter` class

```
final class Counter
{
    private int count = 0;

    public function increment(): void
    {
        this.count++;
    }

    public function currentCount(): int
    {
        return this.count;
    }
}

counter = new Counter();
counter.increment();

assertEquals(1, counter.currentCount());
```

According to the rules for command and query methods, it's clear that `increment()` is a command method, because it changes the state of a `Counter` object. `currentCount()` is a query method, because it doesn't change anything; it just returns the current value of `count`. The good thing about this separation is that given the current state of a `Counter` object, calling `currentCount()` will always return the same answer.

Consider the following alternative implementation of `increment()`.

Listing 6.2 An alternative implementation of `increment()`

```
public function increment(): int
{
    this.count++;

    return this.count;
}
```

This method makes a change and returns information. This is confusing from a client perspective; the object changes even if you just want to look at it.

It's better to have safe methods that can be called any time (and, in fact, can be called any number of times), and other methods that are "unsafe" to call. There are two ways to achieve this:

- Follow the rule that a method should always be either a command or a query method. This is called the *command/query separation principle* (CQS).[1] We applied it in the initial implementation of `Counter` (listing 6.1): `increment()` was a command method, `currentCount()` a query method, and none of the methods of `Counter` were both command and query methods at the same time.

---

[1] Martin Fowler, "CommandQuerySeparation" (2005), https://martinfowler.com/bliki/CommandQuery Separation.html.

- Make your objects immutable (as has been previously advised for almost all objects in your application).

If Counter were implemented as an immutable object, increment() would become a modifier method, and a better, more declarative name for it would be incremented().

Listing 6.3 An alternative Counter implementation

```
final class Counter
{
    private int count = 0;

    public function incremented(): Counter
    {
        copy = clone this;

        copy.count++;

        return copy;
    }

    public function currentCount(): int
    {
        return this.count;
    }
}

assertEquals(
    1,
    (new Counter()).incremented().currentCount()
);
assertEquals(
    2,
    (new Counter()).incremented().incremented().currentCount()
);
```

Is a modifier method a command or a query method?

A modifier method doesn't really return the information you're after. In fact, it returns a copy of the whole object, and once you have that copy, you can ask it questions. So modifiers don't seem to be query methods, but they aren't traditional command methods either. A command method on an immutable object would imply that it changes the object's state after all, which isn't the case. It produces a new object, which isn't far from just answering a query.

Although it's stretching the concept a bit, the incremented() method in listing 6.3 could answer the query "give me the current count, but incremented by 1."

Exercises

1 Which methods are expected to be query methods?

  a `name(): string`
  b `changeEmailAddress(string emailAddress): void`
  c `color(bool invert): Color`
  d `findRecentMeetups(Date today): array`

6.2 *Query methods should have single-type return values*

When a method returns a piece of information, it should return a predictable thing. No mixed types are allowed. Most languages don't even support mixed types, but PHP, being a dynamically typed language does. Take, for example, the following `isValid()` method, which omits a return type, allowing several types of things to be returned. This will be very confusing for its users.

> **Listing 6.4 `isValid()` is a confusing method**

```
/**
 * @return string|bool
 */
public function isValid(string emailAddress)
{
    if (/* ... */) {
        return 'Invalid email address';
    }

    return true;
}
```

If the provided email address is valid, `isValid()` will return true; otherwise it will return a string. This makes it hard to use the method. Instead, make sure always to return values of a single type.

There's another situation to discuss here. Take a look at the following method that doesn't have multiple return types (its single return type is a `Page` object), but it may alternatively return `null`:

```
public function findOneBy(type): Page?
{
}
```

This puts a burden on the caller: they will always have to check whether the returned value is a `Page` object or if it's `null`, and they will need to deal with that.

```
if (page instanceof Page) {
    // ...                        ◁────────┐   page is a Page object and
} else {                                    │   can be used as such.
    // ...                ◁────────┐
}                                  │
                                       page is null, and we have to
                                       decide what to do with it.
```

Returning null from a method isn't always a problem. But you have to make sure that the clients of the method will deal with this situation. For PHP, static analysis tools like PHPStan (https://github.com/phpstan/phpstan) and Psalm (https://github.com/vimeo/psalm) can verify this, and your IDE may also help you with it, telling you when you are risking a possible null pointer exception. For Java, there's the Checker Framework (https://checkerframework.org/), which will provide you with compile-time warnings that clients don't deal with a possible null value.

In most cases, though, it pays to consider alternatives to returning null. For example, the following getById() method, which is supposed to retrieve a User entity by its ID, shouldn't return null if it can't find the user. It should throw an exception. After all, a client expects the User to exist; it's even providing the user's ID. It won't take null for an answer.

Listing 6.5   getById() returns a User or throws an exception

```
public function getById(id): User
{
    user = /* ... */;

    if (!user instanceof User) {
        throw UserNotFound.withId(id);
    }

    return user;
}
```

Another alternative would be to return an object that can represent the null case. Such an object is called a *null object*. Clients won't have to check for null, since the object has the correct type, as defined in the method signature.

Listing 6.6   Return a null object if it makes sense

```
public function findOneByType(PageType type): Page
{
    page = /* ... */;        ◁────── Try to find the Page.

    if (!page instanceof Page) {
        return new EmptyPage();
    }

    return page;
}
```

> ### Show the uncertainty in the name of the method
> You can let a method name indicate the uncertainty about whether or not the method will return a value of the expected type. In the previous examples, we used `get-ById()` instead of `findById()`, to communicate to the client that the method will "get" the `User`, instead of trying to find it and possibly returning empty-handed.

One last alternative for returning `null` is to return a result of the same type, but representing the empty case. If the method is expected to find and return a number of things in an array, return an empty array if you couldn't find anything.

Listing 6.7 Instead of `null`, return an empty list

```
public function eventListenersForEvent(string eventName): array
{
    if (!isset(this.listeners[eventName])) {
        return [];
    }

    return this.listeners[eventName];
}
```

Other return types will have different "empty" cases. For instance, if the return type is `int`, the empty return value might be 0 (or maybe 1), and for strings it might be `' '` (or maybe `'N/A'`).

If you find yourself using an existing method that mixes return types, or that returns `null` when it should return something more reliable, it might be a good idea to write a new method that sets things straight. In the following example, the existing `findOneByType()` method returns a `Page` object or `null`. If we want to make sure that clients don't have to deal with the `null` case and will actually get a `Page` object, we could wrap a call to `findOneByType()` in a new method called `getOneByType`.

Listing 6.8 `getOneByType()` wraps `findOneByType()`, which could return `null`

```
public function getOneByType(PageType type): Page
{
    page = this.findOneByType(type);

    if (!page instanceof Page) {               Don't return null; throw
        throw PageNotFound.withType(type);  ◄─┘ an exception instead.
    }

    return page;
}
```

Exercises

2 What is true about a query method?

   a It should produce an observable side effect.

   b It should not return a mixed type (e.g., `bool|int`).

   c It sometimes makes sense to return `null` from it.

   d It sometimes makes sense to return nothing (`void`) from it.

6.3 *Avoid query methods that expose internal state*

The simplest implementation for query methods is usually to return a property of the object. These methods are known as *getters*, and they allow clients to "get" the object's internal data.

> **"But according to the JavaBean conventions, every property needs a getter!"**
> Indeed, the JavaBean conventions prescribe objects to have a zero-argument constructor and to define both a getter and a setter for every property (http://mng.bz/ 1woy). As you might guess, after reading the previous chapters, every style guide or rule proposed in this book is incompatible with this convention. A zero-argument constructor leads to objects that can be created with an invalid starting state. Allowing every setter to be called separately leads to equally invalid intermediate states. And allowing all of an object's internal data to get out makes it hard to change anything about that data without breaking its clients. The only type of object that could be designed as a JavaBean is a data transfer object (we discussed those in sections 3.13 and 4.3).

For clients, usually the reason to get data is to use it for further calculations, or to make a decision based on it. Since objects are better off keeping their internals to themselves, you should keep an eye on these simple getters and how their return values are used by clients. The things a client does with the information that an object provides can often be done by the object itself.

A first example is the following `getItems()` method, which returns the items in a shopping basket just so the client can count them. Instead of directly exposing the items, the basket could provide a method that counts the items for the client.

Listing 6.9 Providing an alternative to counting items

```
// Before:

final class ShoppingBasket
{
    // ...
```

```
    public function getItems(): array
    {
        return this.items;
    }
}

count(basket.getItems());

// After

final class ShoppingBasket
{
    // ...

    public function itemCount(): int
    {
        return count(this.items);
    }
}

basket.itemCount();
```

The naming of query methods is important too. We didn't use `getItemCount()` or `countItems()` because these method names sound like commands, telling the object to do something. Instead, we named the method `itemCount()`, which makes it look like the item count is an aspect of a shopping basket you can find out about.

How do you handle ambiguous naming?

What if your object has a `name` property? The getter for this property would be called `name()`, but "name" can also be a verb. In fact, we already encountered the same potential confusion when we used the word "count," which can be a verb too.

Although the intended meaning of words will always be up for debate, most of the ambiguity can be resolved by setting the right context. Once you establish a clear difference between query and command methods, it'll be easy to notice when a method is meant to return a piece of information (e.g., return the value of the `name` property), or is meant to change the state of the object (e.g., change the value of the `name` property and return nothing). This will provide the reader with an important clue as to whether the word should be interpreted as a verb (which is most often the case with a command method) or as a noun (which is often the sign of a query method).

With small rewrites like this, you can make an object absorb more and more logic, thereby keeping the knowledge about the concept it represents inside it, instead of scattering little bits of this knowledge all over the code base.

Here's another example: clients call a query method on an object, and then call another method based on the return value of that first call.

Listing 6.10   Clients use the getters of `Product` to make decisions

```
final class Product
{
    public function shouldDiscountPercentageBeApplied(): bool
    {
        // ...
    }

    public function discountPercentage(): Percentage
    {
        // ...
    }

    public function fixedDiscountAmount(): Money
    {

    }
}

amount = new Money(/* ... */);
if (product.shouldDiscountPercentageBeApplied()) {
    netAmount = product.discountPercentage().applyTo(amount);
} else {
    netAmount = amount.subtract(product.fixedDiscountAmount());
}
```

A product has a setting that defines whether a discount percentage should be applied to it. If there's no discount percentage, there can still be a fixed discount.

Clients of Product can calculate a net amount by calling applyDiscountPercentage() first, and using its answer to either apply a discount percentage or a fixed discount.

One way to keep the information about how a discount should be calculated for a given product is to introduce a method with a name that matches this intention: calculateNetAmount().

Listing 6.11   `calculateNetAmount()` offers a better alternative

```
final class Product
{
    public function calculateNetAmount(Money amount): Money
    {
        if (this.shouldDiscountPercentageBeApplied()) {
            return this.discountPercentage().applyTo(amount);
        }

        return amount.subtract(this.fixedDiscountAmount());
    }

    private function shouldDiscountPercentageBeApplied(): bool
    {
        // ...
    }

    private function discountPercentage(): Percentage
    {
        // ...
    }
```

These methods can stay private now, or maybe we could use the properties they expose.

```
        private function fixedDiscountAmount(): Money
        {

        }
}
```
These methods can stay private now, or maybe we could use the properties they expose.

```
amount = new Money(/* ... */);
netAmount = product.calculateNetAmount(amount);
```

Besides no longer needing to repeat this logic at different call sites, this alternative has two more advantages. First, we can stop exposing internal data like the discount percentage and the fixed discount. Second, when the calculation changes, it can be changed and tested in one place.

In short, always look for ways to prevent the need for query methods that expose the object's internal data:

- Make the method smarter, and adapt it to the actual need of its clients.
- Move the call inside the object, letting it make its own decisions.

These approaches will let the object keep its internals to itself, and force clients to use its explicitly defined public interface (see figure 6.1).

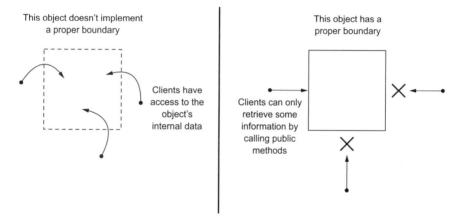

Figure 6.1 An object can be seen as having boundaries. Instead of allowing clients to cross those boundaries to retrieve information from the object, define explicitly which data and which behaviors should be available to clients.

A naming convention for getters

You may have noticed that I don't use the traditional "get" prefix for getters, as in `discountPercentage()` (listing 6.11). This convention shows that the method isn't a command method, but that it simply provides a piece of information. The method name is a description of the piece of information we're looking for, not an instruction for the object to "go get it" for us.

Exercises

3   Take a look at the following `Order` and `Line` classes and how they allow clients to get all the information they need to calculate a total amount for the entire order:

```
final class Line
{
    private int quantity;
    private Money tariff;

    // ...

    public function quantity(): int
    {
        return this.quantity;
    }

    public function tariff(): Money
    {
        return this.tariff;
    }
}

final class Order
{
    /**
     * @var Line[]
     */
    private array lines = [];

    // ...

    /**
     * @return Line[]
     */
    public function lines(): array
    {
        return this.lines;
    }
}

totalAmount = new Money(0);
foreach (order.lines() as line) {
    totalAmount = totalAmount.add(
        new Money(
            line.quantity() * line.tariff()
        )
    );
}
```

Rewrite `Order` and `Line` in such a way that `Order` is no longer forced to expose its internal `lines` array, any of the `Line` objects that are in this array, or the `Line`'s `tariff` and `quantity`.

6.4   *Define specific methods and return types for the queries you want to make*

When you need a specific bit of information, make sure you have a specific question, and that you know what the answer should look like. As an example, if you're working on a piece of code and you need today's exchange rate for USD to EUR, you may discover that there are web services you can call to figure that out, like https://fixer.io/. So you might jump in and write a bit of code that makes the call.

Listing 6.12   The `CurrencyConverter` class

```
final class CurrencyConverter
{
    public function convert(Money money, Currency to): Money
    {
        httpClient = new CurlHttpClient();
        response = httpClient.get(
            'http://data.fixer.io/api/latest?access_key=...' .
                '&base=' . money.currency().asString() .
                '&symbols=' . to.asString()
        );
        decoded = json_decode(response.getBody());
        rate = (float)decoded.rates[to.asString()];

        return money.convert(to, rate);
    }
}
```

There are many issues with this tiny bit of code (we won't deal with the possibility of a network failure, an error response, invalid JSON, a modified response structure, and the fact that a `float` isn't the most reliable data type to use when dealing with amounts of money). At a conceptual level, we're making much too large jumps as well. All we needed at this point in the code is an answer to a question: "What's the current exchange rate for USD to EUR currency conversion?"

Rewriting this question in code results in two new classes: `FixerApi` and `ExchangeRate`. The first has a single method, `exchangeRateFor()`, which represents the question that the `CurrencyConverter` wants to ask. The second class, `ExchangeRate`, represents the answer.

Listing 6.13   The `FixerApi` and `ExchangeRate` classes

```
final class FixerApi
{
    public function exchangeRateFor(          ⟵  We introduce FixerApi.exchangeRateFor()
        Currency from,                            to represent the question being asked:
        Currency to                               "What's the current exchange rate for
    ): ExchangeRate {                             converting from ... to ... ?"
        httpClient = new CurlHttpClient();
        response = httpClient.get(/* ... */);
```

```
        decoded = json_decode(response.getBody());
        rate = (float)decoded.rates[to.asString()];

        return ExchangeRate.from(from, to, rate);
    }
}

final class ExchangeRate          ◁────  This new class will represent
{                                        the answer to the question.
    public static function from(
        Currency from,
        Currency to,
        float rate
    ): ExchangeRate {
        // ...
    }
}                                        CurrencyConverter will get a FixerApi
                                         instance injected, so it can find out the
final class CurrencyConverter     ◁────  current exchange rate when it needs to.
{
    private FixerApi fixerApi;

    public function __construct(FixerApi fixerApi)
    {
        this.fixerApi = fixerApi;
    }

    public function convert(Money money, Currency to): Money
    {
        exchangeRate = this.fixerApi
            .exchangeRateFor(
                money.currency(),
                to
            );

        return money.convert(exchangeRate);
    }
}
```

The "answer" class, ExchangeRate, should be designed to be as useful as possible for
the client that needs it. Potentially, this class can be reused at other call sites, but it
doesn't have to be.

The important part is that the introduction of the exchangeRateFor() method
with a specific return type improves the conversation that's going on in the code.
When reading the code of convert(), we can clearly see that there's a need for information, a question being asked, and an answer being returned, which is then used to
do some more work. Note that so far we've only refactored the code; its structure has
been improved, but it still has the same behavior.

6.5 *Define an abstraction for queries that cross system boundaries*

The question "What's the current exchange rate?" from the previous section is a question that the application itself can't answer, based on what it has in memory. It needs to cross a system boundary to find the answer. In this case, it has to connect to a remote service, reachable through the network. Another example of crossing a system boundary would be when an application reaches out to the filesystem to load or store a file. Or when it uses the system clock to find out the current time.

As soon as an application crosses a system boundary, you should introduce an abstraction, allowing you to hide the low-level communication details of the calls that are going on behind the scenes.

Abstraction in this case means two things, and it can only be successful when you have both ingredients:

- Using a service interface instead of a service class
- Leaving out the implementation details

Introducing a proper abstraction will make it possible to run your code in a test scenario, without making the actual network or filesystem calls. It will also make it possible to swap out implementations without having to modify the client code; you only need to write a new implementation of the service interface.

First we'll discuss an example that fails to introduce a proper abstraction. Let's take another look at the `FixerApi` class. It makes a network call directly, using the `Curl-HttpClient` class.

Listing 6.14 Using a `CurlHttpClient` instance to connect to the API

```
final class FixerApi
{
    public function exchangeRateFor(
        Currency from,
        Currency to
    ): ExchangeRate {
        httpClient = new CurlHttpClient();
        response = httpClient.get(/* ... */);
        decoded = json_decode(response.getBody());
        rate = (float)decoded.rates[to.asString()];

        return ExchangeRate.from(from, to, rate);
    }
}
```

Instead of instantiating and using this specific class, we could define an interface for it and inject an instance of it into the `FixerApi` class, as follows.

Listing 6.15   Adding an `HttpClient` interface and using it in `FixerApi`

```
interface HttpClient
{
    public function get(url): Response;
}

final class CurlHttpClient implements HttpClient
{
    // ...
}

final class FixerApi
{
    public function __construct(HttpClient httpClient)
    {
        this.httpClient = httpClient;
    }

    public function exchangeRateFor(
        Currency from,
        Currency to
    ): ExchangeRate {
        response = this.httpClient.get(/* ... */);
        decoded = json_decode(response.getBody());
        rate = (float)decoded.rates[to.asString()];

        return ExchangeRate.from(from, to, rate);
    }
}
```

First we introduce an interface for HTTP clients.

We also make sure the existing CurlHttpClient implements this new HttpClient interface.

We inject the interface, not the concrete class.

We have to change the code a bit to use the new interface and its get() method.

We can now swap out `HttpClient` implementations because we rely on the interface, not the concrete implementation. This could be useful if you may want to switch to a different HTTP client implementation some day. But we haven't abstracted the most important part yet. What happens if we want to switch to a different API? It's not likely that a different API will send the same JSON response. Or maybe we will want to start maintaining our own local database table with exchange rates. In that case, we wouldn't need an HTTP client anymore.

To remove the low-level implementation details, we need to pick a more abstract name that stands for what we're doing. We're looking for a way to retrieve exchange rates. Where would we get them from? From something that can "provide" them. Or from something that manages them, like a "collection." A good name for this abstraction could be `ExchangeRateProvider`, or simply `ExchangeRates` if we look at this service like a collection of known exchange rates. The following listing shows what this would look like.

Listing 6.16   Introducing the abstract `ExchangeRates` service

```
/**
 * We extract the "question" method and make it a public method on
 * an abstract `ExchangeRates` service:
```

```
 */
interface ExchangeRates
{
    public function exchangeRateFor(
        Currency from,
        Currency to
    ): ExchangeRate;
}
```

> **The existing FixerApi class should implement the new ExchangeRates interface.**

```
final class FixerApi implements ExchangeRates    ◁───┘
{
    private HttpClient httpClient;

    public function __construct(HttpClient httpClient)
    {
        this.httpClient = httpClient;
    }

    public function exchangeRateFor(
        Currency from,
        Currency to
    ): ExchangeRate {
        response = this.httpClient.get(/* ... */);
        decoded = json_decode(response.getBody());
        rate = (float)decoded.data.rate;

        return ExchangeRate.from(from, to, rate);
    }
}
```

> **Instead of a Fixer object, we can now inject an ExchangeRates instance.**

```
final class CurrencyConverter
{
    private ExchangeRates exchangeRates;

    public function __construct(ExchangeRates exchangeRates)   ◁───┘
    {
        this.exchangeRates = exchangeRates;
    }

    // ...

    private function exchangeRateFor(
        Currency from,
        Currency to
    ): ExchangeRate {
        return this.exchangeRates.exchangeRateFor(from, to);   ◁───┘
    }
}
```

> **We use the new service here to get the answer we're looking for.**

As a final improvement, we should inline any existing calls to the private exchange-RateFor() method because it's just a proxy to the ExchangeRates service now.

By defining an interface for the existing class, we performed the first step of a successful abstraction. By hiding all the implementation details behind the interface, we also performed the second step, meaning we now have a proper abstraction for retrieving exchange rates. This comes with two advantages:

- We can easily switch to a different exchange rate provider. As long as the new class implements the `ExchangeRates` interface correctly, the `Currency-Converter` won't have to be modified because it depends on the `ExchangeRates` abstraction.

- We can write a unit test for `CurrencyConverter` and inject a test double for `ExchangeRates`—one that doesn't make an internet connection. This will keep our test fast and stable.

By the way, if you know about the SOLID principles, you've already encountered a similar rule for abstraction of service dependencies, known as the *dependency inversion principle*. You can read more about it in books and articles by Robert C. Martin.[2]

Not every question deserves its own service

In the previous examples, it was clear that the question, "What's the exchange rate?" deserved its own service. It was a question the application itself couldn't answer. In most situations, though, asking a question shouldn't immediately cause a new object to be introduced. Consider these alternatives too:

1 You could introduce better variable names to improve the conversation that's going on inside the code.
2 You could extract a private method, which represents the question and its answer (like we just did by moving logic to the private `exchangeRateFor()` method).

Only if the method becomes too large, needs to be tested separately, or crosses a system boundary should you create a separate class for it. This should keep the number of objects involved limited, and will help keep the code readable; you won't have to click through lots of classes to find out what's going on.

Exercises

4 Which two things would you need to do to create an abstraction for a service?

a Create an abstract class for the service.
b Create an interface for the service.
c Choose higher-level names that leave room for implementers to keep lower-level implementation details to themselves.
d Provide at least two implementations for the abstract service.

---

[2]For instance, Robert C. Martin, "The Dependency Inversion Principle," http://mng.bz/9woa. Other articles about the SOLID principles can be found on http://mng.bz/j50y.

6.6   *Use stubs for test doubles with query methods*

The moment you introduce an abstraction for your queries, you create a useful extension point. You can easily change the implementation details of how the answer will be found. Testing this logic will be easier too. Instead of only being able to test the CurrencyConverter service when an internet connection (and the remote service) is available, you can now test the logic by replacing the injected ExchangeRates service with one that already has the answers and will supply them in a predictable manner.

Listing 6.17   Testing `CurrencyConverter` with `ExchangeRatesFake`

```
final class ExchangeRatesFake implements ExchangeRates
{
    private array rates = [];

    public function __construct(
        Currency from,
        Currency to,
        float rate
    ) {
        this.rates[from.asString()][to.asString()] =
            ExchangeRate.from(from, to, rate);
    }

    public function exchangeRateFor(
        Currency from,
        Currency to
    ): ExchangeRate {
        if (!isset(this.rates[from.asString()][to.asString()])) {
            throw new RuntimeException(
                'Could not determine exchange rate from [...] to [...]'
            );
        }
        return this.rates[from.asString()][to.asString()];
    }
}

/**
 * @test
 */
public function it_converts_an_amount_using_the_exchange_rate(): void
{
    exchangeRates = new ExchangeRatesFake();
    exchangeRates.setExchangeRate(
        new Currency('USD'),
        new Currency('EUR'),
        0.8
    );

    currencyConverter = new CurrencyConverter(exchangeRates);
```

This is a "fake" implementation of the ExchangeRates service, which we can set up to return whatever exchange rates we provide it with.

We can use this fake in the unit test for CurrencyConverter.

Set up the fake ExchangeRates service.

Inject the fake service into CurrencyConverter.

```
    converted = currencyConverter
        .convert(new Money(1000, new Currency('USD')));

    assertEquals(new Money(800, new Currency('EUR')), converted);
}
```

By setting up the test like this, we focus only on the logic of the convert() method, instead of all the logic involved in making the network connection, parsing the JSON response, etc. This makes the test deterministic and therefore stable.

Naming test methods

In listing 6.17, the test method has a name in so-called snake case: lower case with underscores as word separators. If we followed the standard for naming methods, it would have been itConvertsAnAmountUsingTheExchangeRate(). Most standards would also suggest using relatively short names, but it_converts_an_amount _using_the_exchange_rate() is anything but short. Because the purpose of test methods is different from that of regular methods, the solution is not to submit test method names to the same standard, but to set a different standard for them:

1 Test method names describe object behaviors. The best description is an actual sentence.
2 Because they are sentences, test method names will be longer than regular method names. It should still be easy to read them (so use snake case instead).

If you're not used to these rules, a good way to ease into them is to start a test method name with it_. This should get you in the right mood for describing a particular object behavior. Although it's a good starting point, you'll notice that not every test method makes sense starting with it_. For instance, when_ or if_ could work too.

A *fake* is one kind of test double, which can be characterized as showing "somewhat complicated" behavior, just like the real implementation that will be used in production. When testing, you could also use a *stub* to replace a real service. A stub is a test double that just returns hardcoded values. So whenever we'd call the exchangeRateFor() method, it would return the same value, as follows.

Listing 6.18   `ExchangeRatesStub` always returns the same value

```
final class ExchangeRatesStub                      ⊲─┐ This is a sample stub
{                                                     │ implementation of ExchangeRates.
    public function exchangeRateFor(
        Currency from,
        Currency to
    ): ExchangeRate {
        return ExchangeRate.from(from, to, 1.2);   ⊲─┐ The return value
    }                                                 │ is hardcoded.
}
```

An important characteristic of stubs and fakes is that in a test scenario, you can't and shouldn't make any assertions about the number of calls made to them, or the order in which those calls are made. Given the nature of query methods, they should be without side effects, so it should be possible to call them any number of times, even zero times. Making assertions about calls made to query methods leads to tests that don't keep sufficient distance from the implementation of the classes they're testing.

The opposite is the case for command methods, where you do want to verify that calls have been made, how many have been made, and potentially in what order. We'll get back to this in the next chapter.

> **Don't use mocking tools for creating fakes and stubs**
>
> Mocking frameworks are often used to build test doubles on the fly. I recommend against using these frameworks for creating fakes and stubs. They may save you a few lines of boilerplate, but at the cost of code that is hard to read and maintain.
>
> Even if you still prefer to use these mocking tools, I recommend using them only for creating *dummies* (that is, test doubles that don't return anything meaningful and are only there to be passed as unused arguments). For stubs and fakes, mocking tools usually get in the way of good design. They will verify if and how many times a query method has been called, but they often make refactoring harder, because method names often have to be provided as strings, and your refactoring tool may not recognize them as actual method names.

We shouldn't forget to also test the real implementation that uses an HTTP connection to retrieve exchange rates. We have to test that it works correctly. But at that point we're no longer worried about testing the conversion logic itself, but only that the implementation knows how to communicate well with the external service.

Listing 6.19 The test for `FixerApi` will be an integration test

```
/**
 * @test
 */
public function it_retrieves_the_current_exchange_rate(): void
{
    exchangeRates = new FixerApi(new CurlHttpClient());

    exchangeRate = exchangeRates.exchangeRateFor(
        new Currency('USD'),
        new Currency('EUR')
    );

    // Verify the result here...
}
```

You will find that this kind of test still needs some effort to make it more stable. You may have to set up your own exchange rate server that replicates the real one. Or you may be able to use a sandbox environment provided by the maintainers of the real service.

Note that this test doesn't count as a unit test anymore: it doesn't test the behavior of an object in memory. You could call this an *integration test* instead, since it tests the integration of an object with the thing in the world outside that it relies on.

6.7   *Query methods should use other query methods, not command methods*

As we discussed, command methods can have side effects. Command methods change something, save something, send an email, etc. Query methods, on the other hand, won't do anything like that. They will just return a piece of information. Usually, a query method needs some collaborating objects to build up the requested answer. If we get the division between command and query methods right in our code, a chain of calls that starts with a query won't contain a call to a command method. This has to be true, because queries are supposed to have no side effects, and calling a command method somewhere in the chain will violate that rule.

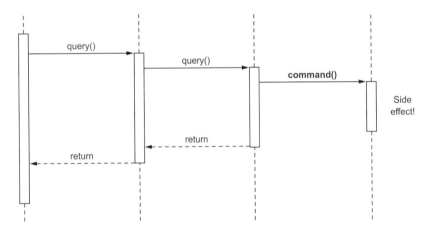

Figure 6.2   There should be no calls to command methods hidden behind a query.

There are some exceptions to this rule. Consider a controller method for a web application, which can be called to register a new user. This method will have a side effect: somewhere down the chain of commands it will store a new user record in the database. This would normally force us to use a `void` return type for the controller itself, but a web application should always return an HTTP response. So the controller will have to return at least something.

Listing 6.20 A controller will always return something

```
final class RegisterUserController
{
    private RegisterUser registerUser;

    public function __construct(
        RegisterUser registerUser
    ) {
        this.registerUser = registerUser;
    }

    public function execute(Request request): Response
    {
        newUser = this.registerUser
            .register(request.get('username'));

        return new Response(200, json_encode(newUser));
    }
}
```

Technically speaking, the controller violates the command/query separation principle, but there's no way around that. At the very least, we should return an empty 200 OK response or something like that. But that won't be very useful for the frontend, which makes the "register user" POST request, and would like to be given a response with a JSON structure representing the newly created user.

To solve this case, you should divide the controller's action into two parts: registering the new user and returning it. Preferably you'd also determine the new ID of the user before calling the RegisterUser service, so the service doesn't have to return anything at all and can be a true command method. This is demonstrated in the following listing.

Listing 6.21 A controller can be separated into command and query parts

```
final class RegisterUserController
{
    private UserRepository userRepository;
    private RegisterUser registerUser;
    private UserReadModelRepository userReadModelRepository;

    public function __construct(
        UserRepository userRepository,
        RegisterUser registerUser,
        UserReadModelRepository userReadModelRepository
    ) {
        this.userRepository = userRepository;
        this.registerUser = registerUser;
        this.userReadModelRepository = userReadModelRepository;
    }
```

```
public function execute(Request request): Response
{
    userId = this.userRepository.nextIdentifier();

    this.registerUser
        .register(userId, request.get('username'));          register() is
                                                              a command
                                                              method.

    newUser = this.userReadModelRepository.getById(userId);   getById()
                                                              is a query
    return new Response(200, json_encode(newUser));           method.
}
}
```

Sometimes, CQS does not make sense

In almost all cases I find that it's best to follow the command/query separation principle, but it should not become a rule that you can't deviate from. In fact, no programming rule should ever be like that.

A common situation where CQS stops being a good rule is in the realm of concurrency. An example would be the following `nextIdentity()` method. It generates a unique ID for an entity that you're going to save. The ID is the next available number in the sequence 1, 2, 3, etc.

```
final class EntityRepository
{
    public function nextIdentity(): int
    {
        // ...
    }
}
```

Two clients that call this method shouldn't receive the same ID, since that might result in them overwriting each other's entity data. Calling `nextIdentity()` should return an integer and at the same time mark the returned integer as "used." However, that would make the method violate CQS: it returns information *and* performs a task, thereby influencing the state of the system in an observable way. Calling the method again will give you a different answer.

You could figure out a way to still follow CQS, but I think that would complicate your code a lot.[a] In a case like this, feel free to let go of CQS and just implement the method in a way that makes sense.

[a]To find out more about this particular situation and possible solutions, take a look at Mark Seemann's article "CQS versus server generated IDs" (2014), http://mng.bz/Q0nQ.

Summary

- A query method is a method you can use to retrieve a piece of information. Query methods should have a single return type. You may still return `null`, but make sure to look for alternatives, like a null object or an empty list. Possibly throw an exception instead. Let query methods expose as little of an object's internals as possible.

- Define specific methods and return values for every question you want to ask and every answer you want to get. Define an abstraction (an interface, free of implementation details) for these methods if the answer to the question can only be established by crossing the system's boundaries.

- When testing services that use queries to retrieve information, replace them with fakes or stubs you write yourself, and make sure not to test for actual calls being made to them.

Answers to the exercises

1 Correct answers: **a**, **c**, and **d**. Answer b has a `void` return type, so it's not a query method.

2 Correct answers: **b** and **c**. A query method is explicitly not supposed to produce a side effect. A query method always has a return value, even if it's `null`, so it can't have a `void` return type.

3 Suggested answer:

```
final class Line
{
    // ...                      ◁——————  It's safe to remove tariff() and
                                         quantity() now, keeping this
                                         data private.
    public function amount(): Money
    {
        return new Money(
            line.quantity() * line.tariff()
        );
    }
}


final class Order                ◁——————  It's safe to remove lines() too,
{                                          keeping the lines array and
    // ...                                 the Line objects private.

    public function totalAmount(): Money
    {
        totalAmount = new Money(0);

        foreach (this.lines() as line) {
            totalAmount = totalAmount.add(
                line.amount()
            );
        }
```

```
            return totalAmount;
        }
    }
```

4   Correct answers: **b** and **c**. An abstract class is not preferable, since it leaves part
    of the implementation defined, and it will be the same for any concrete sub-
    class. Also, you don't have to provide more than one implementation of the
    interface.

Performing tasks

This chapter covers

- Using command methods to perform tasks
- Using events and event listeners to split up larger tasks
- Dealing with failure in command methods
- Introducing abstractions for commands
- Creating test doubles for command calls

Besides retrieving information from objects, you can use objects to perform a variety of tasks for you:

- Send a reminder email
- Save a record in the database
- Change the password of a user
- Store something on disk
- And so on . . .

The following sections provide rules for methods that perform tasks like these.

7.1   Use command methods with a name in the imperative form

We already discussed query methods and how you should use them to retrieve information. Query methods have a specific return type and no side effects, meaning that it's safe to call them several times, and the application's state won't be any different afterwards.

For performing tasks, you should always use a command method, which has a void return type. The name of such a method should indicate that the client can order the object to perform the task that the method name indicates. When looking for a good name, you should always use the imperative form. The following listing shows some examples.

Listing 7.1   Some command methods with imperative names

```
public function sendReminderEmail(
    EmailAddress recipient,
    // ...
): void {
    // ...
}

public function saveRecord(Record record): void
{
    // ...
}
```

7.2   Limit the scope of a command method, and use events to perform secondary tasks

When performing a task, make sure you don't do too much in one method. These are some guiding questions to determine if a method is too large:

- Should or does the method name have "and" in it, to indicate what else it does besides its main job?
- Do all the lines of code contribute to the main job?
- Could a part of the work that the method does be performed in a background process?

The following listing shows a method that does too much. It changes the user's password, but it also sends them an email about it.

Listing 7.2   `changePassword ()` does too much

```
public function changeUserPassword(
    UserId userId,
    string plainTextPassword
): void {
    user = this.repository.getById(userId);
    hashedPassword = /* ... */;
```

```
    user.changePassword(hashedPassword);
    this.repository.save(user);
    this.mailer.sendPasswordChangedEmail(userId);
}
```

This is a very common scenario where the answers to the guiding questions are "yes" in all cases:

- The method name hides the fact that besides changing the user's password it will also send an email. It might as well have been named changeUserPasswordAndSendAnEmailAboutIt().
- Sending the email can't be considered the main job of this method; changing the password is.
- The email could easily be sent in some other process that runs in the background.

One solution would be to move the email-sending code to a new public sendPasswordChangedEmail() method. However, this would transfer the responsibility of calling that method to the client of changeUserPassword(). Considering the bigger picture, these two tasks really belong together; we just don't want to mix them in one method.

The recommended solution is to use events as the link between changing the password and sending an email about it.

Listing 7.3 Using an event to split a task into multiple parts

```
final class UserPasswordChanged          ◄──────┐  The fact that a user changed their
                                                 │  password can be represented by a
{                                                │  UserPasswordChanged event object.
    private UserId userId;

    public function __construct(UserId userId)
    {
        this.userId = userId;
    }

    public function userId(): UserId
    {
        return this.userId;
    }
}

public function changeUserPassword(
    UserId userId,
    string plainTextPassword
): void {
    user = this.repository.getById(userId);
    hashedPassword = /* ... */;
    user.changePassword(hashedPassword);       After changing the
    this.repository.save(user);                password, dispatch a
                                               UserPasswordChanged event so
    this.eventDispatcher.dispatch(     ◄─────┘ other services can respond to it.
        new UserPasswordChanged(userId)
```

```
        );
    }

final class SendEmail
{
    // ...

    public function whenUserPasswordChanged(
        UserPasswordChanged event
    ): void {
        this.mailer.sendPasswordChangedEmail(event.userId());
    }
}
```

SendEmail is an event listener for the UserPasswordChanged event. When notified of the event, this listener will send the email.

You still need an event dispatcher that allows event listener services like SendEmail to be registered. Most frameworks have an event dispatcher that you can use, or you could write a simple one yourself, like the following.

Listing 7.4   A sample `EventDispatcher` implementation

```
final class EventDispatcher
{
    private array listeners;

    public function __construct(array listenersByType)
    {
        foreach (listenersByType as eventType => listeners) {
            Assertion.string(eventType);
            Assertion.allIsCallable(listeners);
        }

        this.listeners = listenersByType;
    }

    public function dispatch(object event): void
    {
        foreach (this.listenersFor(event.className) as listener) {
            listener(event);
        }
    }

    private function listenersFor(string event): array
    {
        if (isset(this.listeners[event])) {
            return this.listeners[event];
        }

        return [];
    }
}

listener = new SendEmail(/* ... */);
dispatcher = new EventDispatcher([
```

```
        UserPasswordChanged.className =>
            [listener, 'whenUserPasswordChanged']
]);

dispatcher.dispatch(new UserPasswordChanged(/* ... */));
```

Because we've registered SendEmail as an event listener for the UserPasswordChanged event, dispatching an event of that type will trigger a call to SendEmail.whenUserPasswordChanged().

Using events like this has several advantages:

- You can add even more effects without modifying the original method.
- The original object will be more decoupled because it doesn't get dependencies injected that are only needed for effects.
- You can handle the effects in a background process if you want.

A possible disadvantage of using events is that the primary action and its secondary effects may be implemented in remote parts of the code base. This could make it hard for a future reader of the code to understand what's going on. You should do two things to overcome this problem:

- Make sure everybody knows that events are used to decouple parts of the application. Someone who tries to understand what the code is doing will then look out for event objects and use the IDE's "find usages" functionality to find other services that are interested in these events.
- Make sure that events are always explicitly dispatched, as is done in listing 7.3. The call to EventDispatcher.dispatch() is a strong signal that more is about to happen.

Exercises

1 Which parts of the following command method could be considered secondary effects that could be handled in an event listener?

```
final class RegisterUser
{
    // ...

    public function register(
        EmailAddress emailAddress
        PlainTextPassword plainTextPassword
    ): void {
        hashedPassword = this.passwordHasher
            .hash(plainTextPassword);

        userId = this.userRepository.nextIdentity();
        user = User.create(userId, emailAddress, hashedPassword);

        this.mailer.sendEmailAddressConfirmationEmail(
```

(continued)
```
            emailAddress
        );

        this.userRepository.save(user);

        this.uploadService.preparePersonalUploadFolder(userId);
    }
}
```

   a Hashing the plain-text password
   b Creating the `User` entity
   c Sending the email address confirmation mail
   d Saving the `User` entity
   e Preparing a personal upload folder for the user

7.3 *Make services immutable from the outside as well as on the inside*

We already covered the rule that it should be impossible to change anything about a service's dependencies or configuration. Once it's been instantiated, a service object should be reusable for performing multiple different tasks in the same way, but using different data or a different context. There shouldn't be any risk that its behavior changes between calls. This is true for services that offer query methods, but also for ones that offer command methods.

Even if you don't offer clients a way to manipulate a service's dependencies or configuration, command methods may still change a service's state in such a way that behavior will be different for subsequent calls. For example, the following `Mailer` service sends out confirmation emails, but it also remembers which users have already received such an email. No matter how many times you call the same method, it will only send out an email once.

Listing 7.5 A `Mailer` service that keeps a list of previous recipients

```
final class Mailer
{
    private array sentTo = [];

    // ...

    public function sendConfirmationEmail(
        EmailAddress recipient
    ): void {
        if (in_array(recipient, this.sentTo)) {       We don't send
            return;                                    the email again.
        }
```

```
            // Send the email here...

            this.sentTo[] = recipient;
        }
    }
```

```
mailer = new Mailer(/* ... */);
recipient = EmailAddress.fromString('info@matthiasnoback.nl');
```
> **This will send out a confirmation email.**

```
mailer.sendConfirmationEmail(recipient);

mailer.sendConfirmationEmail(recipient);
```
> **The second call won't send another email.**

Make sure none of your services update internal state that influences its behavior like this.

A guiding question when deciding whether your service behaves properly in this respect is, "Would it be possible to reinstantiate the service for every method call, and would it still show the same behavior?" For the preceding `Mailer` class, this obviously isn't true: reinstantiating it would cause multiple emails to be sent to the same recipient.

In the case of the stateful `Mailer` service, the question is, "How can we prevent duplicate calls to `sendConfirmationEmail()`?" Somehow the client isn't smart enough to take care of this. What if, instead of providing just one `EmailAddress`, the client could provide an already deduplicated list of `EmailAddress` instances? They could use something like the following `Recipients` class.

> **Listing 7.6 Recipients can provide a list of deduplicated email addresses**

```
final class Recipients
{
    /**
     * @var EmailAddress[]
     */
    private array emailEmailAddresses;

    /**
     * @return EmailAddress[]
     */
    public function uniqueEmailAddresses(): array
    {
        // Return a deduplicated list of of addresses...
    }
}

final class Mailer
{
    public function sendConfirmationEmails(
        Recipients recipients
    ): void {
        foreach (recipients.uniqueEmailAddresses()
```

```
            as emailAddress) {
            // Send the email...
        }
    }
}
```

This would certainly solve the problem and make the `Mailer` service stateless again. But instead of letting `Mailer` make that special call to `uniqueEmailAddresses()`, what we're actually looking for is a list of `Recipients` that couldn't contain duplicate email addresses. You could most elegantly protect this domain invariant inside the `Recipients` class itself.

Listing 7.7   A more effective implementation of `Recipients`

```
final class Recipients
{
    /**
     * @var EmailAddress[]
     */
    private array emailAddresses;

    private function __construct(array emailAddresses)
    {
        this.emailAddresses = emailAddresses;
    }

    public static function emptyList(): Recipients        ◁——  Always start with
    {                                                            an empty list.
        return new Recipients([]);
    }

    public function with(EmailAddress emailAddress): Recipients        ◁——
    {
        if (in_array(emailAddress, this.emailAddresses)) {
            return this;                                    Any time a client wants to add an
        }                                                   email address to it, it will only be
                                                            added if it's not already on the list.
        return new Recipients(
            array_merge(this.emailAddresses),
            [emailAddress]
        );
    }

    public function emailAddresses(): array        ◁——  There's no need for a
    {                                                    uniqueEmailAddresses()
        return this.emailAddresses;                      method anymore.
    }
}
```

No need to add the email address again. (annotation pointing to `return this;`)

Immutable services and service containers

Service containers are often designed to share all service instances once they have been created. This saves the runtime from instantiating the same service again, should it be reused as a dependency of some other service. However, if a service is immutable (as it should be), this sharing isn't really needed. You could instantiate the service over and over again.

Of course, there are services in a service container that shouldn't be instantiated again every time they're used as a dependency. For instance, a database connection object or any other kind of reference to a resource that needs to be created once and then shared between dependent services. In general, however, your services shouldn't need to be shared. If you've followed all of the advice so far, you're doing well already, because immutable services don't need to be shared. They can, but they don't have to.

Exercises

2 What would prevent a service from being immutable?

    a Allowing an optional dependency to be injected by calling a method on it.

    b Allowing a configuration value to be changed by calling a method on it.

    c Offering a query method that itself calls a command method.

    d Having too many constructor arguments.

    e Changing some kind of internal state when a client calls a method on it.

7.4 *When something goes wrong, throw an exception*

The same rule for retrieving information also counts for performing tasks: when something goes wrong, don't return a special value to indicate it; throw an exception instead. As discussed earlier, a method can have precondition checks that throw `Invalid-ArgumentExceptions` or `LogicExceptions`. For the remainder of the failure scenarios, we can't determine upfront if they will occur, so we throw a `RuntimeException`. We've already discussed the other important rules for using exceptions in section 5.2.

Exercises

3 What type of exception would you expect `save()` to throw if it couldn't store a `Product` entity because its ID was already used?

```
interface ProductRepository
{
    public function save(Product product): void;
}
```

(continued)

  a An `InvalidArgumentException`, because the client has provided an invalid `Product` argument.

  b A `RuntimeException`, because whether or not a `Product` entity with that ID already exists can't be decided by just inspecting the arguments.

4 What type of exception would you expect `set()` to throw if an empty string were provided for `key`?

```
interface Cache
{
    public function set(string key, string value): void;
}
```

  a An `InvalidArgumentException`, because the client has provided an invalid argument.

  b A `RuntimeException`, because the client may decide at runtime what the value for `key` should be.

7.5 *Use queries to collect information and commands to take the next steps*

Earlier, when we discussed query methods, we saw how a chain of method calls that starts with a call to a query method won't have a call to a command method inside of it. The command method may produce a side effect, which violates the rule that a query method shouldn't have any side effects.

Now that we're looking at command methods, we should note that the other way around, there's no such rule. When a chain of calls starts with a command method, it's possible that you'll encounter a call to a query method down the line. For instance, the `changeUserPassword()` method we saw earlier starts with a query to the user repository.

Listing 7.8 `changeUserPassword()` starts with a query, then performs a task

```
public function changeUserPassword(
    UserId userId,
    string plainTextPassword
): void {
    user = this.repository.getById(userId);
    hashedPassword = /* ... */;
    user.changePassword(hashedPassword);
    this.repository.save(user);
    this.eventDispatcher.dispatch(
        new UserPasswordChanged(userId)
    );
}
```

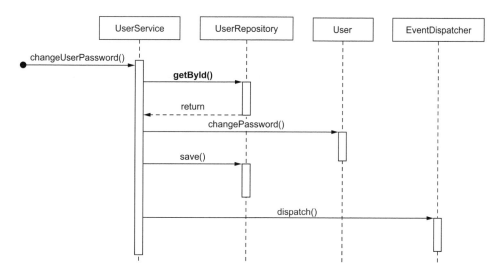

Figure 7.1   **Inside a command method, you may call query methods to retrieve more information.**

The next method call is changePassword() on the user object, then another command on the repository. Inside the repository implementation, there may again be calls to command methods, but it's also possible that query methods are being called there (see figure 7.1).

However, when looking at how objects call each other's command and query methods, be aware of the pattern illustrated in figure 7.2. This pattern of calls often indicates a little conversation between objects that could have been happening inside the called object only. Consider the following example:

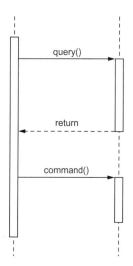

```
if (obstacle.isOnTheRight()) {
    player.moveLeft();
} elseif (obstacle.isOnTheLeft()) {
    player.moveRight();
}
```

The following is an improvement on this piece of code, where the knowledge about which action to take is now completely inside the object.

```
player.evade(obstacle);
```

This object is able to keep this knowledge to itself, and its implementation can evolve freely, whenever it needs to show more complicated behavior.

Figure 7.2   Calling a query method, then a command method on the same object

7.6   *Define abstractions for commands that cross system boundaries*

If a command method has code that reaches out across the application's own boundaries (that is, if it uses a remote service, the filesystem, a system device, etc.), you should introduce an abstraction for it. For instance, the following listing shows a piece of code that publishes a message to a queue, so background consumers can tune into important events inside the main application.

Listing 7.9   `SendMessageToRabbitMQ` publishes messages on a queue

```
final class SendMessageToRabbitMQ
{
    // ...

    public function whenUserChangedPassword(
        UserPasswordChanged event
    ): void {
        this.rabbitMqConnection.publish(
            'user_events',
            'user_password_changed',
            json_encode([
                'user_id' => (string)event.userId()
            ])
        );
    }
}
```

The `publish()` method will reach out to the RabbitMQ server and publish a message to its queue, which is outside of the application's boundaries, so we should come up with an abstraction here. As discussed earlier, this requires an interface and a higher-level concept. For example, preserving the notion that we want to queue a message, we could introduce the following `Queue` abstraction.

Listing 7.10   `Queue` is an abstraction used by `SendMessageToRabbitMQ`

```
interface Queue                          ⟵—— Queue is the abstraction.
{
    public function publishUserPasswordChangedEvent(
        UserPasswordChanged event
    ): void;
}                                                The standard Queue implementation
                                                 is RabbitMQQueue, which contains
final class RabbitMQQueue implements Queue  ⟵─┘ the code we already had.
{
    // ...

    public function publishUserPasswordChangedEvent(
        UserPasswordChanged event
    ): void {
        this.rabbitMqConnection.publish(
            'user_events',
```

```
                    'user_password_changed',
                    json_encode([
                        'user_id' => (string)event.userId()
                    ])
                );
        }
    }


    final class SendMessageToRabbitMQ
    {
        private Queue queue;

        public function __construct(Queue queue)
        {
            this.queue = queue;
        }

        public function whenUserPasswordChanged(
            UserPasswordChanged event
        ): void {
            this.queue.publishUserPasswordChangedEvent(event);
        }
    }
```

The event listener that is supposed to publish a message to the queue whenever a UserPasswordChanged event occurs will use the new abstraction as a dependency.

The first step was to introduce an *abstraction*. Once you start adding more publish ...Event() methods to Queue, you may start noticing similarities between these methods. Then you could apply *generalization* to make these methods more generic. You may need to implement a standard interface for all events.

Listing 7.11 A CanBePublished interface for publishable events

```
interface CanBePublished
{
    public function queueName(): string;
    public function eventName(): string;
    public function eventData(): array;
}


final class RabbitMQQueue implements Queue
{
    // ...

    public function publish(CanBePublished event): void
    {
        this.rabbitMqConnection.publish(
            event.queueName(),
            event.eventName(),
            json_encode(event.eventData())
        );
    }
}
```

It's generally a good idea to start with the abstraction and leave the generalization until you've seen about three cases that could be simplified by making the interface and object types involved more generic. This prevents you from abstracting too early and having to revise the interface and any of its implementations for every new case you want your abstraction to support.

Exercises

5   Why does the task of saving an entity to the database need its own abstraction?

    a   Because one day you may not have that entity anymore.

    b   Because having an abstraction allows you to replace the implementation in a test scenario.

    c   Because you may want to reuse that abstraction to store other types of data.

    d   Because an abstraction uses a higher-level concept to explain what's going on, which makes it easier to read the code, because you can ignore all the lower-level details.

7.7 *Only verify calls to command methods with a mock*

We already discussed that query methods shouldn't be mocked. In a unit test, you shouldn't verify the number of calls made to them. Queries are supposed to be without side effects, so you could make them many times if you want to. Allowing the implementation to do so increases the stability of the test. If you decide to call a method twice instead of remembering its result in a variable, the test won't break.

However, when a command method makes a call to another command method, you may want to mock the latter. After all, this command is *supposed* to be called at least once (you want to verify that, because it's part of the job), but it shouldn't be called more than once (because you don't want to have its side effects being produced more than once too). This is demonstrated in the following listing.

Listing 7.12   Unit testing the `ChangePasswordService` using a mock

```
final class ChangePasswordService
{
    private EventDispatcher eventDispatcher;
    // ...

    public function __construct(
        EventDispatcher eventDispatcher,
        // ...
    ) {
        this.eventDispatcher = eventDispatcher;

        // ...
    }

    public function changeUserPassword(
```

```
            UserId userId,
            string plainTextPassword
        ): void {
            // ...

            this.eventDispatcher.dispatch(
                new UserPasswordChanged(userId)
            );
        }
    }
```

> This defines a true mock object: we verify how many times we expect a method to be called (once), and with which arguments. We don't make assertions about the return value, since dispatch() is a command method.

```
/**
 * @test
 */
public function it_dispatches_a_user_password_changed_event(): void
{
    userId = /* ... */;

    eventDispatcherMock = this.createMock(EventDispatcher.className);  ⟵
    eventDispatcherMock
        .expects(this.once())
        .method('dispatch')
        .with(new UserPasswordChanged(userId));

    service = new ChangePasswordService(eventDispatcherMock, /* ... */);

    service.changeUserPassword(userId, /* ... */);
}
```

There are no regular assertions at the end of this test method, because the mock object itself will verify that our expectations were met. The test framework will ask all mock objects that were created for a single test case to do this.

If you prefer to have some actual assertions in your test case, you could use a *spy* as a test double for `EventDispatcher`. In the most generic form, a spy will remember all method calls that were made to it, including the arguments used. However, in our case, a really simple `EventDispatcher` implementation would suffice.

Listing 7.13 An `EventDispatcher` spy

```
final class EventDispatcherSpy implements EventDispatcher
{
    private array events = [];

    public function dispatch(object event): void
    {                                                      The spy just keeps a
        this.events[] = event;              ⟵            list of the events that
    }                                                      were dispatched to it.

    public function dispatchedEvents(): array
    {
        return this.events;
    }
}
```

```
/**
 * @test
 */
public function it_dispatches_a_user_password_changed_event(): void
{
    // ...
    eventDispatcher = new EventDispatcherSpy();
    service = new ChangePasswordService(eventDispatcher, /* ... */);

    service.changeUserPassword(userId, /* ... */);

    assertEquals(
        [
            new UserPasswordChanged(userId)
        ],
        eventDispatcher.dispatchedEvents()
    );
}
```

◁—— **Now we can make an assertion instead of waiting for the test framework to verify the method calls on our mock.**

Exercises

6   Given the following interface,

```
interface UserRepository
{
    public function save(User user): void;
}
```

if you write a unit test for a class that calls `save()` on its `UserRepository` dependency, what type of test double could you use?

a   Dummy
b   Stub
c   Fake
d   Mock
e   Spy

7   Given the following interface,

```
interface UserRepository
{
    public function getById(UserId userId): User;
}
```

if you write a unit test for a class that calls `getById()` on its `UserRepository` dependency, what type of test double could you use?

a   Dummy
b   Stub
c   Fake
d   Mock
e   Spy

Summary

- Command methods should be used to perform tasks. These command methods should have imperative names ("Do this," "Do that") and they should be limited in scope. Make a distinction between the main job and the effects of this job. Dispatch events to let other services perform additional tasks. While performing its task, a command method may also call query methods to collect any information needed.

- A service should be immutable from the outside, as well as on the inside. Just as with services for retrieving data, services that perform tasks should be reusable many times. If something goes wrong while performing a task, throw an exception (as soon as you know it).

- Define an abstraction for commands that cross a system boundary (commands that reach out to some remote service, database, etc.). When testing command methods that themselves call command methods, you can use a mock or a spy to test calls to these methods. You can use a mocking tool for this or write your own spies.

Answers to the exercises

1. Correct answers: **c** and **e**. All the other options should be considered part of the primary action. c and e are secondary actions or effects of the primary action.

2. Correct answers: **a**, **b**, and **e**. Switching out dependencies or configuration values makes a service object mutable. The number of constructor arguments doesn't have any effect on immutability. The same goes for collaborations with other objects.

3. Correct answer: **b**. The reason has been provided in the answer itself.

4. Correct answer: **a**. The reason has been provided in the answer itself.

5. Correct answers: **b** and **d**. The reason has been provided in the answers. Answer a is wrong because if you get rid of the entity, you also get rid of its repository. Answer c is wrong because that would require us to make the repository generic as well, which is not what we were after here.

6. Correct answers: **d** and **e**. `save()` is a command method, so we use a mock (to assure that a call to that method was made) or a spy (to later find out if that method call was made).

7. Correct answers: **a**, **b**, and **c**. `getById()` is a query method, so we provide a dummy (a nonfunctional object with only the correct type), a stub (an object with the correct type, which can return a previously configured value), or a fake (a more evolved object, with some logic of its own). We don't want to verify actual function calls being made, which is why we don't use a mock or a spy.

Dividing responsibilities

We've looked at how objects can be used to retrieve information or perform tasks. The methods for retrieving information are called query methods, and the ones that perform tasks are command methods.

Service objects may combine both of these responsibilities. For instance, a repository (like the one in the following listing) could perform the task of saving an entity to the database and also retrieving an entity from the database.

Listing 8.1 `PurchaseOrderRepository` can save and retrieve a `PurchaseOrder`

```
interface PurchaseOrderRepository
{
    /**
     * @throws CouldNotSavePurchaseOrder
     */
    public function save(PurchaseOrder purchaseOrder): void;

    /**
     * @throws CouldNotFindPurchaseOrder
     */
    public function getById(int purchaseOrderId): PurchaseOrder;
}
```

Saving and retrieving an entity are more or less each other's inverse operations, so it's only natural to let one object have both responsibilities. However, in most other cases, you will find that performing tasks and retrieving information are better off being divided amongst different objects.

8.1 *Separate write models from read models*

As we saw earlier, there are services and other objects. Some of these other objects can be characterized as *entities*, which model a particular domain concept. In doing so, they contain some relevant data and offer ways to manipulate that data in valid and meaningful ways. Entities can also expose data, allowing clients to retrieve information from them, whether it is exposed internal data (like the date on which an order was placed), or calculated data (like the total amount of an order).

In practice, different clients use entities in different ways. Some clients will want to manipulate an entity's data using its command methods, while others just want to retrieve a piece of information using its query methods. Nevertheless, all these clients will share the same object and potentially have access to all the methods, even when they don't need them or shouldn't have access to them.

You should never pass an entity that can be modified to a client that isn't allowed to modify it. Even if the client doesn't modify it today, one day it might, and then it will be hard to find out what happened. That's why the first thing you should do to improve the design of an entity is separate the *write model* from the *read model*.

We'll explore how this can be done by looking at an example of a `PurchaseOrder` entity. A purchase order represents the fact that a company buys a product from one of its suppliers. Once the product has been received, it's shelved in the company's warehouse. From that moment on, the company has this product in stock. We'll use this example for the rest of this chapter and work out different ways to improve it.

Listing 8.2 The `PurchaseOrder` entity

```
final class PurchaseOrder
{
    private int purchaseOrderId;
    private int productId;
```

```
    private int orderedQuantity;
    private bool wasReceived;

    private function __construct()
    {
    }

    public static function place(
        int purchaseOrderId,
        int productId,
        int orderedQuantity
    ): PurchaseOrder {
        purchaseOrder = new PurchaseOrder();

        purchaseOrder.productId = productId;
        purchaseOrder.orderedQuantity = orderedQuantity;
        purchaseOrder.wasReceived = false;

        return purchaseOrder;
    }

    public function markAsReceived(): void
    {
        this.wasReceived = true;
    }

    public function purchaseOrderId(): int
    {
        return this.purchaseOrderId;
    }

    public function productId(): int
    {
        return this.productId;
    }

    public function orderedQuantity(): int
    {
        return this.orderedQuantity;
    }

    public function wasReceived(): bool
    {
        return this.wasReceived;
    }
}
```

> For brevity, I've used primitive-type values; in practice, value objects are recommended.

In the current implementation, the `PurchaseOrder` entity exposes methods for creating and manipulating the entity (`place()` and `markAsReceived()`), as well as for retrieving information from it (`productId()`, `orderedQuantity()`, and `wasReceived()`).

Now take a look at how different clients use this entity. First, the `ReceiveItems` service will be called from a controller, passing in a raw purchase order ID.

Listing 8.3 The `ReceiveItems` service

```
final class ReceiveItems
{
    private PurchaseOrderRepository repository;

    public function __construct(PurchaseOrderRepository repository)
    {
        this.repository = repository;
    }

    public function receiveItems(int purchaseOrderId): void
    {
        purchaseOrder = this.repository.getById(purchaseOrderId);

        purchaseOrder.markAsReceived();

        this.repository.save(purchaseOrder);
    }
}
```

Note that this service doesn't use any of the getters on `PurchaseOrder`. It's only interested in changing the state of the entity.

Next, let's take a look at a controller that renders a JSON-encoded data structure detailing how much of a product the company has in stock.

Listing 8.4 The `StockReportController` class

```
final class StockReportController
{
    private PurchaseOrderRepository repository;

    public function __construct(PurchaseOrderRepository repository)
    {
        this.repository = repository;
    }

    public function execute(Request request): Response
    {
        allPurchaseOrders = this.repository.findAll();

        stockReport = [];

        foreach (allPurchaseOrders as purchaseOrder) {
            if (!purchaseOrder.wasReceived()) {       ◁──┐ We haven't received the
                continue;                                 │ items yet, so we shouldn't
            }                                             │ add them to the quantity
                                                          │ in stock.
            if (!isset(stockReport[purchaseOrder.productId()] )) {
                stockReport[purchaseOrder.productId()] = 0;
            }                                         ┌── Add the ordered (and
                                                      │   received) quantity to
            stockReport[purchaseOrder.productId()]    ◁──┘ the quantity in stock.
```

We haven't seen this product before ... ┌──▷ (pointing to `stockReport[purchaseOrder.productId()] = 0;`)

```
                    += purchaseOrder.orderedQuantity;
        }

        return new JsonResponse(stockReport);
    }
}
```

This controller doesn't make any change to a `PurchaseOrder`. It just needs a bit of information from all of them. In other words, it isn't interested in the write part of the entity, only in the read part. Besides the fact that it is undesirable to expose more behavior to a client than it needs, it isn't very efficient to loop over all the purchase orders of all time to find out how much of a product is in stock.

The solution is to divide the entity's responsibilities. First, we'll create a new object that can be used to retrieve information about a purchase order. Let's call it `Purchase-OrderForStockReport`.

Listing 8.5   The `PurchaseOrderForStockReport` class

```
final class PurchaseOrderForStockReport
{
    private int productId;
    private int orderedQuantity;
    private bool wasReceived;

    public function __construct(
        int productId,
        int orderedQuantity,
        bool wasReceived
    ) {
        this.productId = productId;
        this.orderedQuantity = orderedQuantity;
        this.wasReceived = wasReceived;
    }

    public function productId(): ProductId
    {
        return this.productId;
    }

    public function orderedQuantity(): int
    {
        return this.orderedQuantity;
    }

    public function wasReceived(): bool
    {
        return this.wasReceived;
    }
}
```

This new `PurchaseOrderForStockReport` object can be used inside the controller as soon as there is a repository that can provide it. A quick and dirty solution would be to let `PurchaseOrder` return an instance of `PurchaseOrderForStockReport`, based on its internal data.

Listing 8.6   A quick solution: `PurchaseOrder` generates the report

```
final class PurchaseOrder
{
    private int purchaseOrderId
    private int productId;
    private int orderedQuantity;
    private bool wasReceived;

    // ...

    public function forStockReport(): PurchaseOrderForStockReport
    {
        return new PurchaseOrderForStockReport(
            this.productId,
            this.orderedQuantity,
            this.wasReceived
        );
    }
}

final class StockReportController
{
    private PurchaseOrderRepository repository;

    public function __construct(PurchaseOrderRepository repository)
    {
        this.repository = repository;
    }

    public function execute(Request request): Response
    {
        allPurchaseOrders = this.repository.findAll();         ← For now, we still load
                                                                 PurchaseOrder entities.
        forStockReport = array_map(                           ←
            function (PurchaseOrder purchaseOrder) {
                return purchaseOrder.forStockReport();
            },
            allPurchaseOrders          We immediately convert them to
        );                                PurchaseOrderForStockReport
                                                            instances.
        // ...
    }
}
```

We can now remove pretty much all of the query methods (`productId()`, `ordered-Quantity()`, and `wasReceived()`) from the original `PurchaseOrder` entity. This makes it a proper write model; it isn't used by clients who just want information from it anymore.

Listing 8.7   `PurchaseOrder` with its getters removed

```
final class PurchaseOrder
{
    private int purchaseOrderId
    private int productId;
    private int orderedQuantity;
    private bool wasReceived;

    private function __construct()
    {
    }

    public static function place(
        int purchaseOrderId,
        int productId,
        int orderedQuantity
    ): PurchaseOrder {
        purchaseOrder = new PurchaseOrder();

        purchaseOrder.productId = productId;
        purchaseOrder.orderedQuantity = orderedQuantity;

        return purchaseOrder;
    }

    public function markAsReceived(): void
    {
        this.wasReceived = true;
    }
}
```

Removing these query methods won't do any harm to the existing clients of
PurchaseOrder that use this object as a write model, like the ReceiveItems service we
saw earlier, as you can see in the following listing.

Listing 8.8   Existing clients use `PurchaseOrder` as a write model

```
final class ReceiveItems
{
    // ...

    public function receiveItems(int purchaseOrderId): void
    {
        purchaseOrder = this.repository.getById(        ◁── This service doesn't
            PurchaseOrderId.fromInt(purchaseOrderId)        use any query method
        );                                                  of PurchaseOrder.

        purchaseOrder.markAsReceived();

        this.repository.save(purchaseOrder);
    }
}
```

Query methods aren't forbidden

Some clients use the entity as a write model but still need to retrieve some information from it. They need this information to make decisions based on it, perform extra validations, etc. Don't feel that you shouldn't add query methods in these cases; query methods aren't by any means forbidden. The point of this chapter is that clients that solely use an entity to retrieve information should use a dedicated read model instead of a write model.

Exercises

1   Is the `salesInvoice` object in the following code a write model or a read model?

```
public function finalize(SalesInvoiceId salesInvoiceId): void
{
    salesInvoice = salesInvoiceRepository.getById(salesInvoiceId);

    if (salesInvoice.wasCancelled()) {
        throw new CanNotFinalizeSalesInvoice
            ::becauseItWasAlreadyCancelled(salesInvoiceId);
    }

    salesInvoice.finalize();

    eventDispatcher.dispatchAll(salesInvoice.recordedEvents());

    salesInvoiceRepository.save(salesInvoice);
}
```

   a A read model
   b A write model

2   Is the `meetup` object in the following code a write model or a read model?

```
public function meetupDetailsAction(Request request): Response
{
    meetup = meetupRepository.getById(request.get('meetupId'));

    return this.templateRenderer.render(
        'meetup-details.html.twig', [
            'meetup' => meetup
        ]
    );
}
```

   a A read model
   b A write model

8.2   *Create read models that are specific for their use cases*

In the previous section, we split the `PurchaseOrder` entity into write and read models. The write model still carries the old name, but we called the read model `Purchase-OrderForStockReport`. The extra qualification `ForStockReport` indicates that this object now serves a specific purpose. The object will be suitable for use in a very specific context, namely arranging the data to produce a useful stock report for the user. The proposed solution isn't optimal yet, because the controller still needs to load all the `PurchaseOrder` entities and convert them to `PurchaseOrderForStockReport` instances by calling `forStockReport()` on them, as in the following listing. This means that the client still has access to the write model, even though our initial goal was to prevent that from happening.

> **Listing 8.9   Creating a stock report still relies on the write model**

```
public function execute(Request request): Response
{
    allPurchaseOrders = this.repository.findAll();        ◁——— We still rely on
                                                               PurchaseOrder
    forStockReport = array_map(                                instances here.
        function (PurchaseOrder purchaseOrder) {
            return purchaseOrder.forStockReport();
        },
        allPurchaseOrders
    );

    // ...
}
```

Another aspect of the design isn't quite right: even though we now have `Purchase-OrderForStockReport` objects, we still need to loop over them and build up another data structure before we can present the data to the user. What if we had an object whose structure matched the way we intended to use it? Concerning the name of this object, there's already a hint in the name of the read model (`ForStockReport`). So let's call this new object `StockReport`, and assume it already exists. The controller would become much simpler, as shown in the next listing.

> **Listing 8.10   `StockReportController` can retrieve the stock report directly**

```
final class StockReportController
{
    private StockReportRepository repository;

    public function __construct(StockReportRepository repository)
    {
        this.repository = repository;
    }

    public function execute(Request request): Response
```

```
        {
            stockReport = this.repository.getStockReport();

            return new JsonResponse(stockReport.asArray());
        }
    }
```

> asArray() is expected to return an array like we the one we created manually before.

Besides `StockReport`, we may create any number of read models that correspond to each of the application's specific use cases. For instance, we could create a read model that's used for listing purchase orders only. It would expose just the ID and the date on which it was created. We could then have a separate read model that provides all the details needed to render a form so the user can update some of the information, and so on.

Behind the scenes, `StockReportRepository` could still create the `StockReport` object based on `PurchaseOrderForStock` objects provided by the write model entities. But there are much better and more efficient alternatives. We'll cover some of them in the following sections.

8.3 *Create read models directly from their data source*

Instead of creating a `StockReport` model from `PurchaseOrderForStock` objects, we could go directly to the source of the data—the database where the application stores its purchase orders. If this is a relational database, there might be a table called `purchase_orders`, with columns for `purchase_order_id`, `product_id`, `ordered_quantity`, and `was_received`. If that's the case, `StockReportRepository` wouldn't have to load any other object before it could build a `StockReport` object; it could make a single SQL query and use that to create the `StockReport`.

Listing 8.11 **`StockReportSqlRepository` creates a stock report using plain SQL**

```
final class StockReportSqlRepository implements StockReportRepository
{
    public function getStockReport(): StockReport
    {
        result = this.connection.execute(
            'SELECT ' .
            ' product_id, ' .
            ' SUM(ordered_quantity) as quantity_in_stock ' .
            'FROM purchase_orders ' .
            'WHERE was_received = 1 ' .
            'GROUP BY product_id'
        );

        data = result.fetchAll();

        return new StockReport(data);
    }
}
```

Creating read models directly from the write model's data source is usually pretty efficient in terms of runtime performance. It's also an efficient solution in terms of development and maintenance costs. This solution will be less efficient if the write model changes often, or if the raw data can't easily be used as-is and needs to be interpreted first.

8.4   Build read models from domain events

One disadvantage of creating the StockReport read model directly from the write model's data is that the application will make the calculations again and again, every time a user requests a stock report. Although the SQL query won't take too long to execute (until the table grows very large), in some cases it'll be necessary to use another approach for creating read models.

Let's take another look at the result of the SQL query we used in the previous example (see table 8.1).

Table 8.1   The result of the SQL query for generating a stock report

product_id	quantity_in_stock
123	10
124	5

How else could we come up with the numbers in the second column, without looking up all the records in the purchase_orders table and summing their ordered_quantity values?

What if we could sit next to the user with a piece of paper, and whenever they marked a purchase order as received, we'd write down the ID of the product and how many items of it were received. The resulting list would look like table 8.2.

Table 8.2   The result of writing down every received product

product_id	received
123	2
124	4
124	1
123	8

Now, instead of having multiple rows for the same product, we could look up the row with the product that was just received, and add the quantity we received to the number that's already in the received column, as in table 8.3.

Table 8.3 The result of combining received quantities per product

product_id	received
123	2 + 8
124	4 + 1

Doing the calculations, this amounts to the same result as when we used the SUM query.

Instead of sitting next to the user with a piece of paper, we should listen in on our PurchaseOrder entity to find out when a user marks it as received. We can do this by recording and dispatching *domain events,* a technique you already saw in section 4.12.

First, we need to let PurchaseOrder record a domain event, indicating that the ordered items were received

Listing 8.12 PurchaseOrder entities record PurchaseOrderReceived events

```
final class PurchaseOrderReceived          ◁── This is the new
{                                               domain event.
    private int purchaseOrderId;
    private int productId;
    private int receivedQuantity;

    public function __construct(
        int purchaseOrderId,
        int productId,
        int receivedQuantity
    ) {
        this.purchaseOrderId = purchaseOrderId;
        this.productId = productId;
        this.receivedQuantity = receivedQuantity;
    }

    public function productId(): int
    {
        return this.productId;
    }

    public function receivedQuantity(): int
    {
        return this.receivedQuantity;
    }
}

final class PurchaseOrder
{
    private array events = [];

    // ...
```

```
    public function markAsReceived(): void
    {
        this.wasReceived = true;

        this.events[] = new PurchaseOrderReceived(
            this.purchaseOrderId,
            this.productId,
            this.orderedQuantity
        );
    }

    public function recordedEvents(): array
    {
        return this.events;
    }
}
```

> We record the
> domain event inside
> PurchaseOrder.

Calling `markAsReceived()` will now add a `PurchaseOrderReceived` event object to the list of internally recorded events. These events can be taken out and handed over to an event dispatcher, as in the following `ReceiveItems` service.

Listing 8.13 `ReceiveItems` dispatches any recorded domain event

```
final class ReceiveItems
{
    // ...

    public function receiveItems(int purchaseOrderId): void
    {
        // ...

        this.repository.save(purchaseOrder);

        this.eventDispatcher.dispatchAll(
            purchaseOrder.recordedEvents()
        );
    }
}
```

An event listener that has been registered for this particular event can take the relevant data from the event object and update its own private list of products and quantities in stock. For instance, it could build up the stock report by maintaining its own stock_report table with rows for every product. It would have to process incoming `PurchaseOrderReceived` events and create new rows or update existing ones in this stock_report table.

Listing 8.14 Using the event to update the stock_report table

```
final class UpdateStockReport
{
    public function whenPurchaseOrderReceived(
```

```
        PurchaseOrderReceived event
    ): void {
        this.connection.transactional(function () {
            try {
                this.connection
                    .prepare(
                        'SELECT quantity_in_stock ' .
                        'FROM stock_report ' .
                        'WHERE product_id = :productId FOR UPDATE'
                    )
                    .bindValue('productId', event.productId())
                    .execute()
                    .fetch();

                this.connection
                    .prepare(
                        'UPDATE stock_report ' .
                        'SET quantity_in_stock = ' .
                        ' quantity_in_stock + :quantityReceived ' .
                        'WHERE product_id = :productId'
                    )
                    .bindValue(
                        'productId',
                        event.productId()
                    )
                    .bindValue(
                        'quantityReceived',
                        event.quantityReceived()
                    )
                    .execute();
            } catch (NoResult exception) {
                this.connection
                    .prepare(
                        'INSERT INTO stock_report ' .
                        ' (product_id, quantity_in_stock) ' .
                        'VALUES (:productId, :quantityInStock)'
                    )
                    .bindValue(
                        'productId',
                        event.productId()
                    )
                    .bindValue(
                        'quantityInStock',
                        event.quantityReceived()
                    )
                    .execute();
            }
        });
    }
}
```

Find out if we have an existing row. → (points to `this.connection .prepare( 'SELECT ...`)

If a row exists for this product, update the existing one and increase the quantity in stock. ← (points to `this.connection .prepare( 'UPDATE ...`)

Otherwise, create a new row and set an initial value for quantity in stock. ← (points to `} catch (NoResult exception) {`)

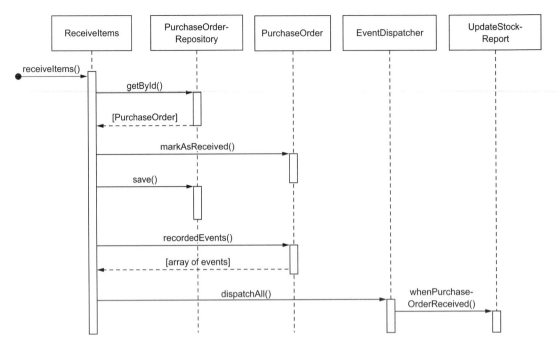

Figure 8.1 The ReceiveItems service makes a change to the PurchaseOrder write model and then dispatches domain events to EventDispatcher to allow other services like UpdateStockReport to listen in on those changes.

Once we have a separate data source for the stock report, we can make Stock-ReportSqlRepository even simpler, because all the information is already in the stock_reports table.

Listing 8.15   The query in StockReportSqlRepository is now much simpler

```
final class StockReportSqlRepository implements StockReportRepository
{
    public function getStockReport(): StockReport
    {
        result = this.connection.execute(
            'SELECT * FROM stock_report'
        );

        data = result.fetchAll();

        return new StockReport(data);
    }
}
```

This kind of simplification may offer you a way to make your read model queries more efficient. However, in terms of development and maintenance costs, using domain events to build up read models is more expensive. As you can see by looking at the examples in this section, more moving parts are involved. If something changes about a domain event, it will take more work to adapt the other parts that depend on it. If one of the event listeners fails, you will need to fix the error and run it again, which requires some extra effort in terms of tooling and operations.

What about event sourcing?

Things will be even more complex if besides using events for building up read models, you also use events for reconstructing write models. This technique is called *event sourcing*, and it fits very well with the idea of separating write models from read models. However, as demonstrated in this chapter, you don't need to apply event sourcing if you're only looking for a better way to divide responsibilities between objects. You can provide clients that only want to retrieve information from an entity with a separate read model by using any of the techniques described here.

Exercises

3   Write down a list of domain events you would need in order to build a read model for a shopping cart with the following features:

    a   A user can add a product to it.
    b   A user can remove a product from it.
    c   A user can change the quantity of a product.

Summary

- For your domain objects, separate write models from read models. Clients that are only interested in an entity because they need data from it should use a dedicated object, instead of an entity that exposes methods for changing its state.
- A read model can be created directly from the write model, but a more efficient way would be to create it from the data source used by the write model. If that is impossible, or the read model can't be created in an efficient way, consider using domain events to build up the read model over time.

Answers to the exercises

1   Correct answer: **b**. The code does retrieve information from the model (it calls the `wasCancelled()` method), but it also modifies the object (it calls its `finalize()` method). This makes it a write model, since a read model would not offer methods to modify the state of the model to regular clients.

2 Correct answer: **a**. In theory it could be a write model, but it really shouldn't be. Its only purpose is to show some information about the meetup by rendering an HTML response for the user.

3 Suggested answer: You would need events that represent each of the things that can happen to the shopping cart. Given the described features, these events could be `ProductWasAddedToCart`, `ProductWasRemovedFromCart`, and `Product-QuantityWasModified`. As always, the advice is to look for domain-specific terms and use the words that your domain experts use. Why is there no event called `CartWasCreated`? Because that's already implied by `ProductWasAddedToCart`.

Changing the behavior of services

You can design your services to be created and used in certain ways. But the nature of a software project is that it will change over time. You'll often modify a class in such a way that, when it's used, it will behave the way you want it to. However, modifying a class comes with a cost: the danger of breaking it in some way. A common alternative to changing a class is to override some of its methods, but this can cause even more trouble. That's why, in general, it's preferable to modify the structure of an object graph instead of the code in a class. It's better to replace parts than to change them.

9.1   *Introduce constructor arguments to make behavior configurable*

We've discussed earlier how services should be created in one go, with all their dependencies and configuration values provided as constructor arguments. When it comes to changing the behavior of a service object, the constructor is again the place to be. Always prefer using a replaceable constructor argument when you want to influence the behavior of a service.

Take for example the following `FileLogger` class, which logs messages to a file.

Listing 9.1   The `FileLogger` class

```
final class FileLogger
{
    public function log(message): void
    {
        file_put_contents(
            '/var/log/app.log',
            message,
            FILE_APPEND
        );
    }
}
```

To reconfigure the logger to log messages to another file, promote the log file path to a constructor argument that gets copied into a property.

Listing 9.2   Use a constructor argument to configure the `FileLogger`

```
final class FileLogger
{
    private string filePath;

    public function __construct(string filePath)
    {
        this.filePath = filePath;
    }

    public function log(message): void
    {
        file_put_contents(this.filePath, message, FILE_APPEND);
    }
}

logger = new FileLogger('/var/log/app.log');
```

Exercises

1 What are good options for making the base URL of the following API client configurable?

```
final class ApiClient
{
    public function sendRequest(
        string method,
        string path
    ): Response {
        url = 'https://api.acme.com' . path;

        // ...
    }
}
```

  a Inject a `Config` object as a constructor argument from which the `ApiClient` can retrieve the base URL.

  b Inject the base URL as a string or a value object into the constructor of `ApiClient`.

  c Add `baseUrl` as an extra parameter to `sendRequest()`.

9.2 Introduce constructor arguments to make behavior replaceable

You saw earlier how every dependency of a service should be injected as a constructor argument. Just as configuration values can be changed, these dependencies can also be replaced.

Consider the following `ParameterLoader`, which can be used to load a list of keys and values ("parameters") from a JSON file.

Listing 9.3 The `ParameterLoader` class

```
final class ParameterLoader
{
    public function load(filePath): array
    {
        rawParameters = json_decode(
            file_get_contents(filePath),
            true
        );

        parameters = [];

        foreach (rawParameters as key => value) {
            parameters[] = new Parameter(key, value);
        }
```

Load parameters from the file and add them to the already loaded ones.

```
            return parameters;
    }
}

loader = new ServiceConfigurationLoader(
    __DIR__ . '/parameters.json'
);
```

Which part of this class should be replaced to support loading an XML or maybe even a YAML file instead? Most of the `ParameterLoader` is pretty generic, except for the call to `json_decode()`. To make this piece replaceable, we need to introduce an abstraction. This means finding a more abstract concept than "decoding a JSON file," and introducing an interface that can represent the abstraction.

The abstract concept is "loading a file," so `FileLoader` would be an appropriate name for an interface that represents this task in code. We'll have a standard implementation for this interface that loads parameters from a JSON file. Let's call this implementation `JsonFileLoader`.

Listing 9.4   The `FileLoader` interface, implemented by `JsonFileLoader`

```
interface FileLoader
{
    public function loadFile(string filePath): array     ◁──┐ Load an array of key/
}                                                            │ value pairs representing
                                                             │ parameters stored in a file
final class JsonFileLoader implements FileLoader            │ at the given location.
{
    public function loadFile(string filePath): array
    {
        Assertion.isFile(filePath);

        result = json_decode(
            file_get_contents(filePath),
            true
        );

        if (!is_array(result)) {
            throw new RuntimeException(
                'Decoding "{filePath}" did not result in an array'
            );
        }

        return result;
    }
}
```

We've used the opportunity to add some precondition and postcondition checks to make the JSON-specific implementation more reliable.

Now we need to make sure that ParameterLoader gets an instance of FileLoader injected as a constructor argument, and we'll replace the existing file-loading code in ParameterLoader with a call to FileLoader.loadFile().

> **Listing 9.5 ParameterLoader depends on a FileLoader instance**

```
final class ParameterLoader
{
    private FileLoader fileLoader;

    public function __construct(FileLoader fileLoader)
    {
        this.fileLoader = fileLoader;
    }

    public function load(filePath): array
    {
        // ...

        foreach (/* ... */) {
            if (/* ... */) {
                rawParameters = this.fileLoader.loadFile(
                    filePath
                );
            }
        }

        // ...
    }
}

parameterLoader = new ParameterLoader(new JsonFileLoader());
parameterLoader.load(__DIR__ . '/parameters.json');
```

With part of the behavior of ParameterLoader abstracted, we can replace it with any other *concrete* implementation, like an XML or YAML file loader.

> **Listing 9.6 Replacing the FileLoader implementation is easy**

```
final class XmlFileLoader implements FileLoader
{
    // ...
}

parameterLoader = new ParameterLoader(new XmlFileLoader());
parameterLoader.load(__DIR__ . '/parameters.xml');
```

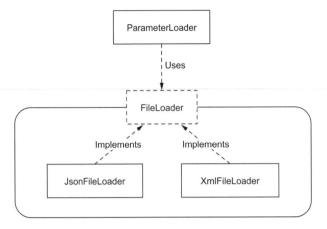

**Figure 9.1   As long as the
FileLoader dependency of
ParameterLoader follows the
contract defined by the interface,
it doesn't matter what goes on
behind the scenes of the real
FileLoader that gets injected.**

Exercises

2   Make the *formatting* and *writing* behaviors of the following Logger class replaceable.

```
final class Logger
{
    private string logFilePath;

    public function __construct(string logFilePath)
    {
        this.logFilePath = logFilePath;
    }

    public function log(string message, array context): void
    {
        handle = fopen(logFilePath);

        fwrite(
            handle,
            message . ' ' . json_encode(context)
        );
    }
}
```

9.3   *Compose abstractions to achieve more complicated behavior*

With the proper abstraction in place, it will be easy to compose multiple concrete
instances into more complicated behavior. For instance, what if you want to support
multiple formats based on the filename's extension? You could accomplish it using
object composition, as follows.

Listing 9.7 `MultipleLoaders` is a `FileLoader` that wraps other `FileLoaders`

```
interface FileLoader
{
    /**
     * ...
     *
     * @throws CouldNotLoadFile
     */
    public function loadFile(string filePath): array
}

final class MultipleLoaders implements FileLoader
{
    private array loaders;

    public function __construct(array loaders)
    {
        Assertion.allIsInstanceOf(loaders, FileLoader.className);
        this.loaders = loaders;
    }

    public function loadFile(string filePath): array
    {
        lastException = null;

        foreach (this.loaders as loader) {
            try {
                return loader.loadFile(filePath);
            } catch (CouldNotLoadFile exception) {
                lastException = exception;
            }
        }

        throw new CouldNotLoadFile(
            'None of the file loaders was able to load file "{filePath}"',
            lastException
        );
    }
}
```

> Add an annotation to the interface, indicating that loading a file may throw a CouldNotLoadFile exception.

> Introduce a new FileLoader that's composed of multiple FileLoader instances. When asked to load a file, it will delegate the call to the loaders until one of them doesn't throw a CouldNotLoadFile.

Note that the new logic is placed outside of `ParameterLoader` itself, which has no idea what's going on behind the `FileLoader` interface it uses.

Instead of simply trying different loaders, you may want a slightly different setup. For instance, one where every loader can be registered for a particular file extension. The following listing shows how to accomplish this (again, using object composition).

Listing 9.8 An alternative `MultipleLoaders` implementation

```
final class MultipleLoaders implements FileLoader
{
    private array loaders;

    public function __construct(array loaders)
```

```
    {
        Assertion.allIsInstanceOf(loaders, FileLoader.className);
        Assertion.allIsString(array_keys(loaders));
        this.loaders = loaders;
    }

    public function loadFile(string filePath): array
    {
        extension = pathinfo(filePath, PATHINFO_EXTENSION);
        if (!isset(this.loaders[extension])) {        ◁────────────────
            throw new CouldNotLoadFile(
                'There is no loader for file extension "{extension}"'
            );
        }

        return this.loaders[extension].loadFile(filePath);
    }
}
```

> this.loaders is supposed to be a map of keys and values, where the key is a file extension and the value is the FileLoader that should be used for loading a file with that extension.

```
parameterLoader = new ParameterLoader(
    new MultipleLoaders([
        'json' => new JsonFileLoader(),
        'xml' => new XmlFileLoader()
    ])
);
parameterLoader.load('parameters.json');
parameterLoader.load('parameters.xml');

parameterLoader.load('parameters.yml');       ◁──────
```

> This will throw a CouldNotLoadFile exception.

As you can see, this setup is now very dynamic. However, always keep in mind that if you're writing this code for your project, you won't usually have to support all these different file formats. Introducing the FileLoader abstraction is a smart thing to do, but writing all these different loader implementations should be considered "generalization before it's needed." *Until it's needed . . .*

9.4   *Decorate existing behavior*

In the previous example, the multiple file loaders for JSON, XML, etc., all return an array of raw parameters (key/value pairs). What if we wanted to allow the user to use environment variables as the values for these parameters? We wouldn't want to copy this replacement logic into all the FileLoader implementations. Instead, we'll want to add the behavior on top of any existing behavior. We can do this using a particular style of composition called *decoration*, demonstrated in the following listing.

Listing 9.9   `ReplaceParametersWithEnvironmentVariables`

```
final class ReplaceParametersWithEnvironmentVariables
    implements FileLoader
{
    private FileLoader fileLoader;
```

```
        private array envVariables;

        public function __construct(
            FileLoader fileLoader,
            array envVariables
        ) {                                              The real file loader is injected
            this.fileLoader = fileLoader;         ◄───   as a constructor argument.
            this.envVariables = envVariables;
        }

        public function loadFile(string filePath): array        We use the
        {                                                        real file loader
            parameters = this.fileLoader.loadFile(filePath);  ◄─  to load the file.

            foreach (parameters as key => value) {
                parameters[key] = this.replaceWithEnvVariable(    ◄──────────────┐
                    value
                );
            }                               Any parameter value that is also the
                                            name of an environment variable will
            return parameters;                be replaced by the latter's value.
        }

        private function replaceWithEnvVariable(string value): string
        {
            if (isset(this.envVariables[value])) {
                return this.envVariables[value];
            }

            return value;
        }
    }

parameterLoader = new ParameterLoader(
    new ReplaceParametersWithEnvironmentVariables(
        new MultipleLoaders([
            'json' => new JsonFileLoader(),
            'xml' => new XmlFileLoader()
        ]),
        [
            'APP_ENV' => 'dev',
        ]
    )
);
```

Decoration is also often used when the cost of using the real service is somewhat high. For instance, if the application has to load and parse the parameters.json file many times, it may be smart to wrap the original service and remember the last result it returned.

Listing 9.10   `CachedFileLoader` calls the real loader only if necessary

```
final class CachedFileLoader implements FileLoader
{
    private FileLoader realLoader;

    private cache = [];

    public function __construct(FileLoader realLoader)
    {
        this.realLoader = realLoader;
    }

    public function loadFile(string filePath): array
    {
        if (isset(this.cache[filePath])) {
            return this.cache[filePath];
        }

        result = this.realLoader.loadFile(filePath);

        this.cache[filePath] = result;

        return result;
    }
}

loader = new CachedFileLoader(new JsonFileLoader());

loader.load('parameters.json');

loader.load('parameters.json');
```

We've loaded this file before, so we can return the cached result.

We haven't loaded this file before, so we do it now.

We keep the result in our cache so we don't have to load the file again next time.

This will forward the call to JsonFileLoader.

The second time we won't hit the filesystem.

The advantage of using composition in this scenario is that the caching logic doesn't have to be duplicated across the different file-loader implementations. In fact, the logic in `CachedFileLoader` is agnostic concerning the `FileLoader` implementation that's being used. This means you can test it separately, and you can also develop it separately. If you want to make the caching logic more advanced, you only have to change the code of this single class dedicated to caching.

Exercises

3   All the `log()` statements in the following code distract from the real purpose of the class: importing a CSV file. Use decoration and composition to move the `log()` statements to separate classes. (Hint: you'll have to introduce a dedicated object for importing a single line so you can decorate it.)

```
final class CsvFileImporter
{
    private Logger logger;

    public function __construct(Logger logger)
    {
        this.logger = logger;
    }

    public function import(string csvFile): void
    {
        this.logger.log('Importing file: ' . csvFile);

        foreach (linesIn(csvFile) as lineNumber => line) {
            this.logger.log('Importing line: ' . lineNumber);

            // import the line
            fields = fieldsIn(line);
            // ...

            this.logger.log('Imported line: ' . lineNumber);
        }

        this.logger.log('Finished importing');
    }
}
```

9.5 Use notification objects or event listeners for additional behavior

We already looked at using event listeners as a technique for separating the main job of a command method from its secondary tasks. If you want to reconfigure services to do other things than they did before, you could use the same technique. As an example, take a look at the ChangeUserPassword service.

Listing 9.11 The `ChangeUserPassword` service

```
final class ChangeUserPassword
{
    private PasswordEncoder passwordEncoder;

    public function __construct(
        PasswordEncoder passwordEncoder,
        /* ... */
    ) {
        // ...
    }

    public function changeUserPassword(
        UserId userId,
```

```
        string plainTextPassword
    ): void {
        encodedPassword = this.passwordEncoder.encode(
            plainTextPassword
        );

        // Store the new password...
    }
}
```

A new requirement for this service is that it should send an email to the user afterward, to tell them that their password has changed (just in case it was a hacker who did it). Instead of adding more code to the existing class and method, this could be a nice opportunity to dispatch an event and set up a listener that will send the email.

> **Listing 9.12 The `UserPasswordChanged` event class and its listener**

```
final class UserPasswordChanged        ◁──┐   Define a new
{                                          │   event type.
    private UserId userId;

    public function __construct(UserId userId)
    {
        this.userId = userId;
    }
}
                                                    ┌   Define a listener
final class SendUserPasswordChangedNotification  ◁──┘   for this event.
{
    // ...

    public function whenUserPasswordChanged(
        UserPasswordChanged event
    ): void {
        // Send the email...
    }
}
```

Finally, we have to rewrite the `ChangeUserPassword` service to dispatch the newly defined `UserPasswordChanged` event.

> **Listing 9.13 `ChangeUserPassword` dispatches a `UserPasswordChanged` event**

```
final class ChangeUserPassword
{
    private EventDispatcher eventDispatcher;

    public function __construct(
        /* ... */,
        EventDispatcher eventDispatcher
    ) {
        // ...
```

```
    }

    public function changeUserPassword(
        UserId userId,
        string plainTextPassword
    ): void {
        encodedPassword = this.passwordEncoder.encode(
            newPassword
        );

        // Store the new password

        this.eventDispatcher.dispatch(
            new UserPasswordChanged(userId)
        );
    }
}
listener = new SendUserPasswordChangedNotification(/* ... */);
eventDispatcher = new EventDispatcher([
    UserPasswordChanged.className => [
        listener,
        'whenUserPasswordChanged'
    ]
]);

service = new ChangeUserPassword(/* ... */, eventDispatcher);

service.changeUserPassword(new UserId(/* ... */), 'Test123');
```

> We have to make sure that the listener is registered in the correct way.

> This will cause a **UserPasswordChanged** event to be dispatched to the **SendUserPasswordChangedNotification** listener.

The advantage of using an event dispatcher is that it enables you to add new behavior to a service without modifying its existing logic. Once it's in place, an event dispatcher offers the option to add new behavior. You can always register another listener for an existing event.

A disadvantage of using an event dispatcher is that it has a very generic name. When reading the code, it's not very clear what's going on behind that call to `dispatch()`. It can also be a bit difficult to figure out which listeners will respond to a certain event. An alternative solution is to introduce your own abstraction.

As an example, take the following `Importer` class that imports CSV files from a given directory and dispatches events to allow other services to listen in on the import process.

Listing 9.14 `Importer` dispatches events

```
final class Importer
{
    private EventDispatcher dispatcher;

    public function __construct(EventDispatcher dispatcher)
    {
        this.dispatcher = dispatcher;
```

```
        }

        public function import(string csvDirectory): void
        {
            foreach (Finder.in(csvDirectory).files() as file) {
                // Read the file
                lines = /* ... */;

                foreach (lines as index => line) {
                    if (index == 0) {
                        // Parse the header
                        header = /* ... */;

                        this.dispatcher.dispatch(
                            new HeaderImported(file, header)
                        );
                    }
                    else {
                        data = /* ... */;

                        this.dispatcher.dispatch(
                            new LineImported(file, index)
                        );
                    }
                }

                this.dispatcher.dispatch(
                    new FileImported(file)
                );
            }
        }
}
```

It turns out that every one of these events has just one listener—one that will write some debug information about the event to a log file. Although this is a very simple task, we have to maintain lots of code for it: we have event and event listener classes to write, and we have to remember to register the listeners in the correct way.

As you know now, most of these listeners do the same kind of job, so instead of spreading this behavior across many classes, we might as well combine it in a single class and introduce our own abstraction for it: ImportNotifications.

> **Listing 9.15   A single abstraction can replace all import events**

```
interface ImportNotifications
{
    public function whenHeaderImported(
        string file,
        array header
    ): void;

    public function whenLineImported(
        string file,
```

```
        int index
    ): void;

    public function whenFileImported(
        string file
    ): void;
}


final class ImportLogging implements ImportNotifications
{
    private Logger logger;

    public function __construct(Logger logger)
    {
        this.logger = logger;
    }

    public function whenHeaderImported(
        string file,
        array header
    ): void {
        this.logger.debug('Imported header ...');
    }

    // And so on...
}
```

Instead of injecting the event dispatcher into the `Importer` class, we can now inject an instance of `ImportNotifications`. And instead of calling `dispatch()`, we should now make a call to the dedicated event method on the injected `ImportNotifications` instance.

Listing 9.16   `Importer` calls `ImportNotifications` instead of `EventDispatcher`

```
final class Importer
{
    private ImportNotifications notify;

    public function __construct(ImportNotifications notify)
    {
        this.notify = notify;
    }

    public function import(string csvDirectory): void
    {
        foreach (Finder.in(csvDirectory).files() as file) {
            // Read the file
            lines = /* ... */;

            foreach (lines as index => line) {
                if (index == 0) {
                    // Parse the header
                    header = /* ... */;
```

```
                    this.notify.whenHeaderImported(
                        file,
                        header
                    )
                }
                else {
                    data = /* ... */;

                    this.notify.whenLineImported(file, index);
                }
            }

            this.notify.whenFileImported(file);
        }
    }
}
```

If besides logging you also want to output the debug information to the screen, you can easily do that in the same class. Or you could add another class and use object composition again to invoke both behaviors instead of just one.

9.6 Don't use inheritance to change an object's behavior

Let's take another look at the `ParameterLoader` example we discussed earlier. What if the original class looked like the one in the following listing?

> **Listing 9.17 A different `ParameterLoader` than the one we saw before**

```
class ParameterLoader
{
    public function load(filePath): array
    {
        // ...

        rawParameters = this.loadFile(filePath);

        // ...

        return parameters;
    }

    protected function loadFile(string filePath): array
    {
        return json_decode(
            file_get_contents(filePath),
            true
        );
    }
}
```

There are two key differences:

- The ParameterLoader class isn't marked as final, meaning that it's possible to define a subclass that extends ParameterLoader.
- There is now a dedicated method for loading the file, and this method is protected, meaning it can be overridden by such a subclass.

With the class internals fully exposed, it's now possible to extend the class, inherit the core logic, and override the file-loading part to make it deal with XML.

Listing 9.18   Loading XML files is possible when we extend `ParameterLoader`

```
final class XmlFileParameterLoader extends ParameterLoader
{
    protected function loadFile(string filePath): array
    {
        rawXml = file_get_contents(filePath);

        // Convert to array somehow

        return /* ... */;
    }
}
```

As you can imagine, this solution doesn't come with all the benefits of the previous one, like the file-loader abstraction itself, which offered clean options for composition, supporting multiple file loaders at once, etc. This alternative solution, where we extend from the existing ParameterLoader class itself, doesn't come with any of that flexibility and reconfigurability. In fact, using class inheritance to change the behavior of an existing object comes with many downsides:

- *Subclass and parent class become tied together*—Changing implementation details that would normally be hidden behind the public interface of the class could now break the implementation of a subclass. Consider what would happen if that protected method's name was changed, or if it got an extra required parameter.
- *Subclasses can override* protected *but also* public *methods*—Subclasses gain access to protected properties and their data types, which have so far been internal information. In other words, a lot of the internals of the object are now exposed.

What if, instead, the parent class offered a so-called *template* method, and allowed the implementer to only provide that method, not exposing any more internals than needed? The following listing shows what this would look like.

Listing 9.19 `ParameterLoader` implementing the template method pattern

```
abstract class ParameterLoader
{
    // ...

    final public function load(filePath): array  ◁──┐
    {
        parameters = [];

        foreach (/* ... */) {
            // ...
            if (/* ... */) {
                rawParameters = this.loadFile(filePath);
                // ...
            }
        }

        return parameters;
    }

    abstract protected function loadFile(string filePath): array;  ◁───
}
```

> Mark all properties "private" to keep them private to the parent class. Mark all methods "final" to make it impossible to override them.

> Only allow one method to be implemented (not overridden).

This is better, but it's still not optimal. We may not have the downsides of inheritance anymore, but we don't have the endless possibilities of using composition either.

Based on this example, we can generalize and claim that everything that can be done with the *template* method pattern can also be achieved with composition. The only thing you need to do is promote the abstract protected method to a regular public method on an injected object. Then you can make the class itself final again. In the case of our ParameterLoader, we already did that.

Listing 9.20 `ParameterLoader` marked `final`

```
final class ParameterLoader
{
    private FileLoader fileLoader;

    public function __construct(FileLoader fileLoader)
    {
        this.fileLoader = fileLoader;
    }

    final public function load(filePath): array
    {
        parameters = [];

        foreach (/* ... */) {
            // ...
            if (/* ... */) {
                rawParameters = this.fileLoader.loadFile(  ◁──
                    filePath
```

> Use the public loadFile() method of the injected FileLoader here, instead of the protected loadFile() method we had earlier.

```
                    );

                    // ...
            }
        }

        return parameters;
    }
}
```

Since many projects still don't mark their classes as "final" by default, you will encounter many frameworks and libraries that allow the behavior of their objects to be modified by extending their classes. Please refrain from doing so. Always choose a solution that uses only `public` methods, preferably those that are part of the published interface of a class. Don't rely on class internals by inheriting them from another class. By doing so, you would be making your solutions more fragile, because you're relying on things that are more likely to change the published, supported API offered by the framework or library.

9.6.1 When is it okay to use inheritance?

Broadly speaking, inheritance should only be used to define a strict hierarchy of types. For example, a content block can be either a paragraph or an image, and you could write, `Paragraph extends ContentBlock` and `Image extends ContentBlock`. In practice, I rarely find a good case for using inheritance. It usually turns out a bit awkward or "forced," and soon it starts to get in the way.

Inheritance is usually used for code reuse, and composition is a much more powerful form of code reuse. However, some object types like entities or value objects don't support dependency injection, so you can't really achieve code reuse via that road. In that case, I recommend using traits. Traits aren't inheritance, because the name of the trait doesn't end up becoming part of the class's hierarchy, like a parent class or an interface would. A trait is plain code reuse—a compiler-level copy/paste of code.

If, for example, you wanted to record domain events in all your entities, you could define the following interface for entities. This will make sure that they all have methods for retrieving those events, and for clearing them after you've dispatched them.

```
interface RecordsEvents
{
    public function releaseEvents(): array;

    public function clearEvents(): void;
}
```

Because all entities will have the same implementation for these methods, and you don't want to manually copy/paste that implementation into all of the entity classes, you could use a `trait`:

```
trait EventRecordingCapabilities
{
    private array events;

    private function recordThat(object event): void
    {
        this.events[] = event;
    }

    public function releaseEvents(): array
    {
        return this.events;
    }

    public function clearEvents(): void
    {
        this.events = [];
    }
}
```

Entities only have to implement this interface and use the accompanying trait, and they will have "event recording capabilities":

```
final class Product implements RecordsEvents
{
    use EventRecordingCapabilities;

    // ...
}
```

9.7   *Mark classes as final by default*

For services, we already made the case for marking classes as `final`: changing behavior by using object composition, instead of inheritance, is the better, more flexible way. If you go this way, there's no need to allow a class to be extended at all. These objects can keep their internals to themselves and only allow clients to use behavior that is part of their public interface. That means every class can, and should be, marked `final`. This will make it clear to the client that the class isn't meant to be extended, its methods aren't meant to be overridden. It will force users to look for better ways to change its behavior.

For other types of objects, like entities and value objects, the question should be asked also: do they also have to be `final`? Yes, they do. These objects represent domain concepts and the knowledge you have gained about them. It would be weird to override part of the behavior of classes by extending from them. If you've learned something about the domain that makes you want to change the behavior of an entity, you shouldn't create a subclass to change its behavior, but change the entity itself.

The only exception to the rule is when you want to declare a hierarchy of objects. In that case, extending from a parent class can indicate the relation between these objects: the subclass should be considered a special case of the parent class. Then the parent class won't be `final`, because the subclass has to be able to extend it.

9.8 *Mark methods and properties private by default*

So far, all the examples in this book have shown final classes with private properties. As soon as you mark your classes final, you may notice that there is no need to have protected properties anymore. Classes generally won't be used to extend from, so they can keep all of their internals to themselves. The only way in which clients can interact with an object is by constructing it and calling public methods on it. By closing down the class definition itself, you can design some really strong objects. The freedom to change anything about the object's internals, as long as it doesn't break the contract defined by its published interface, is a big win.

Exercises

4 For the following class, there are no classes that extend it, nor has it been designed to be extended. What should you change about the class definition?

```
class Product
{
    protected int $id;
    protected string description;

    // ...
}
```

  a The class should be marked as abstract.
  b The class should be marked as final.
  c The properties should be marked as private.
  d The properties should be marked as public.

5 What is wrong with the following code?

```
class Preferences
{
    private string preferencesFilePath;

    public function __construct(string preferencesFilePath)
    {
        this.preferencesFilePath = preferencesFilePath;
    }

    public function getPreference(
        string preference,
        bool defaultValue
    ): bool {
        preferences = this.loadPreferences();

        if (isset(preferences[preference])) {
            return preferences[preference];
        }

        return defaultValue;
    }
```

(continued)

```
        protected function loadPreferences(): array
        {
            return json_decode(
                file_get_contents(preferencesFilePath)
            );
        }
    }

    final class DatabaseTablePreferences extends Preferences
    {
        private Connection connection;

        public function __construct(Connection connection)
        {
            this.connection = connection;
        }

        protected function loadPreferences(): array
        {
            return this.connection.executeQuery(
                'SELECT * FROM preferences'
            ).fetchAll();
        }
    }
```

  a `DatabaseTablePreferences` uses inheritance to change the behavior of a service.
  b `Preferences` should extend `DatabaseTablePreferences` instead.
  c `Preferences` should dispatch events to allow loading preferences from a different location.
  d Loading the preferences should be delegated to a dedicated service with its own interface.

Summary

- When you feel the need to change the behavior of a service, look for ways to make this behavior configurable through constructor arguments. If this isn't an option because you want to replace a larger piece of logic, look for ways to swap out dependencies, which are also passed in as constructor arguments.
- If the behavior you want to change isn't represented by a dependency yet, extract one by introducing an abstraction: a higher level concept and an interface. You will then have a part you can replace, instead of modify. Abstraction offers the ability to compose and decorate behaviors, so they can become more complicated without the initial service knowing about it (or being modified for it).

- Don't use inheritance to change the behavior of a service by overriding its methods. Always look for solutions that use object composition. In fact, completely close all your classes down for inheritance: mark them as `final` and make all properties and methods `private`, unless they are part of the public interface of the class.

Answers to the exercises

1   Correct answer: **b.** Injecting a generic `Config` object is not a smart idea (see also section 2.3). Injecting a configuration value specifically for the base URL makes a lot of sense. And although passing it as an argument to `sendRequest()` is an option, it would force all clients to know this value. This is bad for the maintainability of the code, but is also very inconvenient for its clients.

2   Suggested answer: The formatter of log messages and the writer of log messages should have their own interfaces and standard implementations based on the code that is already in `Logger`:

```
interface Formatter
{
    public function format(
        string message,
        array context
    ): string;
}

final class JsonEncodedContextFormatter implements Formatter
{
    public function format(string message, array context)
    {
        return message . ' ' . json_encode(context);
    }
}

interface Writer
{
    public function write(string formattedMessage): void;
}

final class FileWriter implements Writer
{
    public function write(string formattedMessage): void
    {
        handle = fopen(logFilePath);
        fwrite(formattedMessage);
    }
}

final class Logger
{
    private Formatter formatter;
    private Writer writer;
```

```
    public function __construct(
        Formatter formatter,
        Writer writer
    ) {
        this.formatter = formatter;
        this.writer = writer;
    }

    public function log(string message, array context): void
    {
        this.writer.write(
            this.formatter.format(message, context)
        );
    }
}
```

3   Suggested answer: The following code shows a possible solution. Since it requires a lot of code just to get rid of the logging statements, you may look into an aspect-oriented programming (AOP) solution for your programming language. AOP tools allow you to hook into existing method calls and run code before or after the original method.

The LineImporter interface defines an extension point for importing a line.

```
interface LineImporter       ←──────
{
    public function import(int lineNumber, string line): void;
}


final class DefaultLineImporter implements LineImporter
{
    public function import(int lineNumber, string line): void
    {
        // import the line
        fields = fieldsIn(line);      ←──────
        // ...
    }
}
```

DefaultLineImporter contains the original code for importing a line.

```
final class LoggingLineImporter implements LineImporter
{
    private LineImporter actualLineImporter
    private Logger logger;

    public function __construct(
        LineImporter actualLineImporter
        Logger logger
    ) {
        this.actualLineImporter = actualLineImporter;
        this.logger = logger;
    }

    public function import(int lineNumber, string line): void
```

LoggingLineImporter adds logging before and after actually importing a line.

```
        {
            this.logger.log('Importing line: ' . lineNumber);

            this.actualLineImporter.import(lineNumber, line);

            this.logger.log('Imported line: ' . lineNumber);
        }
}
```

> **The FileImporter interface allows the original CsvFileImporter to be decorated.**

```
interface FileImporter                          ◁─────
{
    public function import(string file): void;
}

final class CsvFileImporter implements FileImporter
{
    private LineImporter lineImporter

    public function __construct(LineImporter lineImporter)
    {
        this.lineImporter = lineImporter;
    }
```

> **The original CsvFileImporter implements FileImporter.**

```
    public function import(string file): void
    {
        foreach (linesIn(csvFile) as lineNumber => line) {    ◁─────
            this.lineImporter.import(lineNumber, line);
        }
    }
}


final class LoggingFileImporter implements FileImporter    ◁─────
{
    private Logger logger;
    private FileImporter actualFileImporter
```

> **LoggingFileImporter adds logging before and after importing a file.**

```
    public function __construct(
        FileImporter actualFileImporter,
        Logger logger
    ) {
        this.actualFileImporter = actualFileImporter;
        this.logger = logger;
    }

    public function import(string csvFile): void
    {
        this.logger.log('Importing file: ' . csvFile);

        this.actualFileImporter.import(csvFile);

        this.logger.log('Finished importing');
    }
}

logger = // ...
```

```
importer = new LoggingFileImporter(
    new CsvFileImporter(
        new LoggingLineImporter(
            new DefaultLineImporter(),
        logger
    )
),
    logger
);
importer.import(/* ... */);
```

Instantiating the importer is more complicated, but its usage has not changed.

4 Correct answers: **b** and **c**. Marking the class as abstract would mean the opposite, namely that it's intended to be extended. Marking the properties as public fully exposes them to clients of `Product`, which is almost never desirable.

5 Correct answers: **a** and **d**. Using inheritance to change the behavior of a service is not recommended. Extending the other way around doesn't improve the situation, nor does using events. An event is meant to be a notification, allowing other services to take further action, not to change the behavior of the service itself. Instead of using inheritance, the `Preference` class should indeed delegate the loading of the preferences to another service—one that can be replaced and/or decorated.

A field guide to objects

So far we've discussed style guidelines for object design. These are meant to be general-purpose rules that can be applied everywhere, but this doesn't mean that all the objects in your application will look the same. Some objects will have lots of query methods and some will have only command methods. Some will have a mix of both, but with a certain ratio of them. You may find that different types of objects often share certain characteristics, which results in pattern names to be invented for them. For instance, developers will talk about "entities," "value objects," or "application services" to indicate the *nature* of the object they're talking about.

The last part of this book discusses some common types of objects you may find in an application and how you can recognize them in their natural habitat. In this sense, the following sections form a "field guide" for objects. If you find an object that doesn't really fit into a certain category, this guide may help you decide whether or not the object should be redesigned to fit in better with the rest of its species. On the other hand, if you encounter an object that doesn't look like any of the objects described in this chapter, don't worry. As long as it abides by the guidelines for object design in this book, it's perfectly fine.

Figure 10.1 offers a quick overview of the types of objects we'll encounter in the following sections. If you find yourself lost in the woods, please refer to it.

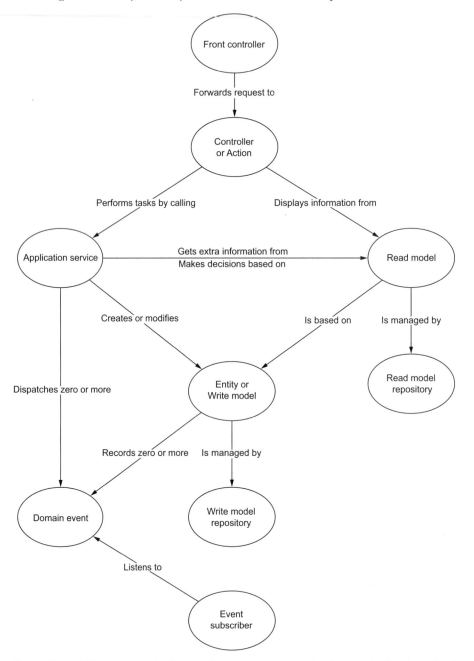

Figure 10.1   Different types of objects and how they work together in a regular (web) application

10.1 Controllers

In an application, there's always some sort of *front controller*. This is where all the requests come in. If you use PHP, this could be your index.php file. In Java's Spring framework, the `DispatcherServlet` plays this role—based on the request URI, its method, and headers, etc., the call will be forwarded to a *controller*, where the application can do anything it needs to do before it can return a proper response. For command-line (CLI) applications, the "front controller" would be the executable you'd call, such as bin/console, artisan, etc. Based on the arguments that the user provides, the call will be forwarded to something like a *command* object, where the application can perform the task requested by the user.

Though they are technically quite different, console commands are conceptually quite similar to web controllers. They both do work that was requested from outside the application by a person, or some other application, that sent a web request or ran the console application. So let's call both console commands and web controllers "controllers."

Controllers typically have code that reveals where the call came from. You'll find mentions of a `Request` object, request parameters, forms, HTML templates, a *session* maybe, or *cookies* (see figure 10.2). All of these are web concepts. The classes used here often originate from the web framework that your application uses.

Other controllers mention command-line arguments, options, or flags and contain code for outputting lines of text to the terminal and formatting them in ways that the terminal can understand (see figure 10.3). These are all signs for the reader that this class takes input from and produces output for the command line.

Because controllers talk about the particular delivery mechanism that initiated a call to them (the web, the terminal), controllers should be considered *infrastructure* code. They facilitate the connection between the client, who lives in *the world outside*, and the *core* of the application.

When a controller has examined the provided input, it will take whatever information it needs, and then call either an *application service* or a *read model repository*. An application service will be called when the controller is supposed to produce some

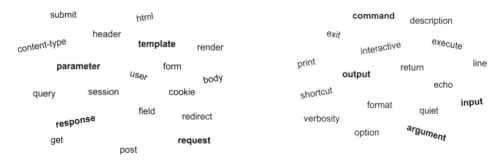

Figure 10.2 A word cloud of the terms you'll find in a web controller

Figure 10.3 A word cloud of the terms you'll find in a console command

kind of effect, such as when it's supposed to make a change to the application's state, to send out an email, etc. A read model repository will be used if the controller is supposed to return some information that the client requested.

An object is a controller if . . .
- a front controller calls it, and it's therefore one of the entry points for the graph of services and their dependencies (see section 2.12),
- it contains infrastructure code that reveals what the delivery mechanism is, and
- it makes calls to an application service or a read model repository (or both).

A typical web controller would look something like the one in the following listing. (The framework used in these examples is Symfony (https://symfony.com/), a solid framework for PHP web applications.)

Listing 10.1 A typical web controller

```
namespace Infrastructure\UserInterface\Web;

use Infrastructure\Web\Form\ScheduleMeetupType;
use Symfony\Bundle\FrameworkBundle\Controller\AbstractController;
use Symfony\Component\HttpFoundation\RedirectResponse;
use Symfony\Component\HttpFoundation\Response;
use Symfony\Component\HttpFoundation\Request;

final class MeetupController extends AbstractController
{
    public function scheduleMeetupAction(Request request): Response
    {
        form = this.createForm(ScheduleMeetupType.className);

        form.handleRequest(request);

        if (form.isSubmitted() && form.isValid()) {
            // ...

            return new RedirectResponse(
                '/meetup-details/' . meetup.meetupId()
            );
        }

        return this.render(
            'scheduleMeetup.html.twig',
            [
                'form' => form.createView()
            ]
        );
    }
}
```

The alternative controller for the command line might look something like the following.

Listing 10.2 A typical command-line controller, or "console command"

```
namespace Infrastructure\UserInterface\Cli;

use Symfony\Component\Console\Command\Command;
use Symfony\Component\Console\Input\InputInterface;
use Symfony\Component\Console\Output\OutputInterface;

final class ScheduleMeetupCommand extends Command
{
    protected function configure()
    {
        this
            .addArgument('title', InputArgument.REQUIRED)
            .addArgument('date', InputArgument.REQUIRED)
            // ...
        ;
    }

    public function execute(
        InputInterface input,
        OutputInterface output
    ) {
        title = input.getArgument('title');
        date = input.getArgument('date');

        // ...

        output.writeln('Meetup scheduled');
    }
}
```

10.2 Application services

An application service represents the task to be performed. It gets any dependency injected as a constructor argument. All the relevant data that's needed to perform the task (see section 2.8), including contextual information like the logged-in user ID or the current time, will be provided as method arguments. When the data originates from the client itself, it will be primitive-type data. That way, the controller can provide the application service with the data as it was sent by the client, without converting it first.

The code of an application service should read like a recipe, with all the steps required to do the job. For instance, "Take out an object from this write model repository, call a method on it, and save it again." Or, "Collect some information from this read model repository and send a report to a certain user."

> ### An object is an application service if . . .
> - it performs a single task,
> - it contains no infrastructure code; that is, it doesn't deal with the web request itself, or SQL queries, or the filesystem, etc., and
> - it describes a single use case that the application should have. It will often correspond one-to-one with a feature request from a stakeholder. For example, it should be possible to add a product to the catalog, to cancel an order, to send a delivery note to a customer, etc.

The web controller and console handler we saw in listings 10.1 and 10.2 will take the data from the request (via a form), or from the command-line arguments, and provide it to the application service, which looks something like the following.

Listing 10.3   An application service

```
namespace Application\ScheduleMeetup;

use Domain\Model\Meetup\Meetup;
use Domain\Model\Meetup\MeetupRepository;
use Domain\Model\Meetup\ScheduleDate;
use Domain\Model\Meetup\Title;

final class ScheduleMeetupService
{
    private MeetupRepository meetupRepository;

    public function __construct(MeetupRepository meetupRepository)
    {
        this.meetupRepository = meetupRepository;
    }

    public function schedule(                       ◁── The application service receives
        string title,                                    primitive-type arguments.
        string date,
        UserId currentUserId                         It converts these primitive-type values
    ): MeetupId {                                    to value objects and instantiates a new
        meetup = Meetup.schedule(          ◁──       Meetup entity using these objects.
            this.meetupRepository.nextIdentity(),
            Title.fromString(title),
            ScheduledDate.fromString(date),
            currentUserId
        );                                       It saves the meetup to the
                                                 write model repository.
        this.meetupRepository.save(meetup);  ◁──

        return meetup.meetupId();    ◁──  Finally, it returns the identifier
    }                                      of the new Meetup.
}
```

Sometimes application services are called "command handlers," but they will still be application services. Instead of invoking an application service using primitive-type arguments, you can also call it by providing a *command object*, which represents the client's request in a single object. Such an object is called a *data transfer object* (DTO) because it can be used to carry the data provided by the client and transfer it as one thing from controller to application service. This should be a simple, easy-to-construct object and should contain only primitive-type values, simple lists, and optionally other DTOs if some sort of hierarchy is required.

Listing 10.4   An example of passing a DTO when calling an application service

```
namespace Application\ScheduleMeetup;

final class ScheduleMeetup              ◁─┐  This command contains the
{                                         │  data needed to perform the
    public string title;                  │  task of scheduling a meetup.
    public string date;
}

final class ScheduleMeetupService
{
    // ...

    public function schedule(           ◁─┐  The application service could
        ScheduleMeetup command,           │  then take the data from the
        UserId currentUserId              │  command object.
    ): MeetupId {
        meetup = Meetup.schedule(
            this.meetupRepository.nextIdentity(),
            Title.fromString(command.title),
            ScheduledDate.fromString(command.date),
            currentUserId
        );

        // ...
    }
}
```

The advantage of using a dedicated command object is that it's easy to instantiate it based on deserialized string data, like a JSON or XML request body. It also works well with form libraries, which can map submitted data directly onto command DTO properties.

10.3   *Write model repositories*

Often an application service makes a change to the application's state, and this usually means that a domain object has to be modified and persisted. The application service uses an abstraction for this: a *repository*. To be more specific, a *write model repository*, because it's only concerned with retrieving an entity and storing the changes that are made to it.

The abstraction itself will be an interface that the application service gets injected as a dependency. This interface doesn't expose any details about *how* the object is going to be persisted. It just offers some general-purpose methods like getById(), `save()`, `add()`, or `update()`. A corresponding implementation will fill in the details, such as which SQL queries will be issued, or which ORM will be used to map the object to a row in the database.

> ## An object is a write model repository if . . .
> - it offers methods for retrieving an object from storage and for saving it, and
> - its interface hides the underlying technology that's been used.

As an example, the following listing shows the `MeetupRepository` that the application service in listing 10.3 relies on.

> **Listing 10.5   A write model repository interface and its implementation**

```
namespace Domain\Model\Meetup;

interface MeetupRepository
{
    public function save(Meetup meetup): void;

    public function nextIdentity(): MeetupId;

    /**
     * @throws MeetupNotFound
     */
    public function getById(MeetupId meetupId): Meetup
}

namespace Infrastructure\Persistence\DoctrineOrm;

use Doctrine\ORM\EntityManager;
use Domain\Model\Meetup\Meetup;
use Domain\Model\Meetup\MeetupId;
use Ramsey\Uuid\UuidFactoryInterface;

final class DoctrineOrmMeetupRepository
    implements MeetupRepository            ◁─┐  The default implementation
{                                              of MeetupRepository uses
    private EntityManager entityManager;       Doctrine ORM.
    private UuidFactoryInterface uuidFactory;

    public function __construct(
        EntityManager entityManager,
        UuidFactoryInterface uuidFactory
    ) {
        this.entityManager = entityManager;
        this.uuidFactory = uuidFactory;
    }

    public function save(Meetup meetup): void
    {
```

```
        this.entityManager.persist(meetup);
        this.entityManager.flush(meetup);
    }

    public function nextIdentity(): MeetupId
    {
        return MeetupId.fromString(
            this.uuidFactory.uuid4().toString()
        );
    }

    // ...
}
```

10.4 Entities

The objects that are being persisted will be the ones the user cares about—the ones
that should be remembered even when the application has to be restarted. These are
the application's *entities*.

   Entities represent the domain concepts of the application. They contain relevant
data and offer useful behavior related to this data. In terms of object design, they will
often have named constructors because this allows you to use domain-specific names
for creating this particular kind of entity (see section 3.9). They will also have modifier
methods, which are command methods that change the entity's state (see section 4.6).
Entities will have only a few, if any, query methods. Retrieving information is usually delegated to a particular kind of object, called a query object. We'll get back to this.

> **Proper entities**
>
> Just like any object, an entity fiercely protects itself against ending up in an invalid
> state. Many entities in the wild shouldn't be considered proper entities, according to
> this definition.

When a state change is allowed, an entity usually produces a domain event representing the change (see section 4.12). These events can be used to find out what exactly
has changed and to announce this change to other parts of the application that want
to respond to it.

> **An object is an entity if . . .**
> - it has a unique identifier,
> - it has a life cycle,
> - it will be persisted by a write model repository and can later be retrieved from it,
> - it uses named constructors and command methods to provide the user with
>   ways to instantiate it and manipulate its state, and
> - it produces domain events when it gets instantiated or modified.

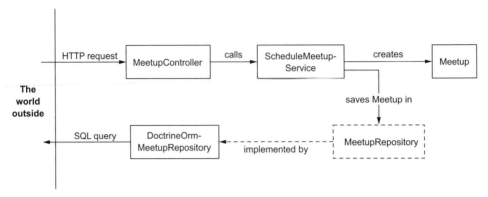

Figure 10.4   How each of the objects discussed so far work together to schedule a meetup

10.5   *Value objects*

Value objects are wrappers for primitive-type values, adding meaning and useful behavior to these values. We discussed them in detail earlier (chapter 3). In the context of the journey from controller to application service to repository, it should be noted that it's often the application service that instantiates value objects and then passes them as arguments to the constructor or a modifier method of an entity. Therefore, they end up being used or stored inside the entity.

However, it's good to remember that value objects aren't meant only to be used in combination with entities. They can be used in any place, and a value object is in fact a preferred way of passing around values.

An object is a value object . . .

- if it's immutable,
- if it wraps primitive-type data,
- if it adds meaning by using domain-specific terms (e.g., this isn't just an `int`, it's a `Year`),
- if it imposes limitations by means of validation (e.g., this isn't just any string, it's a string with an `'@'` in it), and
- it acts as an attractor of useful behavior related to the concept (e.g., `Position.toTheLeft(int steps)`).

The `Meetup` entity we saw being instantiated in listing 10.3, together with its related value objects and domain events, looks something like the following.

Listing 10.6   An entity

```
namespace Domain\Model\Meetup;

final class Meetup
{
```

```
    private array events = [];

    private MeetupId meetupId;
    private Title title;
    private ScheduledDate scheduledDate;
    private UserId userId;

    private function __construct()
    {
    }

    public static function schedule(
        MeetupId meetupId,
        Title title,
        ScheduledDate scheduledDate,
        UserId userId
    ): Meetup {
        meetup = new Meetup();

        meetup.meetupId = meetupId;
        meetup.title = title;
        meetup.scheduledDate = scheduledDate;
        meetup.userId = userId;

        meetup.recordThat(
            new MeetupScheduled(
                meetupId,
                title,
                scheduledDate,
                userId
            );
        );

        return meetup;
    }

    public function reschedule(ScheduledDate scheduledDate): void
    {
        // ...

        this.recordThat(
            new MeetupRescheduled(this.meetupId, scheduledDate)
        );
    }

    public function cancel(): void
    {
        // ...
    }

    // ...

    private function recordThat(object event): void
    {
        this.events[] = event;
```

The following methods are examples of other behavior that this Meetup entity could offer.

```
        }

        public function releaseEvents(): array
        {
            return this.events;
        }

        public function clearEvents(): void
        {
            this.events = [];
        }
    }

    final class Title
    {
        private string title;

        private function __construct(string title)
        {
            Assertion.notEmpty(title);
            this.title = title;
        }

        public static function fromString(string title): Title
        {
            return new Title(title);
        }

        public function abbreviated(string ellipsis = '...'): string
        {
            // ...
        }
    }

    final class MeetupId
    {
        private string meetupId;

        private function __construct(string meetupId)
        {
            Assertion.uuid(meetupId);
            this.meetupId = meetupId;
        }

        public static function fromString(string meetupId): MeetupId
        {
            return new MeetupId(meetupId);
        }
    }
```

We might as well have used a regular public constructor here ...

This is an example of useful behavior that value objects tend to attract.

10.6 Event listeners

We've already encountered domain events. They can be used to notify other services about things that have happened inside the write model. These other services can then perform secondary actions, after the primary work has been done. Since application services are the ones that perform these primary tasks, domain events can be used to notify other services *after* the application service is done. They can also do it at the last moment, just before returning. At that point, an application service could fetch the recorded events from the entity it has modified, and hand them over to the *event dispatcher*, as is shown in the following listing.

Listing 10.7 An application service dispatches domain events

```
final class RescheduleMeetupService
{
    private EventDispatcher dispatcher;

    public function __construct(
        // ...
        EventDispatcher dispatcher
    ) {
        this.dispatcher = dispatcher
    }

    public function reschedule(MeetupId meetupId, /* ... */): void
    {
        meetup = /* ... */;

        meetup.reschedule(/* ... */);

        this.dispatcher.dispatchAll(meetup.recordedEvents());
    }
}
```

> Dispatch any event that has been recorded inside the Meetup entity.

Internally, the dispatcher will forward all events to services called "listeners" or "subscribers," which have been registered for particular types of events.

An event listener could then perform secondary actions, for which it may even call another application service. It can use any other service it needs, such as to send notification emails about the domain event that has just occurred. Take, for example, the following `NotifyGroupMembers` listener, which will notify group members when a meetup has been rescheduled.

Listing 10.8 An event listener responds to domain events

```
final class NotifyGroupMembers
{
    public function whenMeetupRescheduled(
        MeetupRescheduled event
    ): void {
        /*
```

> A convenient naming standard for event listeners is the name of the thing you're going to do (e.g., "notify group members"). The methods will then point out the reasons for doing so (e.g., "when meetup rescheduled").

```
 * Send an email to group members using the information from
 * the event object.
 */
    }
}
```

> ## An object is an event listener . . .
> - if it's an immutable service, with its dependencies injected, and
> - if it has at least one method which accepts a single argument that is a domain event.

10.7   *Read models and read model repositories*

As mentioned earlier, a controller could invoke an application service to perform a task, but it may also invoke a *read model repository* to retrieve information from. Such a repository will return objects. These objects aren't meant to be manipulated, but to read information from. Earlier we called them "query objects"; they have only query methods, meaning that their state can't be influenced by their users.

When the call to the read model repository happens inside the controller, the read model that's returned could be passed to the template renderer, which could generate an HTML response using it. Or it could just as easily be used to generate a JSON-encoded response to an API call. In all these cases, the read model is specifically designed to fit the response that is going to be generated. All the data required for a particular use case should be available inside the read model, and no extra queries should have to be made. Such a read model is a DTO, because it's going to be used to *transfer* data from the core of the application to the world outside. The values that can be retrieved from such a read model should have primitive types.

As an example, take the following read model repository, which returns a list of upcoming meetups. It serves a specific use case and contains only the data required to render a simple list.

Listing 10.9   A read model and its repository

```
namespace Application\UpcomingMeetups;

final class UpcomingMeetup                    UpcomingMeetup is a read model (or
    public string title;                      "view model")—a DTO that carries
    public string date;                       relevant data about upcoming meetups
}                                             to be shown in a list on a web page.

interface UpcomingMeetupRepository            It comes with a repository that returns
{                                             instances of UpcomingMeetup and could
    /**                                       be used by a web controller and passed
     * @return UpcomingMeetup[]               to a template renderer.
     */
    public function upcomingMeetups(DateTime today): array
}
```

```
namespace Infrastructure\ReadModel;

use Application\UpcomingMeetups\UpcomingMeetupRepository;
use Doctrine\DBAL\Connection;

final class UpcomingMeetupDoctrineDbalRepository implements
    UpcomingMeetupRepository
{
    private Connection connection;

    public function __construct(Connection connection)
    {
        this.connection = connection;
    }

    public function upcomingMeetups(DateTime today): array
    {
        rows = this.connection./* ... */;

        return array_map(
            function (array row) {
                upcomingMeetup = new UpcomingMeetup();
                upcomingMeetup.title = row['title'];
                upcomingMeetup.date = row['date'];

                return upcomingMeetup;
            },
            rows
        );
    }
}
```

This implementation of **UpcomingMeetupRepository** fetches data directly from the database. It then creates instances of the **UpcomingMeetup** read model.

An application service itself can also use a read model repository to retrieve information. It then can use the information to make decisions or take further actions. A read model that's used by an application service is often a "smarter" read model than one that's used to generate a response. It uses proper value objects for its return values, instead of primitive-type values, so the application service doesn't have to worry about the validity of the read model. It often feels like such a read model is itself a write model, except there's no way to make changes to it; it's a query object after all.

As for the read model repositories themselves, they should be separated into an abstraction and a concrete implementation. Just like with write model repositories, an interface will offer one or more query methods that can be used to retrieve the read models. The interface doesn't give a hint about the underlying storage mechanism for these models.

An object is a read model repository . . .

- if it has query methods that conform to a specific use case and will return read models, which are also specific for that use case.

An object is a read model . . .
- if it has only query methods, i.e., it's a query object (and is therefore immutable),
- if it's designed specifically for a certain use case, and
- if all the data needed (and no more) becomes available the moment you retrieve the object.

Note that the distinction between a read model repository and a regular service that returns a piece of information isn't that clear. For example, consider the situation where an application service needs an exchange rate to convert a monetary value to a foreign currency. You might say that a service that can provide such information is basically a repository, from which you can get the exchange rate for a given currency conversion. Such a service has access to a "collection" of exchange rates that's defined in some place we don't care about. Still, this service could also be considered a regular service, and it may just as well be called `ExchangeRateProvider` or something like that.

The main idea is that for all these services you need an abstraction (see the following listing for an example) and a concrete implementation, because the abstraction describes what you're looking for, and the implementation describes how you can get it.

Listing 10.10   A regular service

```
namespace Application\ExchangeRates;

interface ExchangeRateProvider
{
    public function getRateFor(
        Currency from,
        Currency to
    ): ExchangeRate;
}

final ExchangeRate
{
    // ...
}
```

The abstraction is the interface that represents the question we're asking.

The types of the return values used by the interface are also part of the abstraction, because we care about how we can use these values, but not about how their data ends up in them.

In terms of their design, some objects aren't very different from others. For example, domain events look a lot like value objects—they are immutable objects holding data that belongs together. The difference between a domain event and a value object is how and where it's used: a domain event will be created and recorded inside an entity and later dispatched; a value object models an aspect of the entity.

10.8   Abstractions, concretions, layers, and dependencies

So far we've encountered different types of objects that you can find in your average web or console application. Besides certain characteristics, like the types of methods these objects have, what kind of information they expose, or what kind of behavior they offer, we should also consider whether they are *abstract* or *concrete*, and in which ways these objects are *dependent* on each other.

In terms of abstraction, we can define the following character traits for the object types we've discussed so far:

- *Controllers are concrete.* They are often coupled to a particular framework and are specific for the delivery mechanism. They don't have, or need, an interface. The only time you'd want to offer an alternative implementation is when you switch frameworks. In that case, you'd want to rewrite these controllers instead of creating a second implementation for them.
- *Application services are concrete.* They represent a very specific use case of your application. If the story of a use case changes, the application service itself changes, so they don't have an interface.
- *Entities and value objects are concrete.* They are the specific result of the developer's understanding of the domain. These types of objects *evolve* over time. We don't provide an interface for them. The same goes for read model objects. We define and use them as they are, never through an interface.
- *Repositories (for write and read models) consist of an abstraction and at least one concrete implementation.* Repositories are services that will reach out and connect to something outside of the application, like a database, the filesystem, or some remote service. That's why they need an abstraction that represents what the service will do and what it will return. The implementation will then provide all the low-level details about how it should do that. The same goes for other service objects that will reach out to some service outside the application. These services will also need an interface and a concrete implementation.

The services for which we have abstractions, according to the preceding list, should be *injected* as abstract dependencies. If we do this, we can form three useful groups, or *layers*, of objects:

1. The *infrastructure* layer:
   - Controllers
   - Write and read model repository *implementations*
2. The *application* layer:
   - Application services
   - Command objects
   - Read models
   - Read model repository *interfaces*
   - Event listeners

3 The *domain* layer:
  – Entities
  – Value objects
  – Write model repository *interfaces*

Considering that the *infrastructure* layer contains the code that facilitates communication with the *world outside*, it can be drawn as a layer around *application* and *domain* (see figure 10.5). Likewise, the *application* uses code in the *domain* layer to perform its tasks, so the domain layer will be the innermost layer of an application.

To show the use of layers in your code, you can make the layer names part of the namespaces of your classes. The code samples in this chapter also use this convention. By injecting abstract dependencies, we can ensure that objects will only depend in one direction: from top to bottom. For instance, an application service that needs a write model repository will depend on that repository's interface, not its concrete implementation. This has two major advantages.

First, we can test the application service code without an actual repository implementation that would need some sort of database that's up and running, with the correct schema, etc. We have interfaces for all these services, and we can easily create test doubles for them.

Second, we can easily switch infrastructure implementations. Our application layer would survive a switch between frameworks (or an upgrade to the framework's next major version), and it would also survive a switch of databases (when you realize you're better off with a graph database than a relational database, for instance) and remove services (when you no longer want to fetch exchange rates from an external service, but from your own local database).

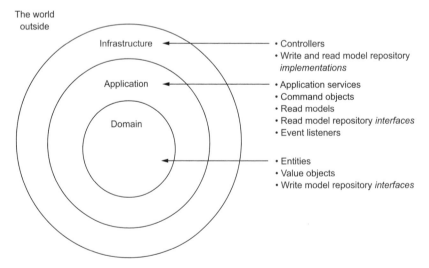

Figure 10.5   Layers can be visualized as concentric circles.

Summary

- An application's front controller will forward an incoming request to one of its controllers. These controllers are part of the application's *infrastructure layer*, and they know how to translate incoming data into a call to an application service or a read model repository, which are both part of the *application layer*.
- An application service will be agnostic regarding the delivery mechanism and can be used just as easily in web or console applications. It performs a single task that could be considered one of the application's use cases. Along the way, it may take an entity from a write model repository, call a method on it, and save its modified state. The entity itself, including its value objects, are part of the *domain layer*.
- A read model repository is a service that can be used to retrieve information. It returns read models that are specific to a use case and that provide all the information that's needed, and nothing more.
- The types of objects described in this chapter naturally belong to layers. A layering system where code only depends on code in lower layers offers a way to decouple domain and application code from the infrastructural aspects of your application.

11

Epilogue

This chapter covers

- Pointers to further reading material about architectural patterns
- Suggestions for improving your testing strategy
- Some hints on domain-driven design and finding out more about it

This book aims to be a style guide. It provides basic rules for object design that will be reflected in the declarations of your classes and methods. For many of these rules, you could build a static analysis tool that emits warnings when you don't follow the rules. Such a tool could, for instance, warn you about methods that make state changes *and* return something. Or about services with methods that change their behavior after construction time.

There are two comments to be made here. First, I think it's important to follow the rules but also to allow yourself to bend them in some special cases, such as when quality doesn't really matter, because you don't have to maintain the code for a long time. Or when, in certain cases, it would take a lot of work to apply *all* the rules, and the benefits don't outweigh the required effort. However, don't be too quick to judge. I'd estimate that in 95% of real-world scenarios, there really isn't a case for taking shortcuts.

Second, these rules aren't all there is to object design. They don't tell you exactly what objects you'll need, what their responsibilities should be, etc. For me, the rules in this book are rules I live by, almost without thinking. And because of this, there's more room for trying things out, for spending mental energy on different things.

In this chapter, I'd like to point out one other topic that helps relieve part of the cognitive burden of application development: architectural patterns. I'd also like to provide two possible topics to dive into after reading this book: testing and domain-driven design (DDD). Both fields can help you discover more about object design.

11.1 Architectural patterns

In the previous chapter, we discussed how certain types of objects form a natural set of layers. Besides using layers to structure the application as a whole (which should be considered an act of architecture), it's important to be aware of the ways in which your application is connected to the world outside. Recognizing the ways in which it communicates and can be communicated with results in a clean separation between code that supports this communication and code that is core to your application. This approach to architecture is called *hexagonal architecture*, or sometimes *ports and adapters*.

On this topic, I recommend taking a look at chapter 4 of Vaughn Vernon's *Implementing Domain-Driven Design* (Addison-Wesley Professional, 2013). A few of my own articles are also relevant to this topic:

- "Layers, ports & adapters—Part 2, Layers," http://mng.bz/2Jao
- "Layers, ports & adapters—Part 3, Ports & Adapters," http://mng.bz/1wMQ
- "When to add an interface to a class," http://mng.bz/POx8

11.2 Testing

In this book we've discussed object design, and we've been looking at a few testing techniques as well. It's very convenient to design objects while testing them. When you adopt a test-first approach, you will find that you write only the code you actually need to implement the desired behaviors. The tests prove that the objects you designed can be used in the ways you imagined. And whenever you think of possible edge cases or encounter bugs in the code behind your objects, you can describe the situation in a test case, see it fail, and then fix it.

11.2.1 Class testing versus object testing

Note that I speak about testing *objects*. I find that developers, myself included, often tend to test *classes*, not objects. This may seem to be a subtle difference, but it has some pretty big consequences. If you test *classes*, you usually test one method of one class with all its dependencies swapped out by test doubles. Such a test ends up being too close to the implementation. You'll be verifying that method calls are made, you'll be adding getters to get data out of the object, etc.

You could consider such tests that test *classes* to be *white box* tests, as opposed to *black box* tests, which are definitely more desirable. A black box test will test an object's behavior as perceived from the outside, with no knowledge about the class's internals. It will instantiate the object with only test doubles for objects that reach across a system boundary. Otherwise, everything is real. Such tests will show that not just a single class, but a larger unit of code, works well as a whole.

Class tests will change all the time, alongside the changes made to the classes themselves. Object tests are more decoupled from the implementation of the object that's being tested, so object tests will be more useful in the long run. In fact, here is a rule for testing that you can follow: write your tests in such a way that as many implementation details as possible could be changed before a change to the test code itself is required.

11.2.2 *Top-down feature development*

Another thing to be aware of when testing software is the level of detail you're working with. I find that developers, myself included, often prefer working on the smaller parts—building blocks that can later be used to complete the feature. You'll often think about everything you're going to need for the full feature and start collecting all the ingredients. Create a repository, a database table, an entity, etc. Once you're trying to connect all the parts, you'll often find that you have to revisit them because you made a few wrong assumptions, and the building blocks don't work well together in the end. This part of your development effort is more or less wasted.

I recommend working the other way around and starting with the bigger picture. Define how the feature will be used: describe user scenarios, make sketches of the interaction, etc. In other words, specify the high-level behavior of the application as you expect it to be after you've finished your work. Don't dive into the low-level details too quickly. Once you know what the application, when treated as a black box, should be capable of, you can descend to deeper layers and write code for everything that's needed.

Specifying application behavior should be done with tests, making this top-down development style fully test-driven. The high-level tests that describe the completed feature won'tpass until all the lower-level tests pass. Figure 11.1 shows how a feature

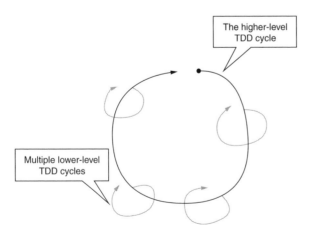

The higher-level
TDD cycle

Multiple lower-level
TDD cycles

Figure 11.1 A higher-level TDD cycle comes to a close after successfully closing several lower-level TDD cycles.

can be finished by making lower-level tests pass, while gradually working toward making the high-level tests pass as well.

A great book that demonstrates this approach is *Growing Object-Oriented Software, Guided by Tests* by Steve Freeman and Nat Pryce (Addison-Wesley Professional, 2009).

If you align this top-down approach to software development with your approach to testing, you can define automatable acceptance criteria that will tell you when you're ready, and that will help you prove that what you have built is what was actually needed.

To find out more about this fascinating topic, take a look at *Specification by Example: How Successful Teams Deliver the Right Software* (Manning, 2011) and *Bridging the Communication Gap: Specification by Example and Agile Acceptance Testing* (Neuri, 2009), both by Gojko Adzic; and *Discovery: Explore Behaviour Using Examples* (BDD Books, 2018) by Gáspár Nagy and Seb Rose (which is part of a series in the making).

11.3 Domain-driven design

If you're looking for more clues about what types of objects you should have in your application, I find domain-driven design (DDD) an excellent area to examine. The idea behind it is to learn about your problem domain and then reflect this knowledge in your application's domain model. A *domain-first approach* leads to a focus on design, taking it away from infrastructural details, like database tables and columns.

Although the strategic aspect of DDD is quite fascinating, you'll find the most useful suggestions, in terms of object design, come from its tactical advice. Take a look at the books *Domain-Driven Design: Tackling Complexity in the Heart of Software* by Eric Evans (Addison-Wesley Professional, 2003) and *Implementing Domain-Driven Design* by Vaughn Vernon (Addison-Wesley Professional, 2013). They contain many practical suggestions for designing entities and value objects, as well as other related types of objects.

11.4 Conclusion

Of course, there's much more to discover about object design and about software development and architecture in general. When it comes to object design, I hope this book has been able to provide you with a good foundation and some useful pointers for learning more. You'll find that there's more to learn every day, so keep experimenting. Best of luck with that!

appendix
Coding standard
for the code samples

The programming language used for the code samples in this book is a generalized object-oriented programming language. Its syntax is a mix of PHP and Java. It has the following properties:

- It's strictly typed. Parameters and return values need explicit return types:

```
public function foo(Bar bar): Baz
{
    // returns an instance of `Baz`
}
```

- Parameters, properties, and return types can allow for null as a value by adding a question mark at the end:

```
public function foo(Bar? bar): Baz?
{
    // allow in instance of `Bar`, or `null`

    // returns an instance of `Baz`, or `null`
}
```

- If you don't add a question mark after a parameter or return value's type, null will not be an accepted value for it:

```
public function foo(Bar bar): Baz
{
    // `bar` will be an instance of `Bar`, and never `null`

    // we have to return an instance of `Baz`
}
```

- void is a special return type that can be used when a function returns nothing:

```
public function bar(): void
{
    // can't return anything
}
```

- Supported types are class names, primitives (string, int, float, bool), arrays (array), callables (callable), and generic objects (object):

```
public function foo(Bar bar, string baz): callable
{
    // return a callable
}
```

- Callables are functions that can be passed to another function:

```
// this executes the callable returned by `foo()`:
this.foo()();
```

- A public object method can be passed as a callable:

```
eventDispatcher.addListener([object, 'methodName']);
```

- An object's constructor method is always called __construct(). Classes can be marked as final to make it impossible to extend them. In object methods, this will be a reference to the object on which the method is called:

```
final class Foo
{
    private string foo;

    public function __construct(string foo)
    {
        this.foo = foo;
    }
}
```

- The constructor will be called *during* object instantiation, not afterward, meaning that throwing an exception inside the constructor will interrupt instantiation and result in a null value being returned:

```
try {
    // When the constructor throws an exception...
    foo = new Foo();
} catch (Exception exception) {
    // `foo` will be `null`
}
```

- Methods and properties can have private, protected, or public scope. The scope relates to the class, not the object, so any object has access to private properties and methods of any other object *of the same type.*

```
final class Foo
{
    private string foo;

    public function equals(Foo other): bool
    {
        return this.foo == other.foo;
    }
}
```

- An interface defines a set of public methods without providing an implementation for them:

```
interface Foo
{
    public function bar(Baz baz): string;
}

final class FooBar implements Foo
{
    public function bar(Baz baz): string
    {
        return 'Hello, world!';
    }
}
```

- The language supports type inference, meaning that the type of a variable is optional if it can be derived from the value that gets assigned to it:

```
final class Foo
{
    private foo;

    public function __construct(string foo)
    {
        /*
         * `foo` is known to be a `string`, so the
         * `foo` property doesn't need to be marked
         * as a `string` too.
         */
        this.foo = foo;

        /**
         * `foo` is known to be a  `string`, so when
         * assigning it to the variable `bar`, you
         * don't need to provide a type for it.
         */
        bar = foo;
    }
}
```

- The `array` type will behave as a list or a map, depending on how you use it:

```
list = [
    'foo',
    'bar'
];
// add another item to `list`:
list[] = 'baz';

map = [
    'foo' => 20,
    'bar' => 30
];
// add another item to `map`:
map['baz'] = 40;
```

- Classes have a namespace, and you can import classes from other namespaces with use statements:

```
namespace Namespace\Subnamespace\Etc;

use From\Other\Namespace\Bar;

final class Foo
{
    public function __construct(Bar bar)
    {
    }
}
```

- Objects have a magic constant that represents the full class name of the object as a string:

```
// This will be `foo`
foo.className
```

- The language has a standard library that offers functions like `strpos()`, `file_get_contents()`, and `json_encode()`, and global constants for influencing the behavior of these functions:

```
originalJsonData = file_get_contents('/path/to/file.json');
decodedData = json_decode(originalJsonData);

jsonDataEncodedAgain = json_encode(
    decodedData,
    JSON_THROW_ON_ERROR | JSON_FORCE_OBJECT?);
```

- You can compare values using ==, which takes the type of the values you're comparing into account. If you're comparing objects, == will only be true if the values refer to the exact same object:

```
'a' == 'a'; // true
'a' == 1; // error
new Foo() == new Foo(); // false

foo = new Foo();
bar = foo;
foo == bar; // true
```

- You can throw any exception, which will stop execution of the code. You can recover from exceptions by catching them. Built-in exception classes can be extended:

```
try {
    // ...

    throw new RuntimeException('Message');

    // this won't be executed
} catch (Exception exception) {
    // do something with the exception if you like
}

final class CustomException extends RuntimeException
{
    // ...
}
```

- You can create a copy of an object by using the `clone` operator:

```
foo = new Foo();
copy = clone foo;
```

index